RIGHTSTART
MATHEMATICS

by Joan A. Cotter, Ph.D.
with Tracy Mittleider, MSEd

LEVEL A LESSONS
Second Edition

A *Activities for Learning, Inc.*

A special thank you to Kathleen Cotter Lawler for all her work on the preparation of this manual.

Note: Rather than use the designations, Kindergarten, First Grade, ect., to indicate a grade, levels are used. Level A is kindergarten, Level B is first grade, and so forth.

Printed in the United States of America

www.RightStartMath.com

For more information: info@RightStartMath.com
Supplies may be ordered from: www.RightStartMath.com

Activities for Learning, Inc.
321 Hill Street
Hazelton, ND 58544-0468
United States of America
888-775-6284 or 701-782-2000
701-782-2007 fax

ISBN 978-1-931980-57-9

May 2017

RightStart™ Mathematics Objectives for Level A

Name _____ Year _____

	Quarter 1	Quarter 2	Quarter 3	Quarter 4
Numeration				
Can recognize quantities to 100 by grouping in 5s & 10s				
Knows even numbers				
Knows odd numbers				
Can count by twos to 100				
Can count by fives to 100				
Can count by tens to 100				
Money				
Knows name and value of penny, nickel, and dime	N/A			
Place Value				
Knows 10 ones is 1 ten	N/A			
Knows 10 tens is 1 hundred	N/A	N/A		
Knows 37 as 3-ten 7	N/A	N/A		
Addition				
Understands addition as combining parts to form a whole	N/A			
Can partition numbers 3–10 into parts	N/A			
Knows number combinations equal to 10	N/A	N/A		
Knows number combinations up to 10	N/A	N/A		
Subtraction				
Understands subtraction as missing addend	N/A	N/A		
Understands subtraction as separating	N/A	N/A		
Problem Solving				
Can solve addition problems	N/A	N/A		
Can solve missing addend problems	N/A	N/A		
Can solve basic subtraction problems	N/A	N/A		
Geometry				
Knows mathematical names for triangle, rectangle, and circle				
Knows mathematical names for cubes, cylinder, sphere, and cone				
Knows parallel and perpendicular lines				
Can continue a pattern on the geoboard	N/A			
Time				
Knows days of the week	N/A			
Knows months of the year	N/A			
Can tell time to the hour	N/A	N/A	N/A	
Can tell time to the half hour	N/A	N/A	N/A	
Measurement				
Can determine length in centimeters and inches	N/A	N/A	N/A	
Fractions				
Can divide into halves and fourths	N/A	N/A	N/A	
Knows unit fractions up to 1/10	N/A	N/A	N/A	

BOOK SUGGESTIONS

Below you will find some book suggestions for the lessons that ask you to read a book.

Lesson 39 and Lesson 70

      Watching the Seasons by Edana Eckart

      The Reasons for Seasons by Gail Gibbons

Lesson 40

      Are You a Bee? by Judy Allen

      Bees! Learn About Bees and Enjoy Colorful Pictures - Look and Learn! (50+ Photos of Bees) by Becky Wolff

Lesson 108

      DK Readers: Telling Time by Patricia J. Murphy

Lesson 112

      Is It Symmetrical? by Nancy Kelly Allen

      Symmetry in Nature by Allyson Valentine Schrier

      What Is Symmetry in Nature? by Bobbie Kalman

MATERIALS NEEDED THAT ARE NOT INCLUDED THE RS MATH SET

Occasionally within the lessons materials list you will see items in bold that are not included in the RS Math Set. Below is a list of the items that will be needed to teach those lessons.

Lessons 3, 67, and 119 – Various Containers of objects for sorting

Lesson 9 – Three different toys

Lessons 9, 12, and 15 – Variety of books, and hardcover books

Lessons 12 and 15 – Two pencils of different length

Lessons 16, 26, 68, 76, 106, and 107 – Glue

Lessons 17, 39, 69, 70, and 71 – Calendar

Lesson 18 – Freestanding folder

Lesson 24 – Container with 11 small slips of paper

Lesson 25 – Valentine heart

Lessons 25, 36, 40, 43, 49, 68, 69, 76, 93, 106, 107, 109, and 113 – Scissors

Lesson 50 – Strings of various length and sand or snow for drawing

Lessons 70, 81, 82, 87, and 103 – Crayons

Lessons 81, 82, and 101 – Blank sheets of paper

Lesson 82 – Stapler

Lesson 90 – Sticky notes

Lesson 91 – Flashlight or some other light source and a bare wall

Lesson 93 – Tape

Lesson 94 – Egg carton with 2 eggs

Lesson 104 – Two identical glasses and water

Lesson 104 – Two 4-inch paper cups and two rubber bands

Lesson 104 – Small objects to weigh

Lesson 119 – Set of measuring cups

How This Program Was Developed

We have been hearing for years that Japanese students do better than U.S. students in math in Japan. The Asian students are ahead by the middle of first grade. And the gap widens every year thereafter.

Many explanations have been given, including less diversity and a longer school year. Japanese students attend school 240 days a year.

A third explanation given is that the Asian public values and supports education more than we do. A first grade teacher has the same status as a university professor. If a student falls behind, the family, not the school, helps the child or hires a tutor. Students often attend after-school classes.

A fourth explanation involves the philosophy of learning. Asians and Europeans believe anyone can learn mathematics or even play the violin. It is not a matter of talent, but of good teaching and hard work.

Although these explanations are valid, I decided to take a careful look at how mathematics is taught in Japanese first grades. Japan has a national curriculum, so there is little variation among teachers.

I found some important differences. One of these is the way the Asians name their numbers. In English we count ten, eleven, twelve, thirteen, and so on, which doesn't give the child a clue about tens and ones. But in Asian languages, one counts by saying ten-1, ten-2, ten-3 for the teens, and 2-ten 1, 2-ten 2, and 2-ten 3 for the twenties.

Still another difference is their criteria for manipulatives. Americans think the more the better. Asians prefer very few, but insist that they be imaginable, that is, visualizable. That is one reason they do not use colored rods. You can imagine the one and the three, but try imagining a brown eight–the quantity eight, not the color. It cannot be done without grouping.

Another important difference is the emphasis on non-counting strategies for computation. Japanese children are discouraged from counting; rather they are taught to see quantities in groups of fives and tens.

For example, when an American child wants to know 9 + 4, most likely the child will start with 9 and count up 4. In contrast, the Asian child will think that if he takes 1 from the 4 and puts it with the 9, then he will have 10 and 3, or 13. Unfortunately, very few American first-graders at the end of the year even know that 10 + 3 is 13.

I decided to conduct research using some of these ideas in two similar first grade classrooms. The control group studied math in the traditional workbook-based manner. The other class used the lesson plans I developed. The children used that special number naming for three months.

They also used a special abacus I designed, based on fives and tens. I asked 5-year-old Stan how much is 11 + 6. Then I asked him how he knew. He replied, "I have the abacus in my mind."

The children were working with thousands by the sixth week. They figured out how to add 4-digit numbers on paper after learning how on the abacus.

Every child in the experimental class, including those enrolled in special education classes, could add numbers like 9 + 4, by changing it to 10 + 3.

I asked the children to explain what the 6 and 2 mean in the number 26. Ninety-three percent of the children in the experimental group explained it correctly while only 50% of third graders did so in another study.

I gave the children some base ten rods (none of them had seen them before) that looked like ones and tens and asked them to make 48. Then I asked them to subtract 14. The children in the control group counted 14 ones, while the experimental class removed 1 ten and 4 ones. This indicated that they saw 14 as 1 ten and 4 ones and not as 14 ones. This view of numbers is vital to understanding algorithms, or procedures, for doing arithmetic.

I asked the experimental class to mentally add 64 + 20, which only 52% of nine-year-olds on the 1986 National test did correctly; 56% of those in the experimental class could do it.

Since children often confuse columns when taught traditionally, I wrote 2304 + 86 = horizontally and asked them to find the sum any way they liked. Fifty-six percent did so correctly, including one child who did it in his head.

This following year I revised the lesson plans and both first grade classes used these methods. I am delighted to report that on a national standardized test, both classes scored at the 98th percentile.

—Joan A. Cotter, Ph.D.

Some General Thoughts on Teaching Mathematics

1. Only five percent of mathematics should be learned by rote; 95 percent should be understood.

2. Real learning builds on what the child already knows. Rote teaching ignores it.

3. Contrary to the common myth, "young children can think both concretely and abstractly. Development is not a kind of inevitable unfolding in which one simply waits until a child is cognitively 'ready.'" —*Foundations for Success* NMAP

4. What is developmentally appropriate is not a simple function of age or grade, but rather is largely contingent on prior opportunities to learn." —Duschl & others

5. Understanding a new model is easier if you have made one yourself. So, a child needs to construct a graph before attempting to read a ready-made graph.

6. Good manipulatives cause confusion at first. If a new manipulative makes perfect sense at first sight, it is not needed. Trying to understand and relate it to previous knowledge is what leads to greater learning. —Richard Behr & others.

7. According to Arthur Baroody, "Teaching mathematics is essentially a process of translating mathematics into a form children can comprehend, providing experiences that enable children to discover relationships and construct meanings, and creating opportunities to develop and exercise mathematical reasoning."

8. Lauren Resnick says, "Good mathematics learners expect to be able to make sense out of rules they are taught, and they apply some energy and time to the task of making sense. By contrast, those less adept in mathematics try to memorize and apply the rules that are taught, but do not attempt to relate these rules to what they know about mathematics at a more intuitive level."

9. Mindy Holte puts learning the facts in proper perspective when she says, "In our concern about the memorization of math facts or solving problems, we must not forget that the root of mathematical study is the creation of mental pictures in the imagination and manipulating those images and relationships using the power of reason and logic." She also emphasizes the ability to imagine or visualize, an important skill in mathematics and other areas.

10. The only students who like flash cards are those who do not need them.

11. Mathematics is not a solitary pursuit. According to Richard Skemp, solitary math on paper is like reading music, rather than listening to it: "Mathematics, like music, needs to be expressed in physical actions and human interactions before its symbols can evoke the silent patterns of mathematical ideas (like musical notes), simultaneous relationships (like harmonies) and expositions or proofs (like melodies)."

12. "More than most other school subjects, mathematics offers special opportunities for children to learn the power of thought as distinct from the power of authority. This is a very important lesson to learn, an essential step in the emergence of independent thinking." —*Everybody Counts*

13. The role of the teacher is to encourage thinking by asking questions, not giving answers. Once you give an answer, thinking usually stops.

14. Putting thoughts into words helps the learning process.

15. Help the children realize that it is their responsibility to ask questions when they do not understand. Do not settle for "I don't get it."

16. The difference between a novice and an expert is that an expert catches errors much more quickly. A violinist adjusts pitch so quickly that the audience does not hear it.

17. Europeans and Asians believe learning occurs not because of ability, but primarily because of effort. In the ability model of learning, errors are a sign of failure. In the effort model, errors are natural. In Japanese classrooms, the teachers discuss errors with the whole class.

18. For teaching vocabulary, be sure either the word or the concept is known. For example, if a child is familiar with six-sided figures, we can give him the word, hexagon. Or, if he has heard the word, multiply, we can tell him what it means. It is difficult to learn a new concept and the term simultaneously.

19. Introduce new concepts globally before details. This lets the children know where they are headed.

20. Informal mathematics should precede paper and pencil work. Long before a child learns how to add fractions with unlike denominators, she should be able to add one half and one fourth mentally.

21. Some pairs of concepts are easier to remember if one of them is thought of as dominant. Then the non-dominant concept is simply the other one. For example, if even is dominant over odd, an odd number is one that is not even.

22. Worksheets should also make the child think. Therefore, they should not be a large collection of similar exercises, but should present a variety. In RightStart™ Mathematics, they are designed to be done independently.

23. Keep math time enjoyable. We store our emotional state along with what we have learned. A person who dislikes math will avoid it and a child under stress stops learning. If a lesson is too hard, stop and play a game. Try the lesson again later.

24. In Japan students spend more time on fewer problems. Teachers do not concern themselves with attention spans as is done in the U.S.

25. In Japan the goal of the math lesson is that the student has understood a concept, not necessarily has done something (a worksheet).

26. The calendar must show the entire month, so the children can plan ahead. The days passed can be crossed out or the current day circled.

27. A real mathematical problem is one in which the procedures to find the answer are not obvious. It is like a puzzle, needing trial and error. Emphasize the satisfaction of solving problems and like puzzles, of not giving away the solution to others.

RightStart™ Mathematics

Ten major characteristics make this research-based program effective:

1. Refers to quantities of up to 5 as a group; discourages counting individually. Uses fingers and tally sticks to show quantities up to 10; teaches quantities 6 to 10 as 5 plus a quantity, for example 6 = 5 + 1.

2. Avoids counting procedures for finding sums and differences. Teaches five- and ten-based strategies for the facts that are both visual and visualizable.

3. Employs games, not flash cards, for practice.

4. Once quantities 1 to 10 are known, proceeds to 10 as a unit. Temporarily uses the "math way" of naming numbers; for example, "1 ten-1" (or "ten-1") for eleven, "1-ten 2" for twelve, "2-ten" for twenty, and "2-ten 5" for twenty-five.

5. Uses expanded notation (overlapping) place-value cards for recording tens and ones; the ones card is placed on the zero of the tens card. Encourages a child to read numbers starting at the left and not backward by starting at the ones.

6. Proceeds rapidly to hundreds and thousands using manipulatives and place-value cards. Provides opportunities for trading between ones and tens, tens and hundreds, and hundreds and thousands with manipulatives.

7. Teaches mental computation. Investigates informal solutions, often through story problems, before learning procedures.

8. Teaches four-digit addition on the abacus, letting the child discover the paper and pencil algorithm.

9. Introduces fractions with a linear visual model, including all fractions from 1/2 to 1/10. "Pies" are not used initially because they cannot show fractions greater than 1. Later, the tenths will become the basis for decimals.

10. Teaches short division (where only the answer is written down) for single-digit divisors, before long division.

Second Edition

Many changes have occurred since the first RightStart™ lessons were begun in 1994. First, mathematics is used more widely in many fields, for example, architecture, science, technology, and medicine. Today, many careers require math beyond basic arithmetic. Second, research has given us new insights into how children learn mathematics. Third, kindergarten has become much more academic, and fourth, most children are tested to ensure their preparedness for the next step.

This second edition is updated to reflect new research and applications. Topics within a grade level are always taught with the most appropriate method using the best approach with the child and teacher in mind.

Daily Lessons

Objectives. The objectives outline the purpose and goal of the lesson. Some possibilities are to introduce, to build, to learn a term, to practice, or to review.

Materials. The Math Set of manipulatives includes the specially crafted items needed to teach RightStart™ Mathematics. Occasionally, common objects such as scissors will be needed. These items are indicated by boldface type.

Warm-up. The warm-up time is the time for quick review, memory work, and sometimes an introduction to the day's topics. The dry erase board makes an ideal slate for quick responses.

Activities. The Activities for Teaching section is the heart of the lesson; it starts on the left page and continues to the right page. These are the instructions for teaching the lesson. The expected answers from the child are given in square brackets.

Establish with the children some indication when you want a quick response and when you want a more thoughtful response. Research shows that the quiet time for thoughtful response should be about three seconds. Avoid talking during this quiet time; resist the temptation to rephrase the question. This quiet time gives the slower child time to think and the quicker child time to think more deeply.

Encourage the child to develop persistence and perseverance. Avoid giving hints or explanations too quickly. Children tend to stop thinking once they hear the answer.

Explanations. Special background notes for the teacher are given in Explanations.

Worksheets. The worksheets are designed to give the children a chance to think about and to practice the day's lesson. The children are to do them independently. Some lessons, especially in the early levels, have no worksheet.

Games. Games, not worksheets or flash cards, provide practice. The games, found in the *Math Card Games* book, can be played as many times as necessary until proficiency or memorization takes place. They are as important to learning math as books are to reading. The *Math Card Games* book also includes extra games for the child needing more help, and some more challenging games for the advanced child.

In conclusion. Each lesson ends with a short summary called, "In conclusion," where the child answers a few short questions based on the day's learning.

Number of lessons. Generally, each lesson is to be done in one day and each manual, in one school year. Complete each manual before going on to the next level. Other than Level A, the first lesson in each level is an introductory test with references to review lessons if needed.

Comments. We really want to hear how this program is working. Please let us know any improvements and suggestions that you may have.

Joan A. Cotter, Ph.D.

info@RightStartMath.com
www.RightStartMath.com

LEVEL A: TABLE OF CONTENTS

Level A: Table of Contents

LEVEL A: TABLE OF CONTENTS

LEVEL A: TABLE OF CONTENTS

LESSON 1: SUBITIZING 1 TO 3

OBJECTIVES:

1. To learn the term *left*
2. To learn finger sets and tally marks for quantities 1 to 3
3. To recognize quantities 1 to 3 without counting

MATERIALS:

1. Music for "Yellow is the Sun" (Appendix p. 1)
2. *Yellow is the Sun* book
3. Colored 1" × 1" tiles
4. Tally sticks (craft sticks)

ACTIVITIES FOR TEACHING:

Left hand. Ask the child to raise her *left* hand. Ask her to point to her left foot, left eye, and other left body parts.

The Yellow is the Sun song and book. Teach the following song with motions. Use only the left hand for numbers 1 to 5.

Yellow is the Sun

Yellow is the sun.
This is only one. (Raise one finger.)

Why is the sky so blue?
Let me show you two. (Raise two fingers.)

Salty is the sea.
One more and it's three. (Raise three fingers.)

Hear the thunder roar.
Here's the mighty four. (Raise four fingers.)

Ducks will swim and dive.
My whole hand makes five. (Raise five fingers.)

Read the book *Yellow is the Sun* to the child.

Quantity of 2. Show two fingers with your left hand and ask the child to show two with her left hand. Place 2 tiles in front of the child. Ask her how many she sees. [2]

Two fingers.　　 **Two tiles.**

Place the tally sticks within reach of the child. Tell her to take 2 tally sticks (without counting). Next ask her to lay them out as shown. Also clap 2 times and ask them how many claps they heard. [2]

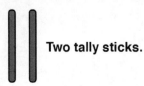 **Two tally sticks.**

EXPLANATIONS:

To learn which is their left hand, some children benefit by wearing a bracelet on their left hand.

Subitizing (SOO bih tighz ing) is perceiving at a glance the number of items without counting. Five-month-old babies can subitize up to three objects and many 12-month-old babies up to four objects. It is easier for children (and adults) to subitize quantities than to count them.

Subitizing allows the child simultaneously to see the whole and the individual items. In counting the child focus on one item at a time. To foster their natural subitizing skills, children should be discouraged from counting small collections.

The left hand is used for numbers less than five to correlate with reading from left to right. It does not matter which fingers of the left hand are used.

For demonstrating fingers 1–5, use your left hand if you are sitting next to a child and your right hand if you are facing the child.

Finger sets, or the use of fingers, to show a quantity gives the child a tactile feel and a visual image of quantity. Many parents use finger sets when they teach their children to show their ages with fingers. We will continue this pattern to 10.

Research shows children who can represent quantities with their fingers score better in upper elementary math.

ACTIVITIES FOR TEACHING CONTINUED:	EXPLANATIONS CONTINUED:

Quantity of 3. Ask the child to show 3 fingers. If she is not sure, show her, but do not count. Ask her to show 3 with the tally sticks.

Three.

Three.

Place 3 tiles in front of the child. Ask: How many do you see? [3]

Three tiles.

Rearrange the tiles and ask: Now how many tiles do you see? [3]

Quantity of 1. Place one tile where the child can see it. Ask: How many? [1] Have her show it with her fingers and with the tally sticks.

Finding given quantities. Ask the child to look around the room and name one of something. [for example, one table]

Repeat for finding two and three objects. [three chairs]

Disagreeing. Place 3 tiles to one side of the child and 2 tiles on the other side. Ask the child if she agrees there are 3 tiles on both sides. [no]

After a short discussion about the number of tiles, add one more tile to the side with 2, and ask her if she agrees now that they both have 3. [yes]

Changing quantities. Start with 3 tiles; ask the child to show the number with her fingers. Now ask her to watch. Remove a tile and ask her to say the new number. [2]

Repeat adding or removing tiles, but do not exceed 3.

In conclusion. Ask the child to show on her fingers: 2, 3, and 1.

It is very important that the child feels comfortable disagreeing with you during math time. The primary role of the teacher is to foster thinking in the child, not merely give information.

For this lesson there is no worksheet. Worksheets are used only when needed in the course of the lesson or when independent work will benefit the child.

LESSON 2: SUBITIZING 4 AND PATTERNING

OBJECTIVES:

1. To learn finger sets and tally marks for 4
2. To recognize quantities 1 to 4 without counting
3. To recognize and continue a simple pattern

MATERIALS:

1. Music for "Yellow is the Sun"
2. *Yellow is the Sun* book
3. Finger cards, cut apart (Appendix p. 2)
4. Tally sticks
5. Tiles

ACTIVITIES FOR TEACHING:

Warm-up. Continue teaching the song, "Yellow is the Sun."

Yellow is the Sun

Yellow is the sun.
This is only one. (Raise one finger.)

Why is the sky so blue?
Let me show you two. (Raise two fingers.)

Salty is the sea.
One more and it's three. (Raise three fingers.)

Hear the thunder roar.
Here's the mighty four. (Raise four fingers.)

Ducks will swim and dive.
My whole hand makes five. (Raise five fingers.)

Read the book *Yellow is the Sun* to the child.

Show the finger card with 2 for one to two seconds and ask the child to show the quantity with his fingers on his left hand and to build it with tally sticks. Repeat with finger cards 1 and 3. Also, clap 2 times. Ask: How many claps did you hear? [2] Repeat with 3.

Subitizing 4. Show 4 with your fingers and ask the child to show 4 with his left hand. Then show 4 tiles and say: This is 4. See the figures below.

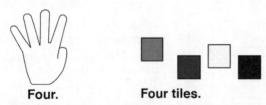

Four.   Four tiles.

Rearrange the 4 tiles and ask how many he sees. Remove 1 tile and ask: How many? [3] Replace it and again ask: How many? [4] Now clap 4 times and ask: How many claps did you hear? [4]

EXPLANATIONS:

It is unimportant which fingers on the left hand the child uses to show the quantities.

The finger, dot, bead, and tally stick cards are found on Appendix pp. 2, 6, 7, and 19. If necessary, copy onto card stock, using one color for the sets of finger cards, another color for the tally sticks, and a third color for the bead pattern cards. You will also need two sets of dot cards, which can be in a fourth color.

| ACTIVITIES FOR TEACHING CONTINUED: | EXPLANATIONS CONTINUED: |

Changing quantities. Tell him to make 4 with 4 tally sticks. Then ask him to remove 2 sticks and say how many? [2] Ask him to add 1 and say how many? [3] Repeat with one more.

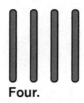

Four.

Introducing patterning. Take a group of tally sticks and lay one out horizontally. Place another next to the first vertically, the third one horizontally and the fourth one vertically. Give the child a tally stick and ask: What do you think comes next? Tell him we will call this the "do-re" (doe-ray) pattern. Tell the child to continue to lay out the pattern.

Continuing the pattern with tally sticks.

Next take out the tiles and lay out a red tile followed by a blue tile and then another red tile. Ask the child which color would come next in the do-re pattern? [blue] Ask him to continue the pattern.

Continuing the do-re (AB) pattern.

Encourage him to make the same pattern with different colors.

In conclusion. Ask the child to say how many fingers he sees while you do the following: Raise 4 fingers, then put 1 down and back up several times. [4, 3, 4, 3, . . .] Ask: Do you hear a do-re pattern? [yes]

Our brains are wired to look for patterns.

Patterns are often named using letters of the alphabet. The letters are used sequentially, naming each different element of the pattern. For example, a strictly alternating pattern is AB. To avoid using the letters of the alphabet for beginning readers, we will use musical scale names to designate pattern names. The names are do (doe), re (ray), mi (me), fa (fah).

You might want to teach him the "Do Re Mi" song from the "Sound of Music."

Conclusions may be a summary of the day's lesson or an expansion of the lesson to challenge higher level thinking.

LESSON 3: SORTING

OBJECTIVES:

1. To practice subitizing quantities 1 to 4
2. To recognize and continue a harder pattern
3. To determine likenesses through sorting

MATERIALS:

1. Music for "Yellow is the Sun"
2. *Yellow is the Sun* book
3. Finger cards
4. Tally sticks
5. Tiles
6. **Various containers of objects for sorting***

ACTIVITIES FOR TEACHING:

Warm-up. Continue teaching the song, "Yellow is the Sun."

Yellow is the Sun

Yellow is the sun.
This is only one. (Raise one finger.)

Why is the sky so blue?
Let me show you two. (Raise two fingers.)

Salty is the sea.
One more and it's three. (Raise three fingers.)

Hear the thunder roar.
Here's the mighty four. (Raise four fingers.)

Ducks will swim and dive.
My whole hand makes five. (Raise five fingers.)

Read the book *Yellow is the Sun* to the child.

Show 3 fingers and ask: How many? [3] Repeat for 4, 2, and 1. Then show the 3 finger card for two seconds and ask the child to show the quantity with her fingers on her left hand and build it with tally sticks. Repeat with the other finger cards.

Patterns. Start a pattern by alternating two colors (different colors from the previous day). Tell the child to take two handfuls of tiles and continue the pattern as long as she can.

The do-re (AB) pattern.

Next show her the following do-re-re pattern. Ask her to copy it and to continue it until she runs out of tiles.

The do-re-re (ABB) pattern.

EXPLANATIONS:

*An item listed in boldface is not part of the RightStart™ materials.

You might want to sing the songs while getting the math materials out. This helps the child mentally prepare for math.

ACTIVITIES FOR TEACHING CONTINUED:

Sorting tiles. Demonstrate sorting with a collection of tiles. First pick up a tile and set it to the side. Next pick up another tile from the collection. If it is the same color as the tile side aside, add it to that pile; if it is a different color, start a new pile.

Continue with a few more tiles before encouraging the child to take over.

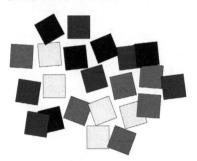

Unsorted tiles.

Sorting tiles.

Sorting other objects. When objects are already sorted, demonstrate removing the objects from their containers and combining them. After sorting, ask the child to return them to their original containers.

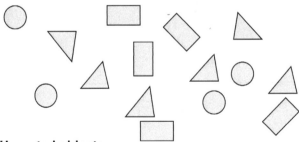

Unsorted objects.

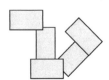

Sorted objects.

In conclusion. Ask the child to show 3 on her fingers. Then ask her to show 4.

EXPLANATIONS CONTINUED:

Young children should sort only two colors to start.

Sorting objects could be colored tiles, as well as crayons, beads, geometric figures, seeds, beans, washers, bolts, pictures of flowers, and pictures of birds. Items can be sorted by color, size, or other attributes.

Alternately, where a container has several different types of objects, (for example, different colored tiles) the child may sort them into different piles and then return all to the original container.

Sorting is an activity with many applications. For example, in science, items can be sorted whether alive or inanimate; in geography, by continent; in music, by composer or period; in everyday life, clean or dirty.

LESSON 4: SUBITIZING 5

OBJECTIVES:
1. To subitize 5
2. To identify without counting 1 to 5 objects
3. To practice sorting

MATERIALS:
1. Finger cards
2. Tiles
3. Tally sticks
4. Multiplication cards (after sorting, use the 2s envelope)*

ACTIVITIES FOR TEACHING:

Warm-up. Continue teaching the song, "Yellow is the Sun."

Show quantities 1 to 4 with your fingers, the finger cards, and the tiles and ask the child to name how many. Also, say quantities between 1 and 4 and ask the child to show with his fingers.

Subitizing 5. Show your hand with all 5 fingers raised and tell the child it is 5. Tell him to show 5. Ask: What is special about 5 on your hand? [whole hand]

Five

Ask the child to lay out 4 tiles and then add 1 more. Ask: How much is it now? [5]

Seeing 5 as having a middle. Ask him to show 5 with his fingers. With the 5 tiles in a row, explain, five has something else special about it: It has a middle. Demonstrate how to find a middle. With a row of 5 tiles, point to the first tile with your left hand and last tile with your right hand. Then simultaneously point to the second and fourth tiles. See the figures below.

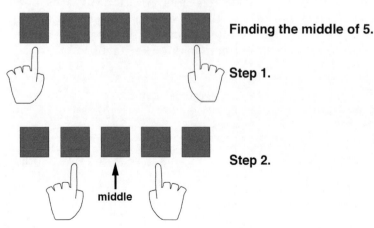

Finding the middle of 5.

Step 1.

Step 2.

middle

EXPLANATIONS:

*Included with the multiplication cards are 10 envelopes, each printed with the multiples of a number from 1–10. Insert into each envelope 10 multiplication cards matching the numbers listed on the front of the envelope.

A new deck of multiplication cards is collated to make this task easy: the first 10 cards go into the 1s envelope; the next 10 cards go into the 2s envelope; and so forth.

ACTIVITIES FOR TEACHING CONTINUED:

EXPLANATIONS CONTINUED:

Ask: Do your fingers have a middle when they show 5? [yes]

Comparing 5 to 4. Remove 1 tile and ask: Do you think 4 has a middle? Repeat the same procedure. See the figures below. Then ask: Do your fingers have a middle when they show 4? [no]

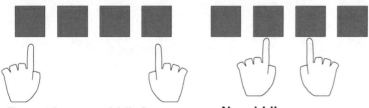

Does 4 have a middle?   **No middle.**

Five with tally sticks. Ask the child to lay out 5 tally sticks. Tell him to watch while we do something to make 5 special. Demonstrate picking up the last tally stick and laying it across the other four as shown.

   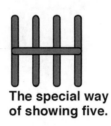

Five tally sticks.   **The special way of showing five.**

Practice. Show fingers 1–5 and ask the child to name the amount. Show 1–5 tiles in various configurations; ask him to show the quantity with his fingers and to say the number. Say a number 1–5; ask him to show his fingers and construct it with tally sticks.

Sorting by number of digits. Find the multiplication card envelope with the multiples of two (2, 4, 6, 8, 10, 12, 14, 16, 18, 20). Lay out the cards so they are not in order. Ask him to sort the cards into two piles, cards with one digit and cards with two digits. See the figure below.

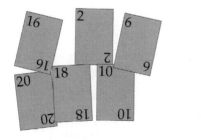

Sorting the multiplication cards into two piles.

In conclusion. Ask the child to show 5 on his fingers. Then ask him to show 4.

Be sure the fifth stick covers the other four sticks. For children the horizontal position is easier than the diagonal position. Also the stick when placed diagonally is too short.

Anna learned how to make 5 with the tally sticks by placing the fifth stick over the other four. That evening at the dinner table, Anna held up four fingers with her left hand and placed her right index finger across the four fingers and proclaimed to everybody, "This is 5"!

LESSON 5: MORE PATTERNING

OBJECTIVES:

1. To review finger sets and tally marks for quantities 1 to 5
2. To continue a simple pattern
3. To learn the terms *up* and *down*

MATERIALS:

1. *Yellow is the Sun* book
2. Two sets of finger cards
3. Tally sticks
4. Tiles

ACTIVITIES FOR TEACHING:	EXPLANATIONS:
Warm-up. Continue reading the book and teaching the song, "Yellow is the Sun."	You might want to sing the songs while preparing the math materials. This helps the child mentally prepare for math.

Yellow is the Sun

Yellow is the sun.
This is only one. (Raise one finger.)

Why is the sky so blue?
Let me show you two. (Raise two fingers.)

Salty is the sea.
One more and it's three. (Raise three fingers.)

Hear the thunder roar.
Here's the mighty four. (Raise four fingers.)

Ducks will swim and dive.
My whole hand makes five. (Raise five fingers.)

Read the book *Yellow is the Sun* to the child.

Show the number three finger card for 2 seconds and ask the child to show the number with her fingers on her left hand. Build it with tally sticks, then show it with tiles. Repeat with other numbers 1 to 5.

Ask her to show 5 with her fingers. Ask: What is special about 5 on your hand? [whole hand, it has a middle]

More patterns. Take a handful of tiles. Demonstrate making the do-re-re (ABB) pattern as shown below. Ask the child to make the same pattern until she runs out of tiles.

The do-re-re pattern.

Next show her the following do-re-mi (ABC) pattern. Ask her to copy it and to continue it until she runs out of tiles.

The do-re-mi pattern.

ACTIVITIES FOR TEACHING CONTINUED:

EXPLANATIONS CONTINUED:

Up and down. With the child standing, say the following nursery rhyme emphasizing *up* and *down*.

Hickory Dickory Dock

Hickory dickory dock,
The mouse ran up the clock. (Raise both arms in the air.)
The clock struck one. (Raise one finger on the left had.)
The mouse ran down. (Put arms down.)
Hickory dickory dock.

Hickory dickory dock,
The mouse ran up the clock. (Raise both arms in the air.)
The clock struck two. (Raise two fingers on the left hand.)
And down he flew. (Put arms down.)
Hickory dickory dock.

Hickory dickory dock,
The mouse ran up the clock. (Raise both arms in the air.)
The clock struck three. (Raise three fingers on the left hand.)
And he did flee. (Put arms down.)
Hickory dickory dock.

Hickory dickory dock,
The mouse ran up the clock. (Raise both arms in the air.)
The clock struck four. (Raise four fingers on the left hand.)
He hit the floor. (Put arms down.)
Hickory dickory dock.

Hickory dickory dock,
The mouse ran up the clock. (Raise both arms in the air.)
The clock struck five. (Raise five fingers on the left hand.)
The mouse took a dive. (Put arms down.)
Hickory dickory dock.

To be sure the child understands the words *up* and *down*, say this nursery rhyme together emphasizing the words up and down. The child could also show on her upraised left hand the number as it is spoken.

Hickory Dickory Dock can be found at Storybook Land in Aberdeen, South Dakota.

In conclusion. Show quantities 1–5 on your hand briefly and ask the child to tell you how many she sees.

12

LESSON 6: SUBITIZING 6

OBJECTIVES:
1. To learn the term *right*
2. To subitize 6 as 5 and 1

MATERIALS:
1. Tiles
2. Tally sticks

ACTIVITIES FOR TEACHING:

Warm-up. Tell the child today we are going to sing the "Yellow is the Sun" song all the way to ten.

Yellow is the Sun

Yellow is the sun.
This is only one. (Raise one finger.)

Why is the sky so blue?
Let me show you two. (Raise two fingers.)

Salty is the sea.
One more and it's three. (Raise three fingers.)

Hear the thunder roar.
Here's the mighty four. (Raise four fingers.)

Ducks will swim and dive.
My whole hand makes five. (Raise five fingers.)

Yellow is the sun.
Six is five and one. (5 fingers on left hand; 1 on right.)

Why is the sky so blue?
Seven is five and two. (5 fingers on left hand; 2 on right.)

Salty is the sea.
Eight is five and three. (5 fingers on left hand; 3 on right.)

Hear the thunder roar.
Nine is five and four. (5 fingers on left hand; 4 on right.)

Ducks will swim and dive.
Ten is five and five. (5 fingers on left hand; 5 on right.)

Show 1 to 5 tiles in various configurations and ask him to show fingers and to say the number. Say a number and ask him to show the equivalent tally sticks.

Left and right. Tell the child to show his left hand. Ask him to show his left hand, knee, foot, and so forth.

Ask the child to raise his *right* hand. Tell him to point to his right foot, right eye, and other right body parts.

EXPLANATIONS:

Seeing quantities between 6 and 9 as 5 plus 1 to 4 makes them visualizable, or imaginable. For example, try to visualize 8 apples without grouping them. Impossible.

Now think of 5 of the apples as red and 3 as green–very possible. Grouping by 5s also prepares the child to think of ten as a unit.

ACTIVITIES FOR TEACHING CONTINUED:	EXPLANATIONS CONTINUED:

Quantity 5. Ask her to show 5 with her fingers. Ask: What is special about 5 on your hand? [whole hand, it has a middle]

Quantity 6. Tell the child that to show the next number, 6, he will need to also use his right hand. Demonstrate showing 5 on the left hand and 1 on the right hand. See the left figure below.

As this point, 6 must be shown as 5 on the left hand and 1 on the right, not for example, as 3 on each hand.

Six.

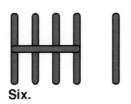

Six.

Now ask the child to make 6 with the tally sticks. If necessary, remind him to make the special 5 with the fifth tally stick horizontal over the vertical four. See the right figure above.

Grouping 6 tiles. Lay out 5 identical tiles and ask: How many do you see? [5] Ask: What would we have if we added 1 more? [6] Add a tile of a different color as shown below and ask the child how much it is. Ask him to make another 6, using two colors.

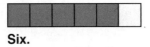

Six.

Claps. Clap once and ask the child: How many did you hear? [1] Next clap twice in quick succession and ask: How many did you hear? [2] Repeat for 3 and 4.

Tell the child to clap his hands as you say a number from 1 to 4. The the clapping should be done quickly without counting.

Now you clap in random order and ask the child to show what he heard with his fingers or tally sticks.

In conclusion. Ask the child to show his left hand, then his right hand. Ask the child to show 6 on his fingers.

LESSON 7: MATCHING

OBJECTIVES:

1. To review finger sets and tally marks for quantities 1 to 6
2. To continue a simple pattern
3. To match objects or cards

MATERIALS:

1. *Yellow is the Sun* book
2. Tiles
3. Tally sticks
4. Finger cards
5. *Math Card Games* book,* N4

ACTIVITIES FOR TEACHING:	EXPLANATIONS:
Warm-up. Continue reading the book and singing the song, "Yellow is the Sun."	*The Fifth Edition of the *Math Card Games* book is needed for this manual.

Yellow is the Sun

Yellow is the sun.
This is only one. (Raise one finger.)

Why is the sky so blue?
Let me show you two. (Raise two fingers.)

Salty is the sea.
One more and it's three. (Raise three fingers.)

Hear the thunder roar.
Here's the mighty four. (Raise four fingers.)

Ducks will swim and dive.
My whole hand makes five. (Raise five fingers.)

Yellow is the sun.
Six is five and one. (5 fingers on left hand; 1 on right.)

Why is the sky so blue?
Seven is five and two. (5 fingers on left hand; 2 on right.)

Salty is the sea.
Eight is five and three. (5 fingers on left hand; 3 on right.)

Hear the thunder roar.
Nine is five and four. (5 fingers on left hand; 4 on right.)

Ducks will swim and dive.
Ten is five and five. (5 fingers on left hand; 5 on right.)

Read the book *Yellow is the Sun* to the child.

Say a number and ask the child to show with her fingers. Show 1 to 6 with your fingers and ask her to show with tiles or tally sticks. Have the child say the number.

EXPLANATIONS (continued):

The book is arranged in chapters as follows:

1. Number Sense (N)
2. Addition (A)
3. Clocks (C)
4. Multiplication (P)
5. Money (M)
6. Subtraction (S)
7. Division (D)
8. Fractions (F)

The games are numbered sequentially within each chapter. For example, A2 is the second game in the Addition chapter and N4 is the fourth game in the previous chapter, Number Sense.

ACTIVITIES FOR TEACHING CONTINUED:

Oral patterns. Demonstrate to the child by saying 1,2,1,2,1, and now ask what comes next in this pattern. [2] Ask what comes next in this pattern: red, white, blue, red, white, blue, red. [white, blue]

Matching. Explain that matching is looking for two items that belong together. Demonstrate matching by setting out 8 tiles, two of each color. Then pick up one color, find its match, and set them aside. Pick up another color and find its match, and so on.

Matching a collection of items.

Matching finger cards. Lay out two sets of finger cards face up in no particular order. Ask the child to find the matches. After she finds a match, ask the child to hop the same number of times the card says. For example, if the card shows 3 fingers, the child hops 3 times. Continue until all the cards are matched.

Finger Card Memory game. Play the Finger Card Memory game found in the *Math Card Games* book, N4.

In conclusion. Hold up 4 fingers and ask: Can you match my fingers by showing the same number with your fingers? Repeat for other numbers.

EXPLANATIONS CONTINUED:

Matching as a life skill can encourage children to look beyond the immediately obvious and to integrate other concepts. Some examples of matching include: a fruit with its seed, pairs of shoes or socks, lower case letters to capital letters, and sports with equipment. It will be used frequently throughout the year for practicing mathematics concepts.

When matching, identical or similar items can be pairs of interesting objects such as colored tiles, beads, seeds, beans, washers, bolts, pictures of flowers, birds, or animals, and cards with numerals.

LESSON 8: SUBITIZING 7 AND THE AL ABACUS

OBJECTIVES:

1. To subitize 7
2. To learn the terms *above* and *below*
3. To learn the terms *top* and *bottom*
4. To enter 1 to 5 beads on the AL Abacus without counting

MATERIALS:

1. *Yellow is the Sun* book
2. Finger cards
3. Tally sticks
4. Tiles
5. AL Abacus

ACTIVITIES FOR TEACHING:	EXPLANATIONS:
Warm-up. Continue reading the book and singing the song, "Yellow is the Sun."	
Show the finger cards 1 to 6 at random for 2 seconds and ask the child to show them on his fingers. Also have him show the number with tally sticks and say the numbers.	
Quantity 7. Show 7 to the child with your fingers. Ask him to show it on his fingers. Also ask him to build it with the tally sticks. Now, ask him to make a 7 with the tiles, using two colors as shown below.	It might help to say "sev-en" as you point to the "two" part of 7.
 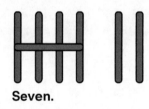 Seven. Seven. 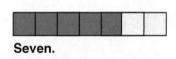 Seven.	As this point, 7 must be shown as 5 on the left hand and 2 on the right, not, for example, as 4 on one hand and 3 on the other.
Above and below. To help the child understand the words *above* and *below*, ask the child is your nose above or below your mouth. Ask: Is your chin above or below your eyes? Repeat with different parts of the face using the words above or below.	The terms *above, below, top,* and *bottom* are part of the spatial terms a child needs to know.
Now have the child show you something under the table or desk. Ask him to name something above his head.	
Top and bottom. Point out examples of *top* and *bottom*, such as "Where is the *top* of the window" and "Where is the *bottom* of the window." Repeat for the top and bottom of a page in a book.	
AL Abacus. Show the child the AL Abacus. Help him learn to handle it with respect, as due any tool. You might give him a few minutes to make patterns and designs.	

| **ACTIVITIES FOR TEACHING CONTINUED:** | **EXPLANATIONS CONTINUED:** |

ACTIVITIES FOR TEACHING CONTINUED:

Entering quantities. Show him how to place the abacus with the circle logo at the top. This means the circle will be on the right and the wires horizontal. Demonstrate clearing the abacus by lifting the left edge so the beads fall toward the side with the circle. See the figure below.

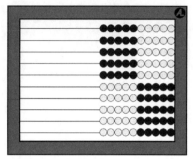

Abacus cleared.

Ask the child to clear the abacus. Ask him to show 2 with his fingers. Ask him to enter 2 on the top wire. See the figures below.

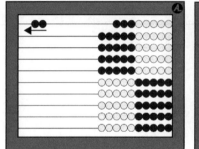 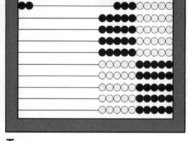

Entering 2 as a unit.   **Two.**

Ask him to clear the abacus. Then ask him to show 3 with fingers and enter 3 on the abacus. Repeat for 5 and ask how he could tell it was 5. [a whole hand, all the dark colored beads on a wire] Lastly, ask him to show 4 and enter 4.

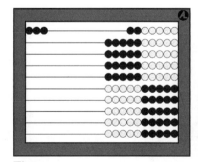 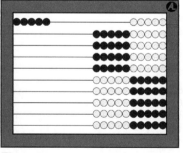

Three.   **Five.**

In conclusion. Show 5 on your fingers and ask: How much is this? [5] Repeat for 7.

EXPLANATIONS CONTINUED:

To enter a quantity on the AL Abacus, move the beads from right to left. This allows the eyes to travel from left to right as in reading.

Quantities are entered on the abacus as a group; they are not counted. If a child counts when entering a quantity, simply say: Okay, now can you enter (3) without counting.

LESSON 9: SUBITIZING 8 AND ORDINAL COUNTING

OBJECTIVES:
1. To subitize 8
2. To use comparison words correctly
3. To introduce ordinal counting

MATERIALS:
1. *Yellow is the Sun* book
2. Tally sticks and Tiles
3. AL Abacus
4. Strips for sorting, cut apart (Appendix p. 3)
5. **A variety of books** & **three different toys**
6. *Math Card Games* book, N4

ACTIVITIES FOR TEACHING:	EXPLANATIONS:
Warm-up. Continue reading the book and singing the song, "Yellow is the Sun."	
Randomly show quantities 1 to 7 on your fingers for 1 to 2 seconds and ask the child to name the quantity.	
Say any number from 1 to 7 and ask the child to show it on her fingers.	
Quantity 8. Show 8 on your fingers and tell her that is 8. Ask her to make 8 with her fingers. Now ask her to make it with the tally sticks. Also ask her to make 8 with the tiles using two colors. See the figures below.	Eight is often the most difficult quantity to subitize.

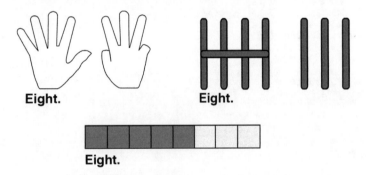

Eight.   Eight.

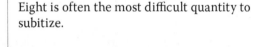

Eight.

Quantities on the abacus. Ask the child to enter on the abacus various quantities from 1 to 7. Then ask her to enter 8. See the figure below.

It is very important that the child enter and read quantities on the abacus without any counting.

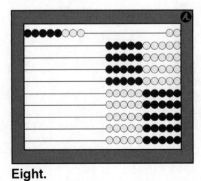

Eight.

Enter various quantities from 1 to 8 and ask her to state the quantity.

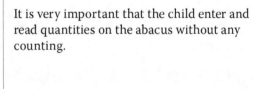

ACTIVITIES FOR TEACHING CONTINUED:	EXPLANATIONS CONTINUED:

Comparison words. Show the child two of the cut out strips of different lengths. See the left figure below. Say: When we talk about two pieces, we say which strip is *longer*. Add a third strip and tell her that when there are three things, we say which piece is *longest*.

Note: There is a duplicate strip that is not needed.

These strips will be used again in a later lessons.

A common error in spoken English is using "longest" when comparing two lengths.

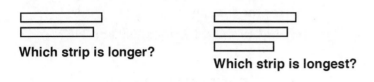

Which strip is longer?

Which strip is longest?

Show her two books and ask: Which of these two books is *thicker*? Pick up a third book and say: Which of these three books is . . . ? [thickest]

Next choose three books, one obviously older than the others. Ask: How could you ask about the books being old? [Which book is oldest?] Set one of the newer books aside and repeat the question? [Which book is older?]

Ordinal counting. This activity can be used for a child to learn to incorporate learning with playing. Ask the child to put 3 toys in a row. Ask the child which toy is first. Which toy is second? Encourage the child to rearrange the toys and to ask similar questions, for example: What position is the ball in?

Ordinal counting is familiar to most children. It has an additional value in beginning mathematics because of the sounds "thir" and "fif," which we need in English to pronounce thirteen, thirty, one-third, as well as fifteen, fifty, and one-fifth.

Finger Card Memory. Play the Finger Card Memory game from the *Math Card Games* book, N4.

In conclusion. Show 8 on your fingers and ask: How much is this? [8] Ask her to show 8.

The first toy should be the one on the child's left because we read from left to right.

LESSON 10: ORDERING

OBJECTIVES:
1. To learn the term *beside*
2. To order by length

MATERIALS:
1. *Yellow is the Sun* book
2. Tally sticks
3. AL Abacus
4. Strips for sorting
5. *Math Card Games* book, N2 and N6

ACTIVITIES FOR TEACHING:	EXPLANATIONS:
Warm-up. Continue reading the book and singing the song, "Yellow is the Sun."	

Warm-up. Continue reading the book and singing the song, "Yellow is the Sun."

Randomly say a quantity from 1 to 8, then ask the child to show the quantity with his fingers and with the tally sticks.

Ask the child to enter various quantities from 1 to 8 on the abacus.

Next ask the child to put 5 beads on the first wire of the abacus. Then ask him to put 8 beads on the 2nd wire. See the left figure below. Ask: Which row is longer? [second] Which row is shorter? [first]

It is very important that the child enter and read quantities on the abacus without any counting.

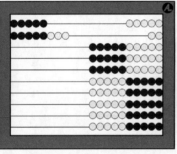 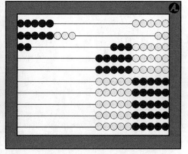

Which row is longer?   **Which row is longest?**

Now have the child enter 2 on the third line. Ask: Now which row is the longest? [second] Which row is the shortest? [third]

The term beside. Sit next to the child and tell him you are sitting *beside* him. Tell him to stand beside the table. Now recite the nursery rhyme Little Miss Muffet; tell him to sit down when he hears *beside*.

Little Miss Muffet and her spider can be seen at Storybook Land in Aberdeen, South Dakota.

ACTIVITIES FOR TEACHING CONTINUED:	EXPLANATIONS CONTINUED:

Little Miss Muffet

Little Miss Muffet sat on a tuffet,
Eating her curds and whey.
Along came a spider who sat down beside her
And frightened Miss Muffet away.

Ordering. Lay out the ten strips with no overlapping. Explain to him that we want to put the strips in order, starting with the longest.

Putting objects in order is an everyday skill, as well as a mathematical skill.

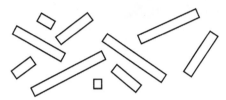

The strips in random order.

Show him how to find the longest; pick up a strip that appears to be the longest and compare it to other long strips. If a longer strip is found, pick it up and lay the other one down.

Lay the longest strip off to the side. Repeat the process, each time choosing the longest of those remaining. It does not matter for the ordering procedure whether the longest is on top or bottom. Ask the child to continue until all are sorted.

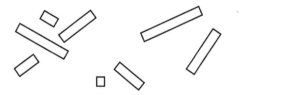

The strips with the two longest in order.

Ask the child to mix up the strips and put them in order again, now starting with the shortest.

Ordering games. Play the Finger Cards in Order game, in the *Math Card Games* book, *N2.* Also play the Tally Cards in Order game, N6.

In conclusion. Show 7 on your fingers and ask: How much is this? [7] Ask him to show 7 on the abacus. Repeat with 8.

LESSON 11: SUBITIZING 9 AND TALLY MARKS

OBJECTIVES:
1. To subitize 9
2. To write tally marks for 1 to 5

MATERIALS:
1. *Yellow is the Sun* book
2. Finger cards
3. Tally sticks
4. AL Abacus
5. Tiles
6. Dry erase board and marker

ACTIVITIES FOR TEACHING:	EXPLANATIONS:
Warm-up. Start by reading the book and singing the song "Yellow is the Sun."	
Show the finger cards 1 to 8 at random for 2 seconds and ask the child to name them and to show them on her fingers. Also show the number with tally sticks.	
Say various numbers from 1–8 and ask her to enter them on the abacus.	
Place 3 different color tiles in a row. Ask the child which color is first in line. Now ask: What color is third? What color is second?	The first tile should be considered as the one on the child's left.
Ask her to make 8 with her fingers. Now ask her to make it with the tally sticks. Also ask her to make 8 with the tiles using two colors. See the figures below.	

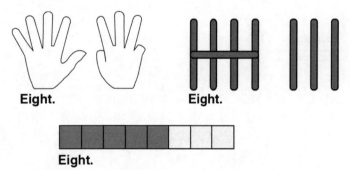

Eight.   **Eight.**

Eight.

Quantity 9. Ask her to make 9 with her fingers and with tally sticks. Also ask her to make 9 with the tiles, using two colors. See the figures below.

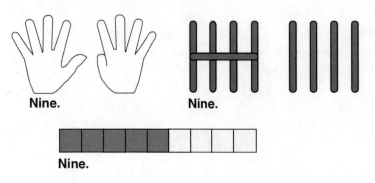

Nine.   **Nine.**

Nine.

ACTIVITIES FOR TEACHING CONTINUED:	EXPLANATIONS CONTINUED:

Ask her to enter 9 on the abacus. It must be entered as a unit.

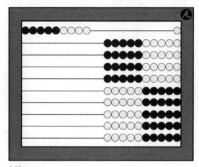

Nine.

Writing tally marks 1 to 5. Ask the child to show 2 with the tally sticks. Then show her how to write the tally marks on the dry erase board, starting at the top and going down. Recall that starting at the top is the correct form for writing any numeral.

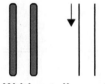

Writing tally marks for 2. Write from top to bottom.

Ask if she could write tally marks for 4. Also ask her to write tally marks for 5. You might want the child to draw from 1 to 5 objects and to write the corresponding tally marks near it.

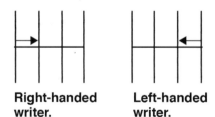

Right-handed writer.	**Left-handed writer.**

Drawing the horizontal line.

In conclusion. Show 9 on your fingers and ask: How much is this? [9] Repeat for 8.

A dry erase board is easier to write on than paper. Therefore, any child experiencing difficulty writing should use a dry erase board and marker.

This is a good time to emphasize how to hold the writing instrument correctly. The thumb and first two fingers grasp the instrument much in the same way as one would grasp a knob that is about 3/8 in. (1 cm) in diameter.

Unfortunately, many children develop bad habits before reaching school age that are difficult or impossible to remedy. The child must want to change; too much intervention can be detrimental.

To emphasize a relaxed hold, tell the child that they should not see any wrinkles on their thumb or finger. Demonstrate various holds, both correct and incorrect, and ask if they are correct.

For drawing the horizontal fifth line, a right-handed child will find it easier to go from left to right while left-handed should write from right to left. If she chooses to use diagonal lines, rather than horizontal lines, that is fine.

LESSON 12: PARALLEL LINES, PLANES, AND MAKING TRIANGLES

OBJECTIVES:
1. To learn the term *parallel*
2. To construct triangles on the geoboard
3. To learn the term *triangle*

MATERIALS:
1. Finger cards and Tiles
2. AL Abacus
3. **Two pencils of unequal length**
4. **Two thin hardcover books or flat objects**
5. Geoboards and rubber bands
6. *Math Card Games* book, N4 and N2

ACTIVITIES FOR TEACHING:	EXPLANATIONS:
Warm-up. Start by singing the song "Yellow is the Sun."	

Warm-up. Start by singing the song "Yellow is the Sun."

Show the finger cards 1 to 9 at random for 2 seconds and ask the child to name them and to show them on his fingers.

Say various numbers from 1–9 and ask him to enter them on the abacus.

Place 3 different color tiles in a row. Ask the child which color is first in line. Now ask: What color is third? What color is second?

Parallel. Using two pencils of unequal lengths, demonstrate a variety of *parallel* lines, as shown below. Tell the child these lines are parallel. Also show him parallel planes and tell him they are parallel planes.

Lines and planes that are parallel.

Sometimes, people think of parallel lines as being the same length, but that is not necessary.

Examples, not definitions, often make it easier for children to learn a concept.

Then hold the them in nonparallel positions and say that these are not parallel.

Lines and planes that are *not* parallel.

Ask the child to find parallel lines and planes in the room or outside.

ACTIVITIES FOR TEACHING CONTINUED:	EXPLANATIONS CONTINUED:

Making triangles. Give the child a geoboard and some rubber bands. Demonstrate making a triangle by looping the rubber band around three pegs that are not in a row. See the figures below. After he has made several triangles, ask: How many sides does each figure have? [3] Tell him they are _triangles_.

Triangles

Finger Card Memory game. Play the Finger Card Memory game found in the _Math Card Games_ book, N4.

Finger Cards in Order game. Play the Finger Cards in Order game in the _Math Card Games_ book, N2.

In conclusion. Have the child show 5 with his fingers. Ask him to point to his finger that is in the middle.

LESSON 13: SUBITIZING 10 AND QUADRILATERALS

OBJECTIVES:

1. To subitize 10
2. To construct quadrilaterals
3. To learn the term *quadrilateral*

MATERIALS:

1. Music for "Writing Numbers" (Appendix p. 4)
2. AL Abacus
3. Tally sticks
4. Tiles
5. Geoboards
6. *Math Card Games* book, N6

ACTIVITIES FOR TEACHING:

Warm-up. Continue singing the song, "Yellow is the Sun."

Introduce the song "Writing Numbers."

Writing Numbers

Before you write a number, stop (Freeze.)
And take a hop to the top. (Raise writing arm.)

Start at the left to make 2, 3, or 4, (Move arm to the left; pump air at 2, 3, 4.)

Also 7, which you can't ignore. (Pump air at 7.)

Start at the right for 5, 6, 8, or 9. (Move arm to the right; pump air at 5, 6, 8, 9.)

Don't lift your pen and you'll do just fine.

Zero and one—not left, not right—a riddle:
They begin at the top, smack in the middle. (Move arm to the middle.)

Joan A. Cotter

Ask her if she found any parallel lines yesterday.

Enter quantities 1–9 on the abacus and ask the child to quickly identify them. Also ask her to enter quantities you name.

Quantity 10. Show her 10 on your hands; ask her to show it on hers. Ask: Why is 10 so special with fingers? [all of them, two 5s] Ask if she thinks she could build 10 with the tally sticks. Ask: What does it looks like? [two 5s] Ask her to make it with the tiles. See the figures below.

EXPLANATIONS:

It is very important that a child learn to write numbers clearly and efficiently. In standard fonts, a 9 is an inverted 6, which is confusing for many children, especially those with dyslexia. The numerals used in Level A are designed to be easy to learn to write and read.

It is important to use the numerals in this manual, and not those in a writing/reading program. This way, the child's numbers will match the worksheets, basic number cards, and place-value cards.

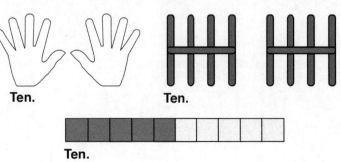

Ten.　　　Ten.

Ten.

| ACTIVITIES FOR TEACHING CONTINUED: | EXPLANATIONS CONTINUED: |

ACTIVITIES FOR TEACHING CONTINUED:

Enter 10 on the abacus and ask: Why is 10 so special on the abacus? [whole row of beads, two 5s] See the figure below.

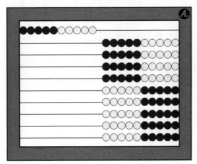

Ten.

Say various numbers from 1–10 for the child to enter on the abacus.

Making quadrilaterals. Give the child a geoboard and some rubber bands. Demonstrate making a quadrilateral by looping the rubber band around 4 pegs that are not in a row. See the figures below.

Quadrilaterals shapes on the geoboards.

After she has made several quadrilaterals, ask: How many sides does each figure have? [4] Tell her they are called *quadrilaterals.*

Tally Cards in Order game. Play Tally Cards in Order game found in the *Math Card Games* book, N6.

In conclusion. Ask the child to show 10 on her fingers. Then ask her to show 9.

EXPLANATIONS CONTINUED:

Be sure the ten is entered as one unit.

The word *quadrilateral* comes from "quad" meaning four and "lateral" meaning side.

Putting objects in order is an everyday skill, as well as a mathematical skill.

LESSON 14: AL ABACUS STAIRS

OBJECTIVES:

1. To build the stairs on the abacus
2. To review the terms *top, bottom, above, below, beside, up,* and *down*

MATERIALS:

1. Finger cards
2. AL Abacus
3. Strips for sorting
4. *Math Card Games* book, N2

ACTIVITIES FOR TEACHING:

Warm-up. Sing "Yellow is the Sun." Then sing "Writing Numbers."

Flash various finger cards 1–10 for 2 seconds, asking the child to identify the quantity.

As a physical activity, have the child jump the same number of times as the number you say from 1 to 5.

I Spy game. This game needs two or more players. Look around the room to find something visible by all players. One player says "I spy with my little eye" and gives a description of an object using the words *top, bottom, above, below, beside, up,* and *down*. Then the person guessing the object takes a turn.

The Abacus song. Give the child an abacus. Sing the following song using the tune of the Hokey Pokey. While singing the song, have the child show the number on the abacus.

The Abacus Song

The one steps in.
The one steps out.
He holds up the number.
And waves it all about.
He clears the number.
And sits back down.
Where is the number two?

The two steps in.
The two steps out . . . .

Continue to 10.

EXPLANATIONS:

You might want to sing the songs while getting the math materials out. This helps the child mentally prepare for math.

This song reminds child that every numeral is written starting at the top. It also teaches which numerals start at the left (2, 3, 4, 7), which start at the right (5, 6, 8. 9), and which start in the middle (0, 9), preventing reversals.

It is also interesting that the numerals that are easier to write start at the left while the harder numerals start at the right.

| ACTIVITIES FOR TEACHING CONTINUED: | EXPLANATIONS CONTINUED: |

ACTIVITIES FOR TEACHING CONTINUED:

Stairs with the strips. Tell the child to put the strips in order with the shortest on top and the longest at the bottom.

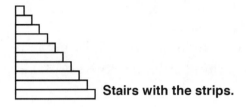

Stairs with the strips.

Ask: Does it look like stairs? Keep it in view while he does the next activity.

Stairs on the abacus. Ask the child to enter 1 on the first wire, 2 on the next wire, and 3 on the next wire. Ask him to continue to 10. See the figure below.

Ask him to name the number of beads from top to bottom. [1, 2, 3, . . . , 10] Ask: How much is on the top wire? [1] How much is on the bottom wire? [10]

Then ask: What does it look like? [stairs] Do you think the two stairs look alike?

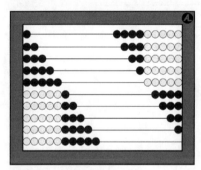

Stairs on the abacus.

Finger Cards in Order game. Play the Finger Cards in Order game as found in the *Math Card Games* book, N2.

In conclusion. Ask the child to show 8 on his fingers. Then ask him to show 9.

EXPLANATIONS CONTINUED:

If a child has difficulty building the stairs on the abacus, try this approach: Ask the child to enter 1, then to copy it onto the next wire and enter one more bead. Continue by copying the last quantity to the next wire and adding one more bead.

LESSON 15: AL ABACUS STAIRS AND PERPENDICULAR

OBJECTIVES:
1. To build the stairs on the abacus
2. To learn the term *perpendicular*

MATERIALS:
1. Finger cards
2. Strips for sorting
3. AL Abacus
4. **Two pencils of different lengths**
5. **Two thin hardcover books or flat objects**
6. *Math Card Games* book, N4

ACTIVITIES FOR TEACHING:	EXPLANATIONS:
Warm-up. Sing "Yellow is the Sun." Then sing "Writing Numbers."	

Warm-up. Sing "Yellow is the Sun." Then sing "Writing Numbers."

Flash various finger cards 1–10 for 2 seconds, asking the child to identify the quantity.

Have the child clap the same number of times as the number you say from 1 to 5.

I Spy game. Play the I Spy game from the previous lesson, using the words top, bottom, above, below, beside, up, and down.

Stairs with the strips. Tell the child to put the strips in order with the shortest on top and the longest at the bottom. Ask: Does it look like stairs? Keep it in view while she does the next activity.

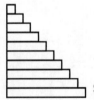
Stairs with the strips.

Stairs on the abacus. Ask the child to enter 1 on the first wire, 2 on the next wire, and 3 on the next wire. Ask her to continue to 10. See the figure below. Then ask: What does it look like? [stairs] Do you think the two stairs look alike?

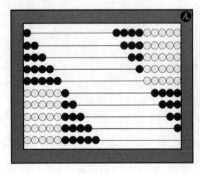
Stairs on the abacus.

Ask her to name the number of beads from top to bottom. [1, 2, 3, . . . , 10] Ask: How much is on the top wire? [1] How much is on the bottom wire? [10]

| ACTIVITIES FOR TEACHING CONTINUED: | EXPLANATIONS CONTINUED: |

Perpendicular. Using two pencils of unequal lengths, demonstrate a variety of *perpendicular* lines, as shown below. Tell the child these lines are perpendicular. Also show her perpendicular planes and tell her they are perpendicular planes.

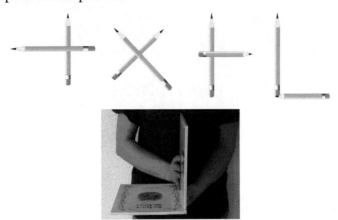

Lines and planes that are perpendicular.

Then hold them in non-perpendicular positions and tell the child they are not perpendicular.

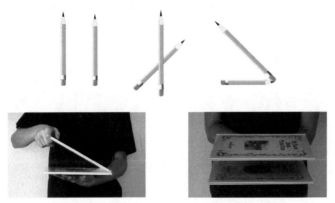

Lines and planes that are not perpendicular.

Finger Card Memory game. Play the Finger Card Memory game found in the *Math Card Games* book, N4.

In conclusion. Ask the child to find perpendicular lines and planes in the room or in nature.

LESSON 16: COMES AFTER GAME, RECTANGLES AND SQUARES

OBJECTIVES:

1. To explore what comes after a number
2. To learn the term *rectangle* as a special *quadrilateral*
3. To identify a *square* as a special rectangle

MATERIALS:

1. AL Abacus
2. Rectangles, cut apart (Appendix p. 5)
3. Worksheet 1, Patterning with Rectangles
4. **Glue**

ACTIVITIES FOR TEACHING:

Warm-up. Sing with the child "Yellow is the Sun" and "Writing Numbers" with the motions.

Writing Numbers

Before you write a number, stop (Freeze.)
And take a hop to the top. (Raise writing arm.)

Start at the left to make 2, 3, or 4, (Move arm to the left; pump air at 2, 3, 4.)

Also 7, which you can't ignore. (Pump air at 7.)

Start at the right for 5, 6, 8, or 9. (Move arm to the right; pump air at 5, 6, 8, 9.)

Don't lift your pen and you'll do just fine.

Zero and one—not left, not right—a riddle:
They begin at the top, smack in the middle. (Move arm to the middle.)

Joan A. Cotter

Flash various quantities 1–10 for 2 seconds, using fingers, or the abacus, asking the child to identify the quantity.

Ask if he has found any perpendicular lines and planes since the last lesson.

Comes After game. Explain that you will say a number and the child will show it with his fingers. Then he adds, or raises, 1 more finger and says the new number. For example, say 2 and he shows 2, add 1 more and say 3. Repeat for numbers 1–9 in random order.

Identifying rectangles. Show the largest two rectangles and say: These are *rectangles*. Ask: Could they also be quadrilaterals? [yes] Then ask: Do they have parallel lines? [yes] Perpendicular lines? [yes] Say: So rectangles are special quadrilaterals.

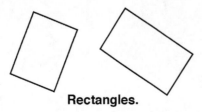

Rectangles.

EXPLANATIONS:

ACTIVITIES FOR TEACHING CONTINUED:

EXPLANATIONS CONTINUED:

Rectangle patterns. Give the child a set of the rectangles. Ask him to put them in some kind of order or pattern. Repeat several times with other orders and patterns.

Possible patterns with a set of the five rectangles.

Squares. After he has worked with the patterns for a while, ask: How many rectangles do you have in a particular pattern? [5] Say: I see something special about one of them. Do you know what it is? [One has all sides the same.] Tell him that special rectangle is also a *square*.

Worksheet 1. Explain to the child that he can paste his favorite pattern on paper. He is to cut out the five rectangles on the right side of the worksheet, and paste the pattern on the left side.

In conclusion. Hold up the large rectangle, ask if this is a square, [no] a rectangle, [yes] a quadrilateral. [yes] Hold up the square and ask the same questions. [yes, yes, yes]

Many people are confused about rectangles. The mathematical definition of a rectangle is a four-sided figure with four right angles and opposite sides equal. Notice this definition also fits a square, which can be described as a special rectangle.

LESSON 17: DAYS OF THE WEEK AND WRITING TALLY MARKS

OBJECTIVES:

1. To begin learning the days of the week
2. To name quantities in order
3. To write tally marks to indicate quantities

MATERIALS:

1. Tally sticks
2. AL Abacus
3. **A calendar showing a full month**
4. Tiles
5. Dry erase board
6. Worksheet 2, Writing Tally Marks

ACTIVITIES FOR TEACHING:	EXPLANATIONS:

ACTIVITIES FOR TEACHING:

Warm-up. Sing with the child "Yellow is the Sun" and "Writing Number" with the motions.

EXPLANATIONS:

Keep in mind that singing the songs while getting the math materials out helps the child mentally prepare for math.

Writing Numbers

Before you write a number, stop (Freeze.)
And take a hop to the top. (Raise writing arm.)

Start at the left to make 2, 3, or 4, (Move arm to the left; pump air at 2, 3, 4.)

Also 7, which you can't ignore. (Pump air at 7.)

Start at the right for 5, 6, 8, or 9. (Move arm to the right; pump air at 5, 6, 8, 9.)

Don't lift your pen and you'll do just fine.

Zero and one—not left, not right—a riddle:
They begin at the top, smack in the middle. (Move arm to the middle.)

Joan A. Cotter

Play the Comes After game with tally sticks. Say a number and ask the child to show it with tally sticks. Then add 1 more stick and say the new number. For example, say 3 and she makes 3, add 1 more and say 4. Repeat for numbers 1–9 in random order.

The Abacus song. Give the child an abacus. Sing the following song using the tune of the Hokey Pokey. While singing the song, have the child show the number on the abacus.

The Abacus Song

The one steps in.
The one steps out.
He holds up the number.
And waves it all about.
He clears the number.
And sits back down.
Where is the number two?

The two steps in.
The two steps out . . . .

Continue to 10.

ACTIVITIES FOR TEACHING CONTINUED:	EXPLANATIONS CONTINUED:

ACTIVITIES FOR TEACHING CONTINUED:

Days of the week. Use a large calendar and point to each column as you say the days of the week. Then using the tune of "Twinkle, Twinkle Little Star," sing the days of the week with these words:

Days of the Week

Sunday, Monday, Tuesday, too.
Wednesday, Thursday—this I knew.
Friday, Saturday that's the end.
Now let's say those days again!
Sunday, Monday, Tuesday, Wednesday, Thursday,
Friday, Saturday!

Naming quantities in order. Ask the child to build the stairs on the abacus. Then say: Start at the top, point to each wire and name the number of beads. [1, 2, . . . , 10]

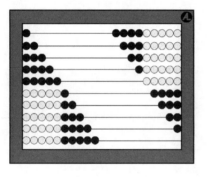

Stairs on the AL Abacus.

Finding the quantity. Using the abacus stairs ask: Can you find the wire that has 5? Repeat for other numbers.

Writing tally marks. Lay out 3 tiles and ask the child to make that number with the tally sticks. Repeat for 6 and 4. Now lay out 2 tiles and ask the child to write that number of tally marks on the dry erase board. Repeat for 5 and 8.

Worksheet 2. Ask the child to name how many (without counting) objects are in each box. Encourage her to work from left to right and top to bottom.

Then tell her to write the tally marks to show how many in each rectangle. Some children might need to construct the quantity with tally sticks before writing them. The solutions are:

IIII	III
HHI	HHI I
HHI HHI	HHI III
HHI II	HHI IIII

In conclusion. Hold up one finger. Have the child name the quantity? [1] Add a second finger. Have the child name the quantity? [2] Continue to 10.

EXPLANATIONS CONTINUED:

Pointing to the corresponding columns will help the child realize the individual words. She will begin to associate each day with a position in the week. For example, Wednesday is the middle day of the week. Ignore the numbers.

It is extremely important that child have access to the entire month. Do not build the month a day at a time.

Notice in this activity that the child is reciting the counting sequence meaningfully.

Be sure the child writes the tally sticks starting at the top.

LESSON 18: MAKING GEOMETRIC FIGURES

OBJECTIVES:

1. To build rectangles, squares, and triangles on geoboards
2. To draw rectangles, squares, and triangles on paper

MATERIALS:

1. Tiles
2. Tally sticks
3. **A freestanding folder**
4. Geoboards
5. Worksheet 3, Geoboard Paper

ACTIVITIES FOR TEACHING:

Warm-up. Sing with the child "Yellow is the Sun," "Days of the Week," and "Writing Numbers."

Play the Comes After game using tiles in two colors. Say a number from 1–10. Ask the child to make them with the tiles using one color for the first 5 and the other color for the second 5, when needed. Then ask him to add 1 more tile and say the new number. For example, say 5 and he makes 5, adds 1 more and he says 6. Repeat for numbers 1–9 in random order.

Guess my number. Construct 4 with the tally sticks. Then place the screen between the tally sticks and the child. Show him that you are adding 1 more stick behind the screen. Ask: How many sticks are hidden? [5] Remove the folder and let him see.

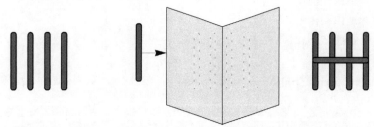

Start with 4 tally sticks. Add 1 more stick behind a screen and ask the child to name the new number.

Repeat by adding 1 more. [6] Continue by adding or removing 1 stick at a time.

Geoboard Rectangle game. Make a rectangle as follows. Start with a rubber-band line anywhere on the geoboard. Ask the child to make another rubber-band line that is perpendicular to your line. His line must start at either end of your line. Next add the third line of the rectangle starting at the end of his line. Ask him to add the last rubber band to complete the rectangle. See the figures at the top of the next page.

EXPLANATIONS:

The person making the first line has many choices, direction and length. The person making the second line has fewer choices. The persons making the last two lines have no choices.

ACTIVITIES FOR TEACHING CONTINUED:

EXPLANATIONS CONTINUED:

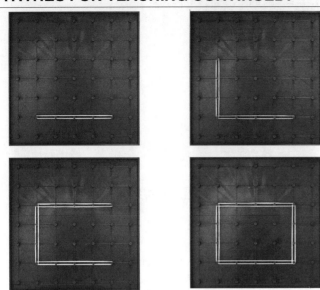

Constructing a rectangle with rubber bands representing the sides.

Repeat the activity but ask the child to make the first line.

Repeat once more: Make the first line and ask him to make the second line so the figure will be a square.

Geoboard Triangle game. Start by asking the child to make the first line of the geoboard triangle. Then you make the second line–not perpendicular. Ask him to make the last line.

Start another triangle, but this time ask him to make his line perpendicular to your line, then complete the triangle. Start a third triangle with one line, then ask: Can you make a triangle with parallel lines? [no] Complete the triangle.

Worksheet 3. The child can make geoboard figures and copy them onto the worksheet. He may also draw them directly on the worksheet. Suggest he make different kinds of triangles, quadrilaterals, including rectangles and squares.

In conclusion. Ask: How many sides are in a rectangle? [4] How many sides are in a triangle? [3]

LESSON 19: MAKING RECTANGLES WITH TILES

OBJECTIVES:

1. To learn the terms *in front of,* and *behind*
2. To make patterns with tiles
3. To build squares and rectangles with tiles

MATERIALS:

1. AL Abacus
2. Tiles

ACTIVITIES FOR TEACHING:	EXPLANATIONS:
Warm-up. Sing with the child "Yellow is the Sun," "Days of the Week," and "Writing Numbers."	
Say a number from 1–10 and ask the child to enter it on the abacus as fast as she can.	If the child needs more practice; spend more time on this activity and/or review it more often with her.
Play the Comes After game using the abacus. Ask the child to enter 5. Then ask: How many will there be if you add 1 more? [6] Ask her to enter 1 more and see if she was right. See the figure below. Repeat for other numbers 1–9 in no particular order.	

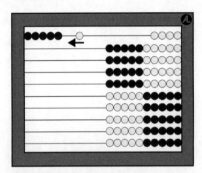

Entering 5 and 1 more.

Terms in front of and behind. While standing with the child, ask the child to stand in front of you. Ask the child to stand behind you.	The terms *above, below, top, bottom, in front of,* and *behind* are part of the spatial terms a child needs to know.
Play the "I Spy" game emphasizing the new words, *in front of* and *behind,* along with the previous words, *top, bottom, above, below, beside, up* and *down.*	
More patterns. Ask the child to make up her own patterns with the tiles. Also ask her to name them. Some possibilities include: do-do-re-re or do-re-mi-re.	

ACTIVITIES FOR TEACHING CONTINUED:	EXPLANATIONS CONTINUED:

Making squares. Show the child one of the tiles. Ask: What shape is this? [square, rectangle, and quadrilateral] Ask for other names until she gives all three. Ask her take 4 tiles and to make a square. See the left figure below.

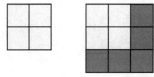

Squares made from the tiles.

Now ask her to make a larger square with the tiles. [3 × 3] See the right figure above. If she is interested, she could use more tiles and make an even larger square. [4 × 4]

Other rectangles. Ask her to make a rectangle using only 6 tiles. Then ask her to use 6 more tiles of a different color and make a different rectangle.

A 2 × 3 and a 3 × 2 rectangle are considered the same rectangle, only rotated.

Two different rectangles made with 6 tiles.

Next ask her to combine the tiles from the last rectangles and make a rectangle using all 12 tiles. Then ask her to make other rectangles. (3 are possible; see figures below.)

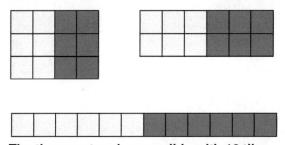

The three rectangles possible with 12 tiles.

In conclusion. Have the child put her hands behind her head and show 5. Then put her hands in front of her head and show what comes after 5. [6]

LESSON 20: WRITING 1 AND 7 & COMBINING TALLY STICKS

OBJECTIVES:

1. To learn to write the numerals 1 and 7
2. To combine two groups of tally sticks

MATERIALS:

1. AL Abacus
2. *Yellow is the Sun* book
3. Tally sticks
4. Worksheet 4, Combining Tally Sticks
5. *Math Card Games* book, N18

ACTIVITIES FOR TEACHING:	EXPLANATIONS:

Warm-up. Sing with the child "Yellow is the Sun," "Days of the Week," and "Writing Numbers."

Ask the child to construct the stairs on the abacus. Then ask him to point to each wire in turn and name the quantity. [1, 2, 3, . . . , 10] Next point to the quantities on the *right* side, starting at the bottom and ask him to name how many on each wire as you proceed toward the top. [1, 2, 3, . . . , 9] Ask him to find both 5s, both 2s, and so forth.

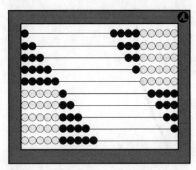

Stairs.

Writing 1. Show the child the "1" page in the *Yellow is the Sun* book. Ask him to practice writing 1s on a flat surface with the first two fingers of his writing hand. If necessary, remind him where to start. [Before you write a number, stop and take a hop to the top.]

Writing 1: straight down.

Writing 7. Next show him the "7" page in the *Yellow is the Sun* book; point out that 7 has two straight lines. Demonstrate writing it while saying, "over, and down," pausing briefly before starting the line going down. Ask the child to practice on a flat surface.

In writing numerals the brief pause between writing different lines is important to prevent rounded corners.

Writing 7: over and down.

| ACTIVITIES FOR TEACHING CONTINUED: | EXPLANATIONS CONTINUED: |

ACTIVITIES FOR TEACHING CONTINUED:

Combining 3 and 2 with tally sticks. Tell the child you will make 3 with the tally sticks and you want him to make 2 with the tally sticks. Then ask him to combine them together and see how much it is. Ask him to describe how he found his answer. Emphasize non-counting strategies.

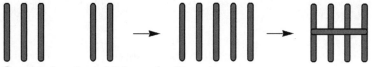

Combining 3 and 2 to make 5.

Combining 4 and 3. Next ask him to make 4 and you will make 3. Again ask him to combine them and find out how many he has. A good strategy to emphasize is taking a stick from the 3 and using it to make the 4 into 5.

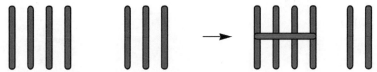

Combining 4 and 3 to make 7.

Combining 4 and 5. As a last example, ask him to combine 4 and 5. Here he could see the answer 9 by reading it backwards, as 5 and 4, or he could remove the crossbar from the 5 and place it on the 4.

Worksheet 4. On this worksheet the child builds the groups with the tally sticks. Then he combines them, organizes them, and writes down the result as tally marks. The problems and solutions are shown below.

2 & 2 gives ||||	5 & 1 gives 卌 |
1 & 4 gives 卌	3 & 3 gives 卌 |
4 & 2 gives 卌 |	2 & 3 gives 卌
3 & 4 gives 卌 ||	4 & 4 gives 卌 |||

More War game. Play the More War game found in the *Math Card Games* book, N18.

In conclusion. Ask the child to show how to write 1 and 7 with his fingers on the flat surface. Enter random quantities on the abacus and have the child name the quantity.

EXPLANATIONS CONTINUED:

✱ Practice this again ✱

Be sure the child does the worksheet independently. The worksheet checks understanding.

LESSON 21: PRESENTING 2s & EVENS AND ODDS

OBJECTIVES:
1. To arrange objects by 2s
2. To learn the terms *even* and *odd*

MATERIALS:
1. AL Abacus
2. Dot cards, cut apart (Appendix p. 6)
3. Tiles

ACTIVITIES FOR TEACHING:	EXPLANATIONS:
Warm-up. Sing with the child "Yellow is the Sun," "Days of the Week," and "Writing Numbers."	
Ask the child to build the stairs on the abacus. Then ask the child to name the quantities from top to bottom. Repeat naming the quantities on the right side of the abacus, starting at the bottom. Point to any quantity on either side of the abacus and ask for the number.	It is vitally important for the child to be able to enter and identify any quantity 1–10 without counting on the abacus before addition is started.
Even. Tell the child: Today we will make new patterns with the tiles. Show the dot card for 4 and ask her to make it with the tiles.	
Then ask the child to watch carefully. With your first two fingers, slowly and deliberately touch both tiles simultaneously in the first row. Then raise your fingers and deliberately touch both tiles in the second row. Ask the child to feel the tiles in the same way. Then say: This is an *even* number.	When learning a concept with only two possibilities, such as even and odd, it is easier to learn if one of them is emphasized and the other as not the first. Here we will emphasize *even*.
Next show her the dot card for 6. Again ask her to copy it with the tiles and to feel the groups of twos. Repeat: This is an *even* number.	Even the word *even* with its two syllables helps give the idea of "twoness."

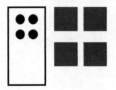

A dot card and tiles showing an *even* number.

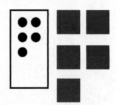

A dot card and tiles showing an *odd* number.

Odd. Now show her the dot card for 5 and ask her to make it with the tiles. Ask her to touch them as before. Ask her if it felt different. [Yes, one finger didn't have a tile for the last row.] Say: This number is *odd*.	The word *even* has an even number of letters and the word odd has an *odd* number.
Ask the child to take 9 tiles and arrange them in twos to find out whether 9 is even or odd. [odd]	

| ACTIVITIES FOR TEACHING CONTINUED: | EXPLANATIONS CONTINUED: |

Sorting the dot cards. Ask the child to sort the dot cards into two piles, the evens and the odds. Then ask: How many cards show even numbers? [5] How many cards show odd numbers? [5]

Entering 2s. Ask the child to enter 2 on the abacus and to say how much it is. [2] Ask the child to enter another 2 and say how much it is. [4] Continue to 10. Then ask her to do it again by herself. [2, 4, 6, 8, 10]

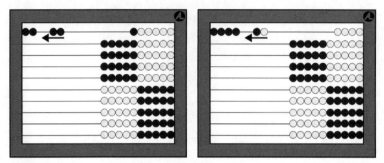

Adding 2s to make even numbers.

In conclusion. Ask the child to write 1 and 7 with her fingers on the a flat surface. Enter random quantities on the abacus, tell the child to name the quantity, and say if it is even or odd.

LESSON 22: ZERO AND EVENS ON THE AL ABACUS

OBJECTIVES:

1. To introduce zero
2. To learn to write the numeral 0
3. To enter quantities on the abacus grouped in twos

MATERIALS:

1. AL Abacus
2. Dry erase board
3. Dot cards

ACTIVITIES FOR TEACHING:	EXPLANATIONS:
Warm-up. Sing with the child "Yellow is the Sun," "Days of the Week," and "Writing Numbers."	

Warm-up. Sing with the child "Yellow is the Sun," "Days of the Week," and "Writing Numbers."

Play the Comes After game with Sunday through Friday.

Enter 2 on the abacus and ask the child to name the number—without counting. [2] Add 2 more and ask him to name the number. [4] Continue adding 2s to 10. [6, 8, 10]

Zero. Enter 2 on the abacus and ask: How many beads are entered? [2] Move a bead to the right and repeat: How many beads are entered? [1] Move the last bead to the right and say: Now there are *zero* beads entered.

Zero is a difficult concept. It took Europeans 900 years to fully accept it. Originally it was only a placeholder, not a symbol for none. We must be careful to help the child understand this dual role. Zero means nothing only when it stands alone.

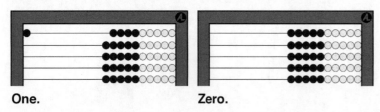

One.　　　　Zero.

Zero activity. With the child seated, ask him to raise his hand 2 times. Ask him to clap 4 times and then to tap his foot 1 time. Finally, ask him to jump up 0 times. Mildly insist that the child do so. Ask: Why don't you get up? [zero times means none]

Writing zero. Ask the child where to start when we write a 1. [in the middle] Ask him what other number starts in the middle? [zero] Review the last line of the song: Zero and one—not left, not right—a riddle. They begin at the top, smack in the middle.

Demonstrate writing 0 on the dry erase board. See the figure below. Ask him to practice with his fingers on a flat surface.

  Writing 0: Go around.

A right-handed child should draw counter clockwise. A left-handed child will find it easier to draw clockwise.

ACTIVITIES FOR TEACHING CONTINUED:	EXPLANATIONS CONTINUED:

Evens on the abacus. Point to the 4 dot card; say: Let's show this on the abacus. Enter 2 beads on the first wire and 2 more on the second wire. See below.

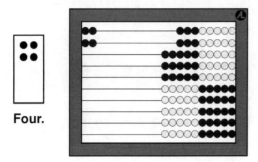

Four.

Show the 10 dot card. Ask: How much it is? [10] Ask him to enter it on the abacus so it looks the same as the card.

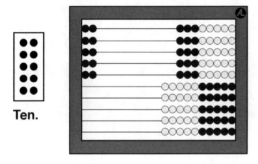

Ten.

In conclusion. Ask the child to draw a zero on a flat surface and to enter zero on the abacus. [nothing to enter]

LESSON 23: WRITING 4 AND TAKE AND GIVE

OBJECTIVES:

1. To learn to write the numeral 4
2. To learn the Take and Give procedure on the abacus

MATERIALS:

1. AL Abacus
2. *Yellow is the Sun* book
3. Dot cards

ACTIVITIES FOR TEACHING:	EXPLANATIONS:
Warm-up. Sing with the child "Yellow is the Sun," "Days of the Week," and "Writing Numbers."	

Warm-up. Sing with the child "Yellow is the Sun," "Days of the Week," and "Writing Numbers."

Play the Comes After game with Sunday through Friday.

Enter 2 on the abacus and ask the child to name the number—without counting. [2] Add 2 more and ask her to name the number. [4] Continue adding 2s to 10. [6, 8, 10]

The Abacus song. Sing the song to the tune of the Hokey Pokey, using the abacus to show the numbers.

The Abacus Song

The one steps in.
The one steps out.
He holds up the number.
And waves it all about.
He clears the number.
And sits back down.
Where is the number two?

The two steps in.
The two steps out. . . .

Writing 4. Ask the child to write the numbers 1 and 7 on a flat surface with her fingers. Challenge her by saying that writing 4 is harder. Ask her to find the "4" page in the *Yellow is the Sun* book; ask: How many lines does numeral 4 have? [3] Demonstrate writing it while saying: Down (pause), over (pause), and down again. Say the words while the child makes some 4s on a flat surface.

 **Making a 4:
down,
over,
and down again.**

The pause is important for a sharp corner.

ACTIVITIES FOR TEACHING CONTINUED:	EXPLANATIONS CONTINUED:

Then ask the child to watch while you make some 4s, to see if you are doing it right. Deliberately make errors: start at the bottom or at the right or retrace. End with the child making a few more 4s a flat surface.

Take and Give. Show the 10 dot card. Ask: How much it is? [10] Ask him to enter it on the abacus so it looks the same as the card. Tell him there is another way to find out how much it is.

We "Take" the beads from the fifth wire and "Give" them to the top wire. With your left hand, move the 2 beads on the fifth wire to the right while simultaneously moving 2 beads on the top wire to the left. See the figures below. Repeat for the fourth, third, and second wires. Ask: How many to we have? [10] Now point to the 10 dot card and ask: So how much is it? [10]

Any number of beads can be "moved" at a time as long as the amounts are the same for both hands.

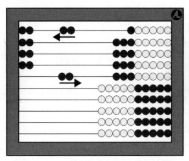

Move 2 from 5th wire to top wire using Take and Give.

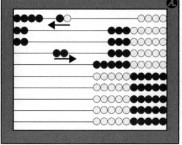

Move 2 from the 4th wire to top wire.

Give the child the 7 dot card and ask her to enter it on abacus and to use Take and Give to find out how much. Repeat for the 8 and 9 cards.

In conclusion. Ask the child to write zero and 4 on a flat surface. Ask: Can you enter zero on the abacus? [nothing to enter]

LESSON 24: WRITING 3 & MORE EVENS AND ODDS

OBJECTIVES:

1. To learn to write the numeral 3
2. To understand zero as nothing
3. To see the even and odd patterns
4. To practice recognizing the quantities on the dot and bead cards

MATERIALS:

1. AL Abacus and Tiles
2. *Yellow is the Sun* book
3. **Container with 11 small slips of paper***
4. Dot cards
5. Bead cards, cut apart (Appendix p. 7)
6. *Math Card Games* book, N17

ACTIVITIES FOR TEACHING:	EXPLANATIONS:
Warm-up. Sing with the child "Yellow is the Sun," "Days of the Week," and "Writing Numbers."	*Write numeral 1, 3, 4, 7, 0, and tally marks for 2, 5, 6, 8, and 9 on the papers, and fold them in half.
Write the numbers that the child has learned to write so far: 1, 4, 7 and 0; point to each one and ask him to name it. Then ask him to show writing them on a flat surface as you say them.	
Flash various quantities 1 to 10 for 2 seconds using fingers or the abacus; ask him to name the quantity.	It is very important for the child to be able to identify quantities without counting

Writing 3s. Show the child the "3" page in the *Yellow is the Sun* book. Tell the child that 3 has two parts, almost the same: We make part of a circle twice, or two times. Have him practice making the curved sections on a flat surface, using his two "writing fingers." Emphasize starting at the left.

ɔ 3 Writing 3: around and around.

Zero game. Ask the child to take a slip of paper from the container and read it silently, but not show it to you. He then enters on the abacus the quantity indicated by his slip. Respond by saying the quantity entered and verify with the slip of paper. Reverse roles and clear the abacus between turns. Upon getting a zero, pretend to enter a zero.

The Zero game helps the child appreciate the nothingness of 0. This game was adapted from a game devised by Maria Montessori.

Entering odds. Ask the child to enter 1 on the abacus and to say how much it is. [1] Now ask the child to enter 2 more and say how much it is. [3] Continue to 9. Then ask him to do it again by himself. [1, 3, 5, 7, 9]

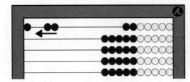

Adding 2s to make odd numbers.

ACTIVITIES FOR TEACHING CONTINUED:	EXPLANATIONS CONTINUED:

Alternating evens and odds. Ask to child to take five tiles in his favorite color and another five tiles in his least favorite color. Ask him to put the dot cards in order from 1 to 10. Then ask him to put his favorite-colored tiles below each even dot card. Then ask him to put the other tiles below each odd dot card.

Ask: How many even cards do you have? [5] Ask: How do you know? [the number of tiles]

Now ask him to move his even cards and tiles up about an inch; show him an inch with your fingers. Ask him if he sees a pattern and to explain it? [do re]

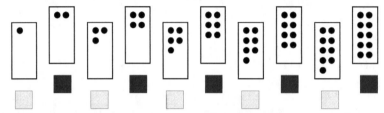

The dot cards with the even numbers raised.

Ask the child to name the even cards. [2, 4, 6, 8, 10] Then ask him to name the odd cards. [1, 3, 5, 7, 9]

Matching bead cards to dot cards. Using a set of dot cards and a set of bead cards, have the child lay out the dot cards in no order. Then he takes a bead card, finds its match among the dot cards, and lays the card below it. See the figure below.

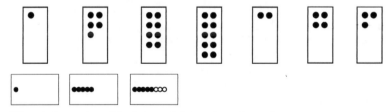

The dot cards with the matching bead cards.

Dot Card and Bead Card Memory. Lay the dot cards out on the left and the bead cards on the right face down. The child first turns over a dot card, says the number aloud, and looks for its match among the bead cards. For more detailed instructions, see the *Math Card Games* book, N17.

In conclusion. Ask the child to demonstrate writing a 3 on a flat surface. Ask: How many hands do you have? [2] How many whiskers do you have? [0]

LESSON 25: WRITING 2, TENS & EQUILATERAL TRIANGLES

OBJECTIVES:
1. To learn to write the numeral 2
2. To introduce tens
3. To introduce *equilateral triangles*

MATERIALS:
1. AL Abacus
2. **A valentine or heart**, to be folded in half
3. *Yellow is the Sun* book
4. Tally sticks
5. Worksheet 5, Equilateral Triangles
6. **Child's scissors**

ACTIVITIES FOR TEACHING:

Warm-up. Sing "Yellow is the Sun," "Days of the Week," and "Writing Numbers." Ask the child to trace the shapes of the numbers she knows (1, 3, 4, 7, 0) while singing.

Ask the child to add 1 bead at a time on the abacus while saying how much it is. [1, 2, . . . , 10] Clear, then ask the child to add 2 beads at a time and say how much it is. [2, 4, 6, 8, 10]

Write the numerals that the child has learned so far: 1, 3, 4, 7, and 0; point to each one in turn and ask her to name them.

Writing 2s. Show the child the heart and fold it in half through the middle. Say: This is how we make the first part of the 2. Ask her to trace around its edge using her first two fingers and then on a surface. Ask her to find the "2" page in the *Yellow is the Sun* book. Then ask her to trace the entire 2 saying: Around and over.

 Writing 2: around and over. Think of the heart shape.

Tens on the abacus. Ask the child to enter 1-ten on the abacus. Ask her to enter ten on the next wire. Tell her we will call it "2-ten." See the left figure below.

Ask the child to continue entering tens and naming them up to 9-ten. [3-ten, 4-ten, . . . , 9-ten] Then ask: How could she tell it is 6-ten? [The colors change.] See the right figure below.

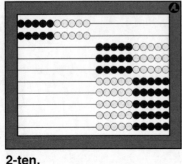
2-ten.

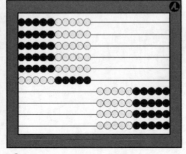
6-ten.

EXPLANATIONS:

The concept of 10, so vital to understanding place value and computation, is difficult to acquire in our culture. The English naming of quantities from 11 to 99, especially 11 to 19, masks the underlying 10 structure.

Twenty will be called "2-ten" for the next several months. The term *2-ten*, rather than *2-tens*, is easier and quicker to say. Also, it is consistent in the way we say *hundred* in two hundred eleven, not two hundreds eleven.

If the child wants to say twenty, tell her that is correct. Then say that people in Japan (also China and Korea) call it 2-ten and that we will do that for a while, too.

Children, generally, do not see the change of color on the abacus after 50 as readily as they do the change after 5.

ACTIVITIES FOR TEACHING CONTINUED:	EXPLANATIONS CONTINUED:

Then, ask the child to enter 10-ten. Ask her why 10-ten is special. [all the beads on the abacus]

Equilateral triangles. Review quadrilateral and triangle by drawing a generic quadrilateral and a triangle. Point to the triangle and ask: Is this a quadrilateral? [no] What is it? [triangle] How can you tell if it is a triangle? [3 sides]

Ask the child to make a triangle with the tally sticks. Then ask her if she could make a different triangle. [no, not if the ends of the sticks are used] Tell her that these are special triangles, called *equilateral triangles*, because all the sides are equal, or the same.

Equilateral triangle.

Worksheet 5. Ask the child to cut out the equilateral triangles. Treat them gently because she will need them the next day.

Ask her to make new shapes and designs with them. A few are shown below.

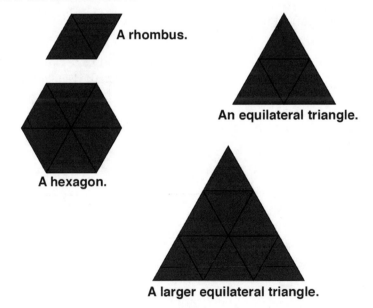

A rhombus.

An equilateral triangle.

A hexagon.

A larger equilateral triangle.

In conclusion. Ask the child to trace a 2 on a flat surface. Ask: How many sides in a triangle? [3]

LESSON 26: WRITING 5, TENS & THE "TEN TRIANGLE"

OBJECTIVES:

1. To write the numeral 5
2. To learn the term *hundred*
3. To construct the first iteration of the "Tens Fractal"

MATERIALS:

1. AL Abacus
2. Yellow is the Sun book
3. Dry erase board
4. Ten cut out triangles from the previous lesson
5. Worksheet 6, Fractal Outline
6. **Glue**

ACTIVITIES FOR TEACHING:	EXPLANATIONS:
Warm-up. Sing "Yellow is the Sun," "Days of the Week," and "Writing Numbers." Ask the child to trace the shapes of the numbers he knows while singing them.	Remember you might want to sign the songs while getting the math materials out. This helps the child mentally prepare for math.

Warm-up. Sing "Yellow is the Sun," "Days of the Week," and "Writing Numbers." Ask the child to trace the shapes of the numbers he knows while singing them.

Ask the child to add 1 bead at a time on the abacus while saying how much it is. [1, 2, . . . , 10] Clear, then ask the child to add 2 beads at a time and say how much it is. [2, 4, 6, 8, 10]

Write the numbers that the child has learned so far: 1, 2, 3, 4, 7, and 0; point to each one in turn and ask him to name them and show the quantity with his fingers.

Writing 5. Ask him to find the "5" page in the *Yellow is the Sun* book. Ask him: Where do we start when writing the 5, left or right? [right] Remind him of the part of the song, "Start at the right for 5, 6, 8, or 9. Don't lift your pen and you'll do just fine."

Demonstrating on the dry erase board, say: Start at the right; then over (pause), down, (pause) and around. Ask the child to practice making 5s.

Remember you might want to sign the songs while getting the math materials out. This helps the child mentally prepare for math.

Writing the numeral 5 with one stroke is more efficient and often more legible. (When the top bar is written last, it may be written too far to the left, making the numeral look more like a 3.)

Writing 5: over, down, and around. Make 5 with one stroke.

Identifying tens on the abacus. Enter 10 on the abacus and ask: How much is entered on the abacus? [10 or 1-ten] Enter another ten and ask: How many tens are entered on the abacus? [2] What do we call it? [2-ten] Enter 2 more tens and ask: How much is entered on the abacus? [4-ten] Repeat for other quantities.

One hundred. Ask the child to enter 10 tens and tell him 10-ten has another name, we call it *hundred*.

Ten arrangement. Ask the child to make a stairs using only the first 4 wires. See the left figure on the next page. Then ask him to use Take and Give to find the number of beads. [10] Emphasize that this is another way to make a 10.

53

| ACTIVITIES FOR TEACHING CONTINUED: | EXPLANATIONS CONTINUED: |

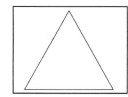

Another way to show a 10.   **1 + 2 + 3 + 4 = 10.**

Next ask him to enter 1 on the top wire, leave a space and enter 2. Repeat for entering 3 and 4. See the right figure above. Ask: What is 1 and 2 and 3 and 4? [10] He can slide the beads to the left to see the ten.

Making the Ten Triangle. Ask the child to arrange the 10 equilateral triangles from the previous day's worksheet as shown in the left figure below. Put 1 triangle in the first row, 2 in the second row, 3 in the third row, and 4 in the last row.

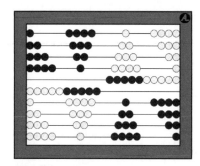

Ten small triangles arranged to form the Ten Triangle.   **Worksheet 6 on which to glue the 10 small triangles.**

Ask him to glue each triangle in place on the outline (Worksheet 6) to make the Ten Triangle.

In conclusion. Make the following arrangement and ask the child to find as many tens as he can. [10]

Finding tens.

Fractals are a new branch of mathematics only a few decades old. There are two types of fractals; regular and random. Scientists use random fractals for computer modeling in order to study some of nature's irregular patterns and structures. Regular fractals, also called geometric fractals, consist of larger structures that are identical in shape to the smaller structure.

The Tens Fractal, a regular fractal, illustrates how our number system is constructed with tens. It starts with 10 small equilateral triangles arranged in the shape of a larger equilateral triangle. This is the Ten Triangle.

Ten of these triangles arranged in the same pattern form the Hundred Triangle. And ten Hundred Triangles form the Thousand Triangle.

Ten Triangle   **Hundred Triangle**

The child will construct the hundred and thousand triangles in later lessons. These triangles are part of the Tens Fractal.

By building this fractal the child will visualize and experience the repeating tens structure of our number system. Another purpose is integrating mathematics and art.

© Activities for Learning, Inc. 2013

LESSON 27: WRITING 6 AND INTRODUCING ADDING

OBJECTIVES:
1. To learn to write the number 6
2. To introduce adding

MATERIALS:
1. AL Abacus
2. *Yellow is the Sun* book
3. Tiles

ACTIVITIES FOR TEACHING:	EXPLANATIONS:
Warm-up. Sing "Yellow is the Sun," "Days of the Week," and "Writing Numbers." Ask the child to trace the shapes of the numbers she knows while singing.	

ACTIVITIES FOR TEACHING:

Warm-up. Sing "Yellow is the Sun," "Days of the Week," and "Writing Numbers." Ask the child to trace the shapes of the numbers she knows while singing.

Then write the numerals 1 to 5, 7, and 0; point a numeral; and ask the child to enter it on the abacus.

Ask the child to add 1 bead at a time on the abacus while saying aloud how much it is. [1, 2, . . . , 10] Ask the child to add 2 beads at a time and say how much it is. [2, 4, 6, 8, 10]

Ask the child to enter 3-ten on the abacus. Repeat for 5-ten and 8-ten. Also enter 4-ten and ask: How much is this? [4-ten] Repeat for 6-ten [6-ten] and 10-ten. [one hundred]

Writing 6. Ask the child to find the "6" page in the *Yellow is the Sun* book. Ask her: Where do we start when writing the 6, left or right? [right] Remind her of the part of the song, "Start at the right for 5, 6, 8, or 9. Don't lift your pen and you'll do just fine."

Then demonstrate writing 6, using the words "around and around" as you do it. Ask the child to practice writing 6s on a flat surface.

Writing 6: around and around.

Counting tiles with the abacus. Tell the child to take a handful of tiles (10 or less) and lay them in a pile on the right. Show her how to move over 1 tile to a pile on the left and to enter 1 bead on the abacus. Ask her to move over another tile and enter 1 more bead. Ask: How many tiles are in the left pile? [2] How many entered on the abacus? [2]

Ask her to continue until all the tiles are moved to the left pile. Then ask: How many beads are entered on the abacus? How many tiles are in the pile? [same number]

EXPLANATIONS:

This activity introduces one-to-one correspondence in a meaningful context.

ACTIVITIES FOR TEACHING CONTINUED:	EXPLANATIONS CONTINUED:

Adding on the abacus. Ask the child to enter 4 beads on the abacus. Ask her to enter 1 more and say: How much is 4 and 1 more? [5]

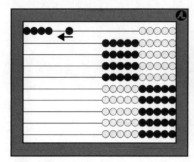 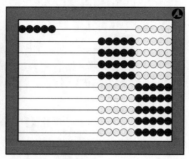

Entering 4 and 1 more.   **4 and 1 added.**

Now have the child enter 5 and 2 more. Ask: How much is 5 and 2? [7] Continue with 3 and 2; but ask: How much is 3 and 2? [5]

Continue by asking the child to add:

      5 and 5 [10]

      1 and 3 [4]

      5 and 3 [8]

      4 and 1 [5]

      6 and 2 [8]

      8 and 1 [9]

      1 and 4 [5]

      5 and 4 [9]

In conclusion. Ask the child to trace a 6 on a flat surface. Ask: What is 2 and 2? [4] Ask: Is 6 an even or odd number? [even]

LESSON 28: WRITING 8 AND EVENNESS

OBJECTIVES:

1. To determine *evenness*
2. To learn to write the number 8
3. To trace on paper the numerals 1–4 and 7

MATERIALS:

1. AL Abacus
2. Dot cards
3. Tiles
4. *Yellow is the Sun* book
5. Worksheet 7, Writing Numbers Starting at the Left

ACTIVITIES FOR TEACHING:	EXPLANATIONS:
Warm-up. Sing "Yellow is the Sun," "Days of the Week," and "Writing Numbers." Ask the child to trace the shapes of the numbers he knows while singing.	

Warm-up. Sing "Yellow is the Sun," "Days of the Week," and "Writing Numbers." Ask the child to trace the shapes of the numbers he knows while singing.

Ask the child to add 1 bead at a time on the abacus while saying how much it is. [1, 2, . . . , 10] Ask the child to add 2 beads at a time and say how much it is. [2, 4, 6, 8, 10]

Ask the child to add on the abacus 1 and 2 and to say how much it is. [3] Repeat for 7 and 3. [10]

Tell the child to enter 2-ten on the abacus, then to enter 2 more tens. Ask: How much do you have now? [4-ten] Repeat for 7-ten and 3-ten. [10-ten, 100]

Ask the child to lay out the dot cards in order in a row. Then ask him to point to and say each even number in order. [2, 4, 6, 8, 10] Repeat for the odd numbers. [1, 3, 5, 7, 9]

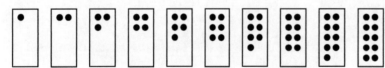

The child find the requested number as fast as he can.

Determining evenness. Ask the child to take a handful or two of tiles. Ask him to group the tiles by twos.

Pairing the tiles and noticing one lacks a partner; thus, the number is odd.

57

ACTIVITIES FOR TEACHING CONTINUED:	EXPLANATIONS CONTINUED:

Ask: Is the number even or odd? [odd for this example] Repeat the activity several times by putting the tiles back and taking a new group.

Writing 8. Say to the child now he will learn to write 8. Ask: Where do we start when writing 8, left or right? [right] Repeat the part of the song, "Start at the right for 5, 6, 8, or 9. Don't lift your pen and you'll do just fine." Ask him to find the "8" page in the *Yellow is the Sun* book.

Demonstrate writing 8 while saying: Down like a 7, around like a 6, and then finish it. See the figures below. Ask him to practice writing it on a flat surface.

   Writing 8: start like a 7, around like 6, and finish it.

Worksheet 7. For this worksheet, the child is to trace the numerals in each row. Remind him to start at the dot. Explain that he is to do only the top half of the worksheet.

In conclusion. Ask the child to trace an 8 on a flat surface. Ask: What is 2 plus 3? [5]

The number 8 seems easier for most children if they start like a 7, curve like a 6, and then finish it as shown, rather than start with an "S."

LESSON 29: GEOBOARD PATTERNS

OBJECTIVES:

1. To construct and continue patterns on geoboards

MATERIALS:

1. AL Abacus
2. Dot cards
3. Geoboards

ACTIVITIES FOR TEACHING:	EXPLANATIONS:
Warm-up. Sing "Yellow is the Sun," "Days of the Week," and "Writing Numbers." Ask the child to trace the shapes of the numbers she knows while singing.	

Warm-up. Sing "Yellow is the Sun," "Days of the Week," and "Writing Numbers." Ask the child to trace the shapes of the numbers she knows while singing.

Ask the child to add 1 bead at a time on the abacus while saying how much it is. [1, 2, . . . , 10] Ask the child to add 2 beads at a time and say how much it is. [2, 4, 6, 8, 10]

Ask the child to add on the abacus 3 and 2 and to say how much it is. [5] Repeat for 8 and 2. [10]

Tell the child to enter 3-ten on the abacus, then to enter 2 more tens. Ask: How much do you have now? [5-ten] Repeat for 8-ten and 2-ten. [10-ten, 100]

Ask the child to lay out the dot cards in order in a row. Then ask her to point to and say each even number in order. [2, 4, 6, 8, 10] Repeat for the odd numbers. [1, 3, 5, 7, 9]

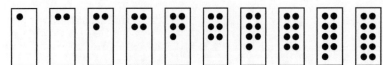

The child finds the requested number as quickly as can.

The Abacus song with dot cards. Have the child lay out the even dot cards. While singing the song, to the tune of the Hokey Pokey, have the child show the correct dot card during the song. Repeat using the odd numbers.

The Abacus Song

The two steps in.

The two steps out.

He holds up the number.

And waves it all about.

He clears the number.

And sits back down.

Where is the number four?

The four steps in. . . .

ACTIVITIES FOR TEACHING CONTINUED:

EXPLANATIONS CONTINUED:

Geoboard patterning. Put the first pattern on your geoboard. Ask the child to copy the pattern and to continue it. Repeat for patterns 2 and 3.

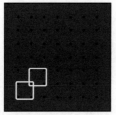

Pattern 1.

Pattern 1 continued.

Pattern 2.

Pattern 3.

Explain that the next two patterns are *growing* patterns; each new element is larger than the last.

Pattern 4.

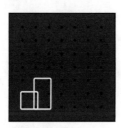

Pattern 5.

Previous patterns have been repeating patterns. Growing patterns—Pattern 4 and Pattern 5— are another type of pattern.

Hint: when the smallest rubber bands are still too long, hold the stretched rubber band against a peg with two fingers of one hand and twist the rubber band with the other hand; then double it over to the previous peg.

For pattern 6, the child continues her own pattern. Ask her to discuss her results.

Pattern 6.

In conclusion. Ask the child to trace an 8 on a flat surface. Ask: What is 2 and 2? [4]

LESSON 30: WRITING 9 AND NUMBER SEQUENCING

OBJECTIVES:

1. To learn to write 9
2. To match numbers with quantities
3. To practice the number sequence

MATERIALS:

1. AL Abacus
2. *Yellow is the Sun* book
3. Worksheet 7, Writing Numbers Starting at the Left
4. Set of basic number cards 1 to 10
5. Tally sticks

ACTIVITIES FOR TEACHING:

EXPLANATIONS:

Warm-up. Sing "Yellow is the Sun," "Days of the Week," and "Writing Numbers." Ask the child to trace the shapes of the numbers he knows while singing.

Ask the child to add 1 bead at a time on the abacus while saying how much it is. [1, 2, . . . , 10] Ask the child to add 2 beads at a time and say how much it is. [2, 4, 6, 8, 10]

Ask the child to add on the abacus 4 and 2 and to say how much it is. [6] Repeat for 5 and 4. [9]

Tell the child to enter 4-ten on the abacus, then to enter 2 more tens. Ask: How much do you have now? [6-ten] Repeat for 7-ten and 3-ten. [10-ten, 100]

Write the numbers that the child has learned: 1 to 8, and 0; point to each one and ask him to name them.

Writing 9. Ask the child to show 9 with his fingers. Say that 9 is the last number that we are going to learn to write. Find the "9" page in the *Yellow is the Sun* book. Also tell him that the hardest thing to remember when writing a 9 is to keep the pencil on the paper, not to lift until the very end. Demonstrate while saying the words: Around and then down. Now practice it on a flat surface.

  Write 9: around and then down.

Worksheet 7. Ask the child to finish the second half of the worksheet that was started in a prior lesson.

Numbers in order. Give the child the set of basic number cards. Lay the cards out in random order. Ask him to put them in order as follows: enter 1 on the abacus and look for the card saying 1.

Add another bead. Note there are 2 beads and look for the card with 2. See the figure on the next page. Continue to 10.

ACTIVITIES FOR TEACHING CONTINUED:

EXPLANATIONS CONTINUED:

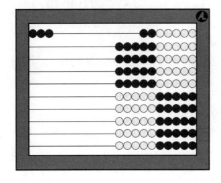

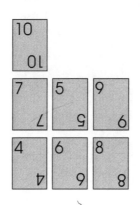

If necessary, tell the child that he should look only at the number on the top left of the card, not the upside down number at the bottom.

For the child still learning to read the numbers, give him a copy of the Tally Sticks and Numbers Chart in the *Math Card Games* book, appendix p. 5.

Tally to ten. Give the child 55 tally sticks and tell him he is to make all the numbers from one to ten. Also ask him to put the matching basic number card next to the tally sticks.

This activity takes considerable space and is best done on a rug.

One child was surprised to find that he needed all 55 tally sticks to make the numbers.

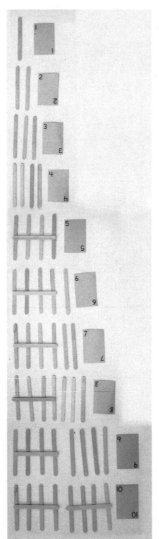

In conclusion. Ask the child to trace a 9 on a flat surface. Ask: What is 9 and 1 more? [10]

LESSON 31: ASSESSMENT 1

OBJECTIVES:
1. To assess understanding

MATERIALS:
1. Dot cards
2. Assessment Checklist 1 (Appendix p. 8)
3. Set of basic number cards 1 to 10
4. Geoboards

ACTIVITIES FOR TEACHING:	EXPLANATIONS:
Warm-up. Sing "Yellow is the Sun," "Days of the Week," and "Writing Numbers." Ask the child to trace all the shapes of the numbers while singing.	

Ask the child to lay out the dot cards in order in a row. Then say a number and the child finds the card and sets it aside. Continue saying the numbers until all the cards are picked up.

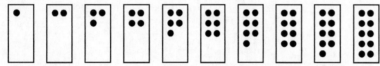

The child finds the requested number as quickly as she can.

Ask the child to add on the abacus 3 and 2 and to say how much it is. [5] Repeat for 8 and 2. [10]

Tell the child to enter 3-ten on the abacus, then to enter 2 more tens. Ask: How much do you have now? [5-ten] Repeat for 8-ten and 2-ten. [10-ten, 100]

Write the numbers 0-9. Point to each one and ask her to name them.

Assessing using games. Have the assessment checklist (Appendix p. 8) next to you while you play the following games. Use the checklist to track what the child understands.

At this age, assessing with games is more reliable than any paper and pencil tests. Children's confidence in playing a game shows level of mastery.

ACTIVITIES FOR TEACHING CONTINUED:

EXPLANATIONS CONTINUED:

Matching dots to numbers. Use one set of basic number cards and one set of dot cards. Ask the child to lay out the basic number cards in no particular order. Then ask her to spread out the dot cards to the side. She starts at the left, reads the first number 6, (in this example) and searches for the matching dot card and lays it under the basic number card. She continues by reading the other number cards. See the figure below.

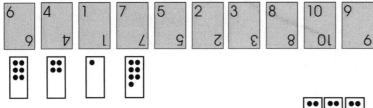

Matching dot cards to number cards.

Matching numbers to dots. This activity is similar to the above activity. Now the dot cards are laid out and the child searches for the matching number.

Understanding figures on Geoboards. On the geoboard ask the child to first build a triangle. Now have her make a rectangle, square and quadrilateral.

Making geoboard patterns. Have the child make a do-re (AB) pattern on the geoboard using the shapes she made above. For example, square, triangle, square, triangle. See figure below.

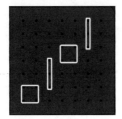

Do-re pattern on the geoboard.

In conclusion. Ask the child to trace an 8 on a flat surface. Ask: What is 2 and 6? [8]

If there are concepts that the child struggles with, review by playing the games.

LESSON 32: PARTITIONING 5

OBJECTIVES:
1. To partition 5
2. To learn that the "+" sign means "and"
3. To practice matching numbers to quantities

MATERIALS:
1. AL Abacus
2. *Math Card Games* book, N17

ACTIVITIES FOR TEACHING:	EXPLANATIONS:

ACTIVITIES FOR TEACHING:

Warm-up. Sing "Yellow is the Sun," "Days of the Week," and "Writing Numbers." Ask the child to trace the shapes of all the numbers while singing.

Ask the child to add 1 bead at a time on the abacus while saying how much it is. [1, 2, . . . , 10] Ask the child to add 2 beads at a time and say how much it is. [2, 4, 6, 8, 10]

Ask the child to add on the abacus 4 and 2 and to say how much it is. [6] Repeat for 7 and 2. [9]

Tell the child to enter 4-ten on the abacus, then to enter 2 more tens. Ask: How much do you have now? [6-ten] Repeat for 7-ten and 2-ten. [9-ten]

Ask the child to build the stairs on the abacus. Then say this fun nursery rhyme, "One, Two, Three, Four, Five," with him while asking him to touch the appropriate wires on the abacus.

One, Two, Three, Four, Five

One, two, three, four, five,
Once I caught a fish alive,
Six, seven, eight, nine, ten,
Then I let it go again.

Partitioning 5 on the abacus. Ask the child to enter 5 on the abacus. Then ask him to enter 5 on the second wire. Tell him we want to break the second 5 into two parts. Move 1 bead a little to the right as shown below. Ask: What are the parts of 5? [4 and 1]

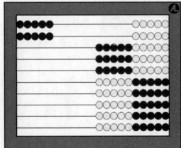

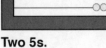
Two 5s.

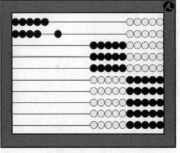
Five partitioned into 4 and 1.

EXPLANATIONS:

The word *partition* is used here to mean to divide into parts. Indeed, the child can hear the word *part* in partition.

For breaking a number into parts, sometimes the word "decompose" is used. Unfortunately, this word often has a negative connotation. For this reasons, RightStart™ will use the term "partition" for splitting numbers into their parts.

It is interesting to note that "decompose" is a mathematical term used in very advanced mathematics.

| ACTIVITIES FOR TEACHING CONTINUED: | EXPLANATIONS CONTINUED: |

Ask the child to enter a 5 on the third line. Then ask him to move 2 beads to the right. Continue with partitioning 5 on the fourth and fifth lines.

Then ask him to name the parts of five while you write them down. Use the "+" sign and tell him that it means *and*. Ask the child to find all the parts. Ignore the 0 combinations if he does not mention them.

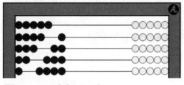

Five partitioned.

(5 + 0)
4 + 1
3 + 2
2 + 3
1 + 4
(0 + 5)

Some children may want to do a sixth row with 0 and 5, or even 5 and 0.

Partitioning 5. Ask the child to show partitioning 5 with his hands . See the pictures below.

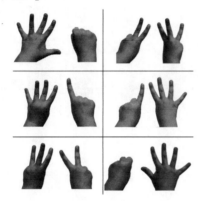

Memory with Different Sets of Cards game. Play the Memory with Different Sets of Cards game found in the *Math Card Games* book, N17.

These games provide practice in reading the numbers from 1–10.

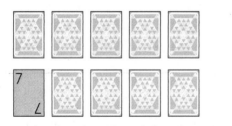 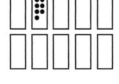

It can also be played with bead cards, tally stick cards, or finger cards.

In conclusion. Ask the child to name the ways to partition 5.

LESSON 33: PART-WHOLE CIRCLE SETS

OBJECTIVES:

1. To introduce part-whole circle sets
2. To practice recognizing the written sequence 1–10

MATERIALS:

1. AL Abacus
2. Worksheet 8, Writing Numbers Starting at the Right
3. The Part-Whole Circle Set (Appendix p. 9)
4. Tiles
5. *Math Card Games* book, N12 and N13

ACTIVITIES FOR TEACHING:	EXPLANATIONS:

ACTIVITIES FOR TEACHING:

Warm-up. Sing "Days of the Week." Also sing "Writing Numbers," during which the child traces the shapes of the numbers.

Ask the child to add on the abacus 5 and 3. [8] Then ask her to add 5 + 5. [10]

Tell the child to enter 5-ten on the abacus, then to add 3-ten. Ask: How much do you have now? [8-ten] Repeat for 5-ten and 5-ten. [10-ten, one hundred]

Ask the child to clear the abacus. Then as she recites the "One, Two, Three, Four, Five," rhyme, ask her to build the stairs while saying the corresponding words.

One, Two, Three, Four, Five

One, two, three, four, five,
Once I caught a fish alive,
Six, seven, eight, nine, ten,
Then I let it go again.

Worksheet 8. For this worksheet, the child is to trace the numerals in each row. Remind her to start at the dot. Explain she is to do only the top half of the worksheet.

Part-whole circle set. Show the child a part-whole circle set (Appendix p. 9). Explain that the whole goes in the largest circle and the parts go in the smaller circles.

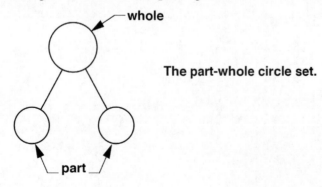

The part-whole circle set.

Say: Take 5 tiles and put them in the circle for the whole. Then ask her to take 5 more tiles and put part in each of the smaller circles. Two examples are on the next page.

EXPLANATIONS:

Research shows that children using part-whole circles are better able to solve problems.

67

ACTIVITIES FOR TEACHING CONTINUED:

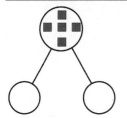 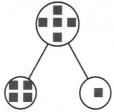 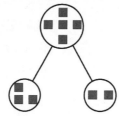

The whole is 5.   Parts are 4 and 1.   Parts are 3 and 2.

Now ask her find other ways to make parts. [0 and 5, 1 and 4, 2 and 3, 3 and 2, 4 and 1, 5 and 0]

Finding the missing part or whole. Say: Let's make 4 to be the whole and 2 to be a part. Put 4 in the whole-circle and 2 in a part-circle. See the figures below. Ask the child: What is the other part?

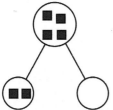   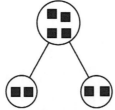

Find the missing part.   The missing part is 2.

Set up some other examples of the part-whole circle set with one circle empty (see below). Ask the child to fill in the missing circle with tiles.

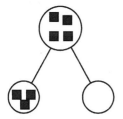   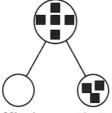   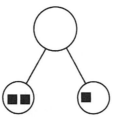

Missing part is 1.   Missing part is 2.   Whole is 3.

Mixed-Up Cards game. In this game a set of basic number cards is laid out in order; another set is mixed-up. For instructions, see the *Math Card Games* book game, N12.

Mystery Card game. Here the child must think of the missing card. See the *Math Card Games* book game, N13.

In conclusion. Show the child the part-whole circle set. Put 5 tiles in the large circle. Ask: What could the parts be? [0 and 5, 1 and 4, 2 and 3, 3 and 2, 4 and 1, or 5 and 0]

EXPLANATIONS CONTINUED:

These games will help the child learn the written number sequence 1–10.

© Activities for Learning, Inc. 2013

LESSON 34: PARTITIONING PROBLEM

OBJECTIVES:

1. To introduce *greater than* and *less than*
2. To solve a problem using part-whole circle sets

MATERIALS:

1. AL Abacus
2. Tiles
3. The Part-Whole Circle Set
4. *Math Card Games* book, N14 and N15
5. Worksheet 8, Writing Numbers Starting at the Right

ACTIVITIES FOR TEACHING:	EXPLANATIONS:
Warm-up. Sing "Days of the Week." Also sing "Writing Numbers," during which the child traces the shapes of the numbers on a flat surface.	
Tell the child that he will play a new game called Comes After. Explain that you will say a number and he is to say what number comes next. For example, say 2 and he says 3. Repeat for numbers 7, [8] 1, [2] 4, [5] and 9. [10]	
Also play the Comes After game for the days of the week. Say Sunday and the child says Monday. Repeat for Tuesday [Wednesday] and Monday. [Tuesday]	
Tell the child to enter 5-ten on the abacus, then to add 2-ten. Ask: How much do you have now? [7-ten] Repeat for 9-ten and 1-ten. [10-ten, one hundred]	
Ask the child to show the ways to partition 5 on the abacus.	
Greater than and less than. Place 6 tiles on the child's left and 2 tiles on the right. Ask: Which pile is greater? [left]	
Discuss the meaning of opposite by giving examples; hot is the opposite of cold; up is the opposite of down; and front is the opposite of back. Tell him the opposite of *greater than* is *less than*. Ask again which pile is greater. [left] Ask: Which pile is less than? [right]	
Move 1 tile from the left pile and place it on the right. Ask: Which is less than? [right] Move another tile from the left to the right. Again ask: Which is less than? [neither, the same] Once more move 1 tile from the left to the right and ask: Which is less than? [left] Ask which is greater than. [right]	
Partitioning problem. Tell the child that we have a partitioning problem to solve. Give the problem:	You may want to change the names in a story problem to those more familiar to the child.
Morgan has 5 dog treats to give to dogs named Daisy and Flash. How many dog treats could Morgan give to Daisy and how many to Flash?	

| ACTIVITIES FOR TEACHING CONTINUED: | EXPLANATIONS CONTINUED: |

Tell him that we are going to use tiles to represent dog treats. Ask: How many treats did Morgan have? [5] Ask him to put the 5 tiles in the whole-circle as shown in the left figure below.

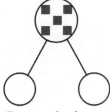 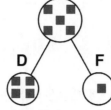 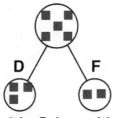

5 treats is the whole. **4 for Daisy and 1 for Flash.** **3 for Daisy and 2 for Flash.**

Ask him to take 5 more tiles and partition them between the dogs. [Shown above are 4 & 1 and 3 & 2.] Ask: Which dog has more? Which dog has less?

Record the results as shown below; write "D" (for Daisy) above the first column and "F" (for Flash) above the second column.

D	F
4	1
3	2
2	3
1	4
0	5
5	0

Now ask him to do a different grouping. After he has correctly demonstrated it, record it. Repeat until he has found all possible ways. If he doesn't suggest using a zero, ask: What about zero?

To help him learn to check the reasonableness of his solutions, discuss why someone would give all the treats to one dog. [One dog did a trick or one dog is gone.]

Harder Mixed-Up Cards game. This game is similar to Mixed-Up cards, but only one set of cards is used. See *Math Card Games* book game, N14.

Missing Card game. Play this game like Mystery Card except the gap is removed. See *Math Card Games* book game, N15.

Worksheet 8. Ask the child to finish the second half of the worksheet that was started in the previous lesson.

In conclusion. Ask the child to name the ways to partition 4. [3 and 1, 2 and 2, 1 and 3, 4 and 0, 0 and 4]

LESSON 35: MORE PART-WHOLE CIRCLE SETS

OBJECTIVES:

1. To use numerals with the part-whole circle sets
2. To use the part-whole circle sets to solve simple problems

MATERIALS:

1. AL Abacus
2. Dry erase board
3. *Math Card Games* book, N34

ACTIVITIES FOR TEACHING:	EXPLANATIONS:
Warm-up. Sing "Days of the Week." Also sing "Writing Numbers," during which the child traces the shapes of the numbers on a flat surface.	

Warm-up. Sing "Days of the Week." Also sing "Writing Numbers," during which the child traces the shapes of the numbers on a flat surface.

Play the Comes After game (described in the previous lesson). Ask: What number comes after 3? [4] Repeat for numbers 9, [10] 2, [3] 8, [9] and 7. [8]

Also play the Comes After game for the days of the week. Ask: What day comes after Monday? [Tuesday] Repeat for Sunday [Monday] and Thursday. [Friday]

Tell the child to enter 5-ten on the abacus then to add 2-ten. Ask: How much do you have now? [7-ten] Repeat for 7-ten and 3-ten. [10-ten, one hundred]

Partitioning 4. Ask the child to draw a part-whole circle set on the dry erase board. Then say: Let's partition 4. Write 4 in the whole-circle.

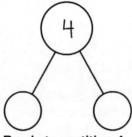

Ready to partition 4.

Ask her to partition the 4 on the abacus then write the parts in the part-whole circle set. The 1 and 3 partition is shown below.

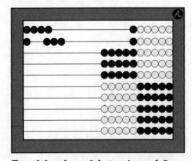

Partitioning 4 into 1 and 3.

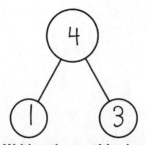

Writing the partitioning.

Tell the child to find another partition for 4. Then she can erase the 1 and 3 and write the new partitions. Ask the child to find all the partitions.

ACTIVITIES FOR TEACHING CONTINUED:

If the child omitted partitioning with zero, ask her to write 4 in the left part-circle. Then ask: What is the other part? [0] Repeat for 4 in the right part-circle.

Adding. Give the child the following problem:

Robin had 5 pennies and found 3 more pennies. How many pennies does Robin have now?

Read it twice to the child. Ask: Are the 5 pennies a part or a whole? [part] Ask the child to write it in a part-circle. See the figure below. Ask: Are the 3 pennies a part or a whole? [part] Write it in the other part-circle.

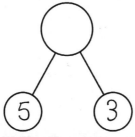
Writing the parts.

Ask the child to enter the parts on the abacus and find the whole. [8] See figure below. Ask her to write 8 in the whole-circle.

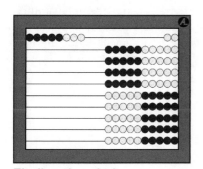
Finding the whole.

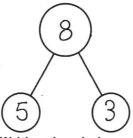
Writing the whole.

Change the problem. Tell her that Robin found 4 pennies and not 3. Ask the child to change the numbers in the circles. [parts are 5 and 4, whole is 9]

Repeat the steps for another problem:

Jessica ate 5 raisins yesterday and 5 more raisins today. How many raisins did Jessica eat altogether?

Ask: What are the parts? [5 and 5] What is the whole? [10 raisins]

Swim to Ten game. Play the Swim to Ten game in the *Math Cards Games* book, N34.

In conclusion. Ask the child to name the different ways to partition 3? [0 and 3, 1 and 2, 2 and 1, 3 and 0]

EXPLANATIONS CONTINUED:

Solving problems using the part-whole model may seem difficult at first. The child may need a number of examples before she understands.

A problem where more is added to existing objects is easier than a problem that combines two sets of objects.

LESSON 36: ONES & FINDING AND READING TENS

OBJECTIVES:

1. To introduce the term *tomorrow*

2. To introduce the term *ones*

3. To practice distinguishing between written 1s and 10s

4. To build the Hundred Triangle, the second iteration of the Tens Fractal

MATERIALS:

1. AL Abacus

2. Place-value cards

3. *Math Card Games* book, N43 Level 1

4. Worksheet 9-1, Ten Triangles

5. **Child's scissors**

6. Worksheet 9-2, Fractal Outline

ACTIVITIES FOR TEACHING:	EXPLANATIONS:
Warm-up. Sing "Days of the Week." Also sing "Writing Numbers," during which the child traces the shapes of the numbers on a flat surface.	
Play the Comes After game. Ask: What number comes after 2? [3] Repeat for numbers 9, [10] 5, [6] 3, [4] and 8. [9]	
Also play the Comes After game for the days of the week. Ask: What day comes after Friday? [Saturday] Repeat for Wednesday [Thursday] and Tuesday. [Wednesday] Tell them the day after today is called *tomorrow*.	
Ones. Enter 2-ten on the abacus and ask: What do we call it? [2-ten] Now enter 2 and ask: What do we call it? [two] Tell him sometimes we call it 2 *ones*. Explain that each bead is called a one, so 2 beads is 2 ones. Ask him to enter 3 ones, then 7 ones, and finally 5 ones.	Place value is the single most important concept in arithmetic; without place value arithmetic cannot be understood. Children must not be asked to discover this magnificent achievement of humankind, but be carefully taught its significance early in their mathematical development.
Recording tens. Review by entering 1s and 10s on the abacus and asking the child to name the quantities. For example, enter 3, 3-ten, 6-ten, 2, and the like. Enter 2-ten and show him the place-value card for 20 saying: This is how we write 2-ten. Point to the 2 while saying two and to the 0 while saying ten.	

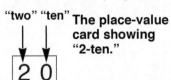 "two" "ten" The place-value card showing "2-ten."

 "ten" "ten" Emphasizing "10-ten" with the place-value card showing 100.

Numbers need to be read from left to right. Children should not be taught to start at the "ones place."

Next show the place-value card 30. Point to the individual digits while the child reads it. [three-ten] Also ask him to enter it on the abacus. Repeat for other tens up to 10-ten. For 10-ten, point to the 10 on the left while saying ten and to the 0 while saying ten as shown above.

Find the place-value card. Ask the child to spread out the place-value cards (1–9 and 10–90) so he can see all of them, but in no order. See the figure on the next page.

ACTIVITIES FOR TEACHING CONTINUED:

40		7		90		2		50		3
80		70		5		6		60		1
8		4		10		30		20		9

A layout for place-value card activities.

Enter 4 on the abacus and ask him to find the matching card. When he finds the card, he sets it aside. Repeat for 8.

Enter 2-ten on the abacus and ask him to find that card and set it aside. Continuing entering quantities, both ones and tens, on the abacus until all the cards are picked up.

Can You Find game. This game, found in the *Math Card Games*, N43 is similar to the previous game, but the abacus is not used. With the cards laid out, ask: Where is 6-ten? The child searches for it and removes it. Continue by asking for 3, 5 ones, 4-ten and so on. Vary your voice to heighten the excitement.

Building the Hundred Triangle. Ask the child to cut out the Ten Triangles (not the tiny triangles). After they are cut out, ask: Can you show me 2-ten? [two tens triangles] Can you show me 4-ten? [4 triangles] Can you show me ten? [1 ten triangle]

Arrange the 10 Ten Triangles as shown in the figures below. Put 1 triangle in the first row, 2 in the second row, 3 in the third row, and 4 in the fourth row.

Ask him to glue each triangle in place on the outline to make the Hundred Triangle. It may be easier to start at the bottom row.

Ten Ten Triangles form the Hundred Triangle.

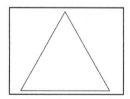

Worksheet 9-2 on which to glue the 10 Ten Triangles.

Ask the child to compare this Hundred Triangle to the Tens Triangle he did previously.

In conclusion. Ask: Where do you see ten dark triangles? [any of the triangles grouped in tens] How many little dark triangles in the whole fractal? [1 hundred]

EXPLANATIONS CONTINUED:

Some children may find hearing the quantity easier than seeing it on the abacus.

The Hundred Triangle is the second iteration of the Tens Fractal, which was started in previously. Save this worksheet.

In a future lesson the child will make the third iteration, the Thousand Triangle.

LESSON 37: EQUAL AND PLUS

OBJECTIVES:
1. To make the even stairs
2. To introduce the term *equal*
3. To introduce the term *plus*

MATERIALS:
1. AL Abacus
2. Tiles
3. *Math Card Games* book, N22

ACTIVITIES FOR TEACHING:	EXPLANATIONS:
Warm-up. Sing "Days of the Week." Also sing "Writing Numbers," during which the child traces the shapes of the numbers on a flat surface.	
Play the Comes After game. Ask: What number comes after 4? [5] Repeat for numbers 7, [8] 1, [2] and 9. [10]	
Also play the Comes After game for the days of the week. Ask: What day comes after Tuesday? [Wednesday] Repeat for Monday, [Tuesday] Sunday, [Monday] and Saturday. [Sunday] What day is today? What day is tomorrow?	The day following Saturday has not been discussed before because the rhyme ends with Saturday. Some children may need to be prompted for the answer.
Ask the child to enter 4 on the abacus. Then ask her to enter 4-ten. Ask her to enter 3-ten and one more ten; ask: How much do you have now? [4-ten]	
Name the Rule game. Tell the child we are going to play a new game. I will name some items and you tell me what they have in common. Start by naming all the objects in the room that have red in them. Then ask the child: Can you name the rule that I used to decide what objects I named? [those with red] Repeat, perhaps, for those objects that are made of wood or that are round.	
The evens stairs. Tell the child we will build a different kind of stairs. Have her enter 2 on the first wire and 4 on the second wire. See the left figure on the next page. Ask: Which row has less? [first] Which row has more? [second]	
Ask the child to enter 6 on the third wire. Ask her to continue the pattern for two more wires. See the right figure on the next page. Ask: How many beads are on the third row? [six] How many beads are on the fourth row? [eight] How many beads are on the fifth row? [ten]	The terms *fourth* and *fifth* have not been used before.

ACTIVITIES FOR TEACHING CONTINUED:

EXPLANATIONS CONTINUED:

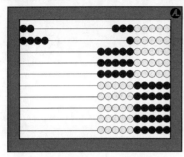

Start of the twos stairs.

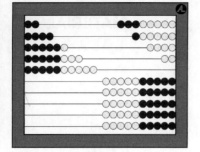

The evens stairs.

Ask the child to say the number on each wire from top to bottom. [2, 4, 6, 8, 10] Ask: What is special about these numbers? [evens]

Equal. Ask the child to take a handful of tiles. Take the same number of tiles. Ask if the two groups have the same number of tiles? [yes] Tell her that when the number is the same, the math word we use is *equal*. Equal means "the same" or "the same as."

The number of tiles in each pile is *equal*.

This time you take a handful of tiles. Ask the child to take an equal number. Also ask her to enter the number on the abacus.

Plus. Tell the child that there is another word that she can learn, *plus*. Instead of saying 4 and 2 is 6, the mathematical words are 4 plus 2 equals 6. Ask the child to enter 6 and 4 on the abacus and to state it in mathematical words. [6 plus 4 equals 10] Repeat for 4 and 3. [4 plus 3 equals 7]

Dot card game. Play the dot card activities in the *Math Card Games* book, N22.

In conclusion. Ask the child: What is 3 and 2? [5] What is 4 plus 3? [7] Raise 4 fingers on your hands and ask the child: Can you show an equal number of fingers?

LESSON 38: COMBINING 10s AND 1s

OBJECTIVES:	**MATERIALS:**
1. To make the odd stairs	1. AL Abacus
2. To introduce combining 10s and 1s	2. Dot cards

ACTIVITIES FOR TEACHING:	**EXPLANATIONS:**

Warm-up. Sing "Days of the Week." Also sing "Writing Numbers," during which the child traces the shapes of the numbers on the flat surface.

Play the Comes After game. Ask: What number comes after 4? [5] Repeat for numbers 7, [8] 1, [2] and 9. [10]

Also play the Comes After game for the days of the week. Ask: What day comes after Tuesday? [Wednesday] Repeat for Monday, [Tuesday] Sunday, [Monday] and Saturday. [Sunday] What day is today? What day is tomorrow?

Ask the child to enter 6 on the abacus. Then ask him to enter 6-ten. Ask him to enter 5-ten and one more ten; ask: How much do you have now? [6-ten]

The Abacus Song with dot cards. Ask the child to lay out the even dot cards. While singing the song, to the tune of the Hokey Pokey, have the child show the correct dot card during the song. Repeat using the odd numbers.

The Abacus Song

The two steps in.
The two steps out.
He holds up the number.
And waves it all about.
He clears the number.
And sits back down.
Where is the number four?

The four steps in. . . .

Make the odd stairs. Tell the child we will build a different kind of stairs. Have him enter 1 on the first wire and 3 on the second wire. See the left figure on the next page. Ask: Which row has less? [first] Which row has more? [second]

Ask the child to enter 5 on the third wire. Ask him to continue the pattern for two more wires. See the right figure on the next page. Ask: How many beads are on the

ACTIVITIES FOR TEACHING CONTINUED:

third row? [five] How many beads are on the fourth row? [seven] How many beads are on the fifth row? [nine]

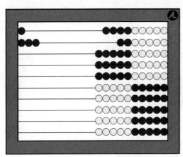 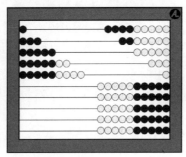

Start of the odd stairs.　　**The odd stairs.**

Ask the child to say the number on each wire from top to bottom. [1, 3, 5, 7, 9] Ask: What is special about these numbers? [odds]

Ask him if he sees anything special about the beads on the right side. [odd numbers from bottom to top]

Tens and ones. Ask each child to enter 3-ten plus 2 ones. See the figure below. Tell him we call it 3-ten 2. Ask them to enter 4-ten plus 6 and to give its name. [4-ten 6] Repeat, giving each child a turn to answer, for 8-ten plus 1 [8-ten 1] and 6-ten plus 7. [6-ten 7]

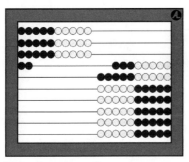

Entering 3-ten 2.

Ask the child to enter numbers such as 2-ten 7, 5-ten 9, 8-ten 1, 6-ten 2, 9-ten 4, and 1-ten 3 on the abacus.

In conclusion. Ask the child: What is 2 and 2? [4] What is 3 plus 3? [6] Raise 6 fingers on your hands and ask the child: Can you show an equal number of fingers?

EXPLANATIONS CONTINUED:

As stated previously, the concept of 10, so vital to understanding place value and computation, is difficult to acquire in our culture. The English naming of quantities from 11 to 99, especially 11 to 19, masks the underlying 10 structure and is very confusing for children.

The term 2-ten will be used temporarily. This term 2-ten, rather than two tens, is easier to say. Also, it is consistent in the way we say hundred as in two hundred thirty-seven, rather than two hundreds thirty-seven.

LESSON 39: COMPOSING TENS AND ONES

OBJECTIVES:

1. To introduce 12 months and a year
2. To introduce the term *yesterday*
3. To count by 2s
4. To compose 10s and 1s using the place-value cards

MATERIALS:

1. AL Abacus
2. **A calendar with 12 months**
3. **A book about the seasons* (optional)**
4. Place-value cards
5. *Math Card Games* book, N43 Level 2

ACTIVITIES FOR TEACHING:	EXPLANATIONS:
Warm-up. Teach the child the new song, "The Months." Sing it to the tune of "Michael Finnegan."	*Two book suggestions: *Watching the Seasons* by Edana Eckart and *The Reasons for Seasons* by Gail Gibbons.

The Months

January, February, March, and April,
May, June, July, and August,
September, October, November, December.
These are the months of the year.

Tell the child to enter 2-ten 3 on the abacus. Ask: What number comes after 2-ten 3? [2-ten 4] Tell them to enter 3-ten 7. Ask: What number comes after 3-ten 7? [3-ten 8]

Comes Before game. Ask the child to say the names of the days of the week. Then play the Comes Before game with the days of the week. For example, say: What day comes before Monday? [Sunday] What day is today? What day is tomorrow? What day was *yesterday*? Explain that yesterday is the day before today.

Calendar of a year. Show the child a calendar and explain that a year has 1-ten 2 months. Discuss the seasons, and if available, read a book about the seasons.

This is a good time to introduce seasons as part of a year.

More Than problem. Ask the child: What quantities can you enter on the top row of the abacus that are more than 5? [6, 7, 8, 9, 10]

Counting by 2s. Ask the child to build the even stairs. Then ask her to read the quantities entered from top to bottom. [2, 4, 6, 8, 10] Tell her that is called *counting by twos*. See the left figure below.

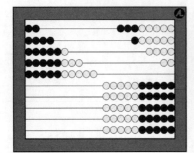

The twos stairs.

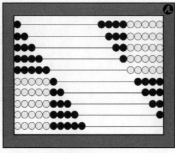

The ones stairs.

ACTIVITIES FOR TEACHING CONTINUED:	EXPLANATIONS CONTINUED:

Ask her: Can you *count by ones* from 1 to 10? [1, 2, 3, 4, 5, 6, 7, 8, 9, 10] She may want to built the stairs as shown in the right figure on the previous page.

Naming 10 quantities. Ask the child to enter 6-ten on the abacus. Then to enter 4 more on the next wire. Ask how much she has entered. [6-ten 4] Repeat for several more combinations, such as 8-ten 7, 9-ten 6, and 4-ten 8.

Composing numbers with place-value cards. Ask the child to spread out the 10s and 1s from the place-value cards. Enter 3-ten 2 on the abacus and ask her to read the quantity. [3-ten 2] Then ask her to find place-value cards matching the quantities. Look for the 3-ten card then the 2 card. Show her how to overlap the cards as shown below. Finally, ask her to read the cards. [3-ten 2]

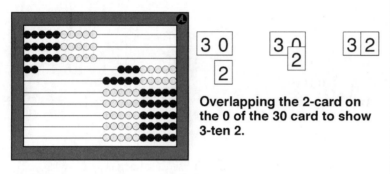

Overlapping the 2-card on the 0 of the 30 card to show 3-ten 2.

For the second example, ask the child to enter 7-ten 3. Then ask her to find the matching cards, to overlap and to read them.

Tell the child to think of a number. Then she says it, enters it, composes it, and reads it. Ask her to do several other numbers.

Can You Find game. Play the Can You Find game in the *Math Card Games* book, N43 Level 2.

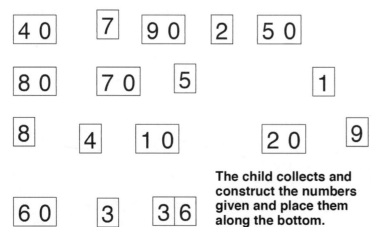

The child collects and construct the numbers given and place them along the bottom.

In conclusion. How much is 4-ten and 3? [43]

LESSON 40: INTRODUCING THE MATH BALANCE & HEXAGONS

OBJECTIVES:
1. To introduce the math balance
2. To learn the term *hexagon*
3. To combine hexagons

MATERIALS:
1. AL Abacus
2. Math balance and 3 weights
3. Worksheet 10, Hexagons
4. **A book or pictures about bees and their honeycombs* (optional)**
5. **Scissors**

ACTIVITIES FOR TEACHING:	EXPLANATIONS:
Warm-up. Sing with the child the song, "The Months" to the tune of "Michael Finnegan."	*Two suggestions: *Are You a Bee?* Judy Allen and *Bees! Learn About Bees and Enjoy Colorful Pictures* by Becky Wolff

The Months

January, February, March, and April,
May, June, July, and August,
September, October, November, December.
These are the months of the year.

Ask the child to say the names of the days of the week. Then play the Comes Before game with the days of the week. Ask: What day comes before Saturday? [Friday] What day is today? What day was yesterday? What day is tomorrow?

Ask the child to count by ones to 10. [1, 2, 3, 4, 5, 6, 7, 8, 9, 10] Also ask him to count by twos to 10. [2, 4, 6, 8, 10]

Child can use the abacus to help with counting.

Ask the child to enter on the abacus combinations such as 2-ten 4, 4-ten 9, 9-ten 9, and 1-ten 2.

Ask the child: Do you see any parallel lines or planes? Do you see any perpendicular lines or planes?

Math balance. Tell the child we are going to explore the math balance. Give the child two weights and ask him to put one on each side to make it balance. Avoid giving hints. When he has made it balance, ask him to find another way to make it balance.

After the math balance is assembled, check to be sure it is level. If necessary, adjust it by moving the little white weights under the yellow beam.

All the weights are the same; ignore the number embossed on them.

An interesting note: for their first attempt, many children choose the 10s, while adults usually choose low numbers.

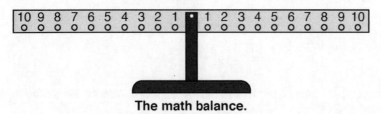

The math balance.

Next give him a third weight and ask him to put 1 weight on one side and 2 weights on the other side to make it balance. One possibility is shown on the next page. Ask him to find other ways. Encourage him to experiment to discover how it works.

A person can make this discovery only once so do not let anyone else spoil it.

ACTIVITIES FOR TEACHING CONTINUED:

An example of balancing with three weights.

Cutting out hexagons. Worksheet 10 has two groups of five hexagons. Tell him: These figures are called *hexagons*. Ask: How many hexagons are on the page? [10] Ask: If you cut out 5 how many will be left to cut out? [5] Now share the task of cutting.

Worksheet 10.

Honeybees. While the child finishes cutting out the hexagons, you could read a book about bees. Emphasize how the bees build their honeycombs in the shape of regular hexagons. Ask him to arrange some hexagons in the same way. See the left figure below.

He could also make a ten-fractal. See the right figure below.

Arranging hexagons to fill up space.

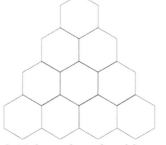

A 10-fractal made with hexagons.

Inspecting hexagons. Ask: Does a hexagon have perpendicular lines? [no] Ask: Does a hexagon have parallel lines? [yes] How many sets of parallel lines? [3 sets] How many sides does a hexagon have? [6]

In conclusion. Ask the child what is 4-ten and 6 and have them enter it on the abacus. [4-ten 6]

EXPLANATIONS CONTINUED:

Children love exploring this concept with other combinations.

These hexagons will be used again in later lessons.

LESSON 41: PARTITIONING ON THE MATH BALANCE

OBJECTIVES:
1. To partition with the math balance
2. To learn to write the "=" and the "+" signs
3. To discover doubles

MATERIALS:
1. AL Abacus
2. A hexagon (from Worksheet 10)
3. Math balance and 3 weights
4. Dry erase board

ACTIVITIES FOR TEACHING:	EXPLANATIONS:
Warm-up. Sing with the child the song, "The Months" to the tune of "Michael Finnegan."	

Teach the rhyme, "One, Two, Buckle my Shoe."

One, Two, Buckle my Shoe
One, two, buckle my shoe.
Three, four, shut the door.
Five, six, pick up sticks.
Seven, eight, lay them straight.
Nine, ten, a big, fat hen.

Ask the child to enter on the abacus combinations such as 3-ten 7, 2-ten 6, 8-ten 9, and 1-ten 4.

Show a hexagon to the child. Ask: Does a hexagon have perpendicular lines? [no] Ask: Does a hexagon have parallel lines? [yes] How many sets of parallel lines? [3 sets] How many sides does a hexagon have? [6]

Show 5 on your fingers and ask: Can you enter an equal amount on the abacus? Then ask her to enter 5 plus 1 more. Ask: How many do you have now? [6] Next ask her to enter 6 plus 1 more. How many do you have? [7]

Partitioning 5. Ask the child to place a weight on the 5 on the left side of the math balance. Then ask her to make it balance with two weights on the right side. See the figure below.

Remember, a person can make this discovery only once so do not let anyone else spoil it.

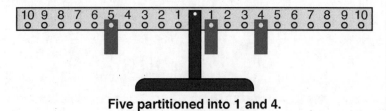

Five partitioned into 1 and 4.

ACTIVITIES FOR TEACHING CONTINUED:

After she has made it balance, say: Let's write this down. Point to the left side of the dry erase board and ask the child to write 5. Then write "=" after the 5, explaining that it is the *equal sign*. Explain that the equal sign is written with two parallel lines that are *equal* in length. Then ask the child to write the first number from the right side of the math balance. Write "+" explaining that it is the *plus sign*. Have her complete the equation by writing the other number from the right side. Finally, ask her to say how she balanced it using "+" and "=". [5 = 1 + 4, or 5 = 2 + 3]

$$5 = 1 + 4$$

Ask the child to find another way to make 5 balance. This time she can write the entire equation:

$$5 = 2 + 3$$

Partitioning 6. Tell the child: Let's partition 6. Prompt her to move the left 5 weight to the left 6. Then ask her to make it balance and to write down the results.

$$6 = 1 + 5$$

$$6 = 2 + 4$$

$$6 = 3 + 3$$

Express delight at the two 3s and say: Six has a *double*.

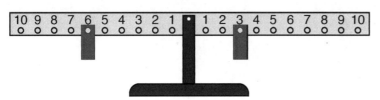

Six has a double (3 and 3).

Partitioning 7–10. Ask: Do you think 7 has a double? Ask her to partition 7. Ask her to write down only the doubles. Continue with 8, 9, and 10.

Doubles mystery. Challenge the child: Can you figure out which numbers have doubles? Let the child discover the answer for herself. Do not give hints. If necessary, let her think about it overnight. [evens]

In conclusion. Ask: Can you name the ways to partition 5 on the math balance? [1 + 4 and 2 + 3]

EXPLANATIONS CONTINUED:

Children in their elementary years often view the = sign as meaning "do something." This limited view interferes with their complete understanding of the concept of equations needed for advanced topics. The mathematical meaning of the equal sign is that the two sides of the equation are equal. Therefore, it is suggested that you do not refer to the equal sign with "makes."

If the child tires of the writing, you could do it for her.

LESSON 42: DOUBLES AND WRITING EQUATIONS

OBJECTIVES:

1. To learn the term *equation*
2. To find and write the first five double equations
3. To introduce the term *sum*

MATERIALS:

1. A hexagon
2. AL Abacus
3. Math balance
4. Dry erase board

ACTIVITIES FOR TEACHING:	EXPLANATIONS:
Warm-up. Tell the child the name of the current month. Then ask him to sing, "The Months" to the tune of "Michael Finnegan."	

The Months

January, February, March, and April,
May, June, July, and August,
September, October, November, December.
These are the months of the year.

Continue teaching the rhyme, "One, Two, Buckle my Shoe."

One, Two, Buckle my Shoe

One, two, buckle my shoe.
Three, four, shut the door.
Five, six, pick up sticks.
Seven, eight, lay them straight.
Nine, ten, a big, fat hen.

Show a hexagon to the child. Ask: Does a hexagon have perpendicular lines? [no] Ask: Does a hexagon have parallel lines? [yes] How many sets of parallel lines? [3 sets] How many sides does a hexagon have? [6]

Ask the child to enter on the abacus 1-ten 7. Ask: What number comes next? [1 ten 8] Enter 5-ten 2 and ask: What number comes next? [5-ten 3] Enter 7-ten 3 and ask: What is next? [7-ten 4] Enter 2-ten 1, and ask: What is next? [2-ten 2]

Play the Continue the Pattern game. Tell the child: I am going to name some numbers and you listen to the pattern and keep going. Start with 2, 3, 4. [5, 6, 7] Next try 3, 4, 5. [6, 7, 8]

ACTIVITIES FOR TEACHING CONTINUED:

Doubles on the math balance. Ask the child to put two weights on the left 1-peg. Then ask him to balance it and write it down on the dry erase board. See the figure below.

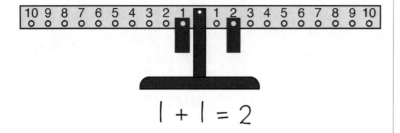

$$1 + 1 = 2$$

Explain that 1 + 1 = 2 is called an *equation*.

Ask him to put two weights on the 2. Ask him to balance it and write the equation.

$$2 + 2 = 4$$

Continue 3, 4, and 5.

$$3 + 3 = 6$$

$$4 + 4 = 8$$

$$5 + 5 = 10$$

After the child has written all five equations ask him to read the equations. Then ask: What did you notice about the *sums*, the number after the equal sign? [even number]

In conclusion. Show the hexagon and ask for its name. [hexagon] Ask: Can you finish the equation 2 + 2 = __? [4]

EXPLANATIONS CONTINUED:

An expression such as 2 + 2 = 4 is properly call an equation—the word equation comes from the word *equal*. The term "number sentence," which sometimes is used, makes no sense grammatically or mathematically and should be avoided. Engineers and scientists do not talk about number sentences. A sentence is a group of words making a complete thought or sentence may refer to a punishment. Some children have thought that writing a number sentence meant spelling out the numbers.

The Common Core State Standards uses equation. However, some older tests still use "number sentence". If the child will be taking such a test, tell him that the person who wrote the test may use the incorrect words "number sentence" instead of equation.

LESSON 43: ELLIPSE AND FOLDING SHAPES

OBJECTIVES:
1. To learn the term *ellipse*
2. To fold figures in half

MATERIALS:
1. Tiles
2. AL Abacus
3. Worksheet 11, Figures to Fold
4. **Scissors**
5. Geometry reflector

ACTIVITIES FOR TEACHING:	EXPLANATIONS:
Warm-up. Ask the child the name of the current month. Then ask her to sing, "The Months" to the tune of "Michael Finnegan."	

The Months

January, February, March, and April,
May, June, July, and August,
September, October, November, December.
These are the months of the year.

Continue teaching, "One, Two, Buckle my Shoe."

One, Two, Buckle my Shoe

One, two, buckle my shoe.
Three, four, shut the door.
Five, six, pick up sticks.
Seven, eight, lay them straight.
Nine, ten, a big, fat hen.

Show a tile to the child. Ask: What shape is this? [square, rectangle, quadrilateral] Ask: Does this tile have parallel lines? [yes] How many sets of parallel lines? [2 sets] Ask: Does this tile have perpendicular lines? [yes] Then ask: How many sets of perpendicular lines? [4 sets] How many sides does this tile have? [4]

Ask the child to enter on the abacus 1-ten 6. Ask: What number comes next? [1 ten 7] Enter 6-ten 2 and ask: What number what comes next? [6-ten 3] Enter 7-ten 1 and ask: What is next? [7-ten 2] Enter 1-ten 1, and ask: What is next? [1-ten 2]

Play the Continue the Pattern game with numbers. Tell the child: I am going to name some numbers and you listen to the pattern and keep going. Start with 1, 2, 3. [4, 5, 6] Next try 5, 6, 7. [8, 9, 10]

| **ACTIVITIES FOR TEACHING CONTINUED:** | **EXPLANATIONS CONTINUED:** |

Worksheet 11. There are four figures on the worksheet. Tell the child to cut out the figures.

Ask the child to name the three figures she knows. [square, quadrilateral, and triangle] Tell her the name of the remaining figure is an *ellipse*.

Folding. Ask the child to fold her ellipse in half so that the edges match. Then tell her to unfold it and fold it a different way. See the figures below. Ask if she can find another way. [no]

 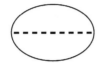

Folding the ellipse in half two ways.

Repeat the folding for the quadrilateral and square. [They can each be folded two different ways.]

Repeat for the triangle. [It can be folded only one way]

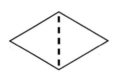 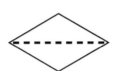

    Folding other figures in half by matching the edges.

Geometry reflector. Encourage the child to explore the figures with the geometry reflector. Ask: What happens if she puts the geometry reflector on a folded line? [It would look the same.]

Ellipse reflected.

In conclusion. Show the ellipse and ask for its name. Ask: Can you finish the equation 4 + 4 = __? [8]

Sometimes an ellipse is called an oval. However, while a racetrack is an oval, it is not an ellipse. The correct mathematical name for this figure is *ellipse*.

LESSON 44: PENNIES & REFLECTIONS

OBJECTIVES:

1. To learn the value of a *penny*
2. To learn the term *cent*
3. To build reflections on geoboards
4. To learn the term *reflection*

MATERIALS:

1. Music for "Three-ten Days Has September" (Appendix p. 10)
2. AL Abacus
3. Math balance
4. Coins
5. Geoboards and Geometry reflector

ACTIVITIES FOR TEACHING:	EXPLANATIONS:
Warm-up. Teach the child this new song, "Three-ten Days Has September." Explain that it tells how many days are in a month.	In future lessons, the child will be making a calendar for the next year. Knowing the number of days in a month will be helpful.

Three-ten Days Has September

Three-ten days has September,
April, June, and November.
The rest have 3-ten 1 to carry,
But only 2-ten 8 for February,
Except in leap year, that's the time
When February has 2-ten 9.

Ask the child to count by ones to 10. Also ask him to count by twos to 10.

Ask the child to enter on the abacus combinations such as 1-ten 4, 2-ten 3, 6-ten 2, and 8-ten 1.

Play the Continue the Pattern game with numbers. Tell the child you are going to name some numbers and he is to listen to the pattern and keep going. Start with 4, 5, 6. [7, 8, 9] Next try 2, 3, 4. [5, 6, 7]

Using the math balance, partition 5. [1 + 4, 2 + 3] Ask the child to partition 6, using three different combinations. [1 + 5, 2 + 4, 3 + 3]

Penny. Tell the child that today he will be working with money. Show him a penny and tell him it is called a *penny* and it is worth 1 *cent*. Ask him to show it with his fingers and to enter that amount on the abacus.

Then show him 2 pennies and ask how much he thinks they are worth. [2 cents] Be sure that he includes the word cents. Ask him to show 2 cents with his fingers and to enter it on the abacus. Continue up to 5 pennies.

Practice. Lay out various coins. Ask the child to pick up three pennies. Return the pennies to the collection. Then ask him to pick up 4 cents. How many pennies are you holding? [4] If desired, repeat with other quantities using the terms pennies and cents.

ACTIVITIES FOR TEACHING CONTINUED:

EXPLANATIONS CONTINUED:

Count by ones. Ask the child to count by 1s by adding 1 bead at a time on the top wire of the abacus. [1, 2, 3, 4, 5, 6, 7, 8, 9, 10] Then tell him: Add 1 more bead on the second wire. Now how much do you have? [1-ten 1] Ask him to add 1 more and say how much it is. [1-ten 2] Continue to 2-ten.

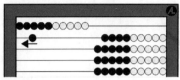 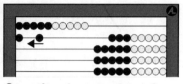

Counting 1 more: 1-ten 1.   **Counting 1 more: 1-ten 2.**

Reflections on the geoboard. Place a rubber band around the geoboard between two columns near the center. See the left figure below. Tell the child: This will be the *line of reflection.*

Tell the child that you going to make a triangle on one side of the line of reflection. See the left figure below. Then tell him you are going to make its *reflection* on the other side. See the second figure below.

The concept of reflection and symmetry is best taught by examples. The definitions are not helpful to children, and many adults.

Ask the child to place the geometry reflector on the line: What do you see? [the reflected triangle]

With reflector.

Original and original and reflection.

Ask him to make some shapes and their reflections on the geoboard. Some examples are shown below.

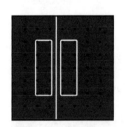  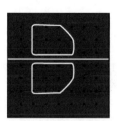

Other examples of reflections.

In conclusion. Ask him if he can find other examples of reflections in the room. [his hands, feet, shoes, two windows side-by-side]

LESSON 45: THE LESS GAME & REFLECTIONS

OBJECTIVES:
1. To introduce the term *less*
2. To build a reflection of a structure

MATERIALS:
1. AL Abacus
2. Math balance
3. Three sets, 1 to 10 of the basic number cards
4. Centimeter cubes
5. Geometry reflector

ACTIVITIES FOR TEACHING:	EXPLANATIONS:

ACTIVITIES FOR TEACHING:

Warm-up. Sing "Three-ten Days Has September."

Three-ten Days Has September
Three-ten days has September,
April, June, and November.
The rest have 3-ten 1 to carry,
But only 2-ten 8 for February,
Except in leap year, that's the time
When February has 2-ten 9.

Ask the child to enter on the abacus combinations such as 1-ten 9, 3-ten 4, 5-ten 1, and 9-ten 9.

Play the Continue the Pattern game with numbers. Start with 2, 3, 4. [5, 6, 7] Next try 5, 6, 7. [8, 9, 10]

Ask the child to use the math balance to partition 4. [1 + 3, 2 + 2] Ask the child to find the three ways to partition 7. [1 + 6, 2 + 5, 3 + 4]

Less. Tell the child the opposite of hot is cold. Then ask: What is the opposite of good, [bad] the opposite of black, [white] the opposite of light, [dark or heavy] and the opposite of fast? [slow] Encourage her to think of other opposites.

Ask the child: What is the opposite of happy? [sad] What is the opposite of sad? [happy] Repeat for short and tall. Ask: What is the opposite of more? Emphasize that it is *less*. Show 3 fingers and say: Three fingers are more than two. Two fingers are less than three. See the figure.

EXPLANATIONS:

These questions are to help the child understand that the opposite of an opposite is the original.

Three is more than two.

Two is less than three.

ACTIVITIES FOR TEACHING CONTINUED:

Ask: Which is less, 4 or 1? [1] Repeat for 2-ten and 3-ten. Ask: Which is less, 4 or 4? [neither, the same]

Conclude by asking: What is the opposite of more? [less] What is the opposite of less? [more]

The Less game. This simple war game uses tally marks for scoring. Use about 30 basic number cards (3 sets, 1–10), divided into two piles. Each player takes a card, turns it over for both to see and says the number aloud. The player having less writes a tally mark. Set the cards aside. Players take turns deciding whose card is less.

In the event the cards played have the same quantity, both players write a tally mark. Continue until one player reaches 10.

Making a copy. Tell the child you will work together on this activity. Each needs 10 cubes. First you build a structure, then ask the child to copy it. When you both agree it is the same, ask the child to build some thing that you copy. The child may continue the activity herself by both constructing and copying an arrangement using the cubes.

Copying an arrangement

Making a reflection. Ask: Does the geometry reflector make an exact copy? [no] Tell the child it makes a reflection. Build a structure and tell her to build a reflection, perhaps by pretending that there is a geometry reflector between the two. When she is finished, ask her to check her structure with the geometry reflector. Next ask the child to build a structure for which you build the reflection.

Copying a reflection.

In conclusion. Ask the child: What do you see when you look in the mirror? [her own reflection}

EXPLANATIONS CONTINUED:

LESSON 46: MORE DOUBLES AND GROUPING

OBJECTIVES:

1. To introduce the doubles 6 + 6 to 9 + 9
2. To practice counting using the abacus
3. To rearrange a group of objects into 5s and 10s

MATERIALS:

1. Math balance
2. Tiles
3. AL Abacus
4. Place-value cards

ACTIVITIES FOR TEACHING:	EXPLANATIONS:
Warm-up. Sing "Three-ten Days Has September." Say the rhyme, "One, Two, Buckle my Shoe." Ask: Which is less, 5 or 2? [2] Repeat for 3-ten and 6-ten. [3-ten] Lastly ask: Which is less, 2 or 2? [neither, the same] What is the opposite of more? [less] What is the opposite of less? [more] Ask the child to use the math balance to partition 6. [1 + 5, 2 + 4, 3 + 3] Ask him: Can you find four ways to partition 8. [1 + 7, 2 + 6, 3 + 5, 4 + 4] Using tiles, make a pattern and have the child make the same pattern. Then make another pattern and have the child make the reflection. **More doubles.** Ask the child to enter 5 on the top two rows of the abacus. Ask: What is 5 + 5? [10] Ask him to enter 1 more on each row. See the figures below. Ask: Can you say the equation that says how much is it altogether? [6 + 6 = 1-ten 2] Ask how he knows. [There is a blue ten and 2 more.]	

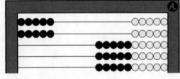

5 + 5 = 10.   **6 + 6 = 1-ten 2**

Again ask the child to add 1 more to each row and say the equation. [7 + 7 = 1-ten 4] Continue to 10 + 10.

More doubles on the balance. Review by asking the child to place 2 weights on the right 1-peg and a third weight on the left to balance it, and to say the equation. [1 + 1 = 2] Repeat for 2; place 2 weights on the right 2-peg and the third weight on the left to balance it. Say the equation. [2 + 2 = 4] Repeat for 3, 4, and 5.

| ACTIVITIES FOR TEACHING CONTINUED: | EXPLANATIONS CONTINUED: |

Have the child put two weights on the 6-peg on the right side. Ask him to make it balance. Let him struggle for a while. (Two 6s on the left is not a solution.) Suggest he use a weight on the 10-peg and another somewhere else. [1-ten and 2] Ask the child to show the solution with the place-value cards. See the figure below. Repeat for 7 + 7, 8 + 8, and 9 + 9.

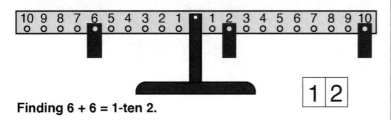

Finding 6 + 6 = 1-ten 2.

Research shows that a child will have better recall for something he learned after a bit of struggle.

Counting with the abacus. Ask the child to take several handfuls of tiles. Ask him to count the tiles by moving them over one at a time and entering the quantity on the abacus while saying the number.

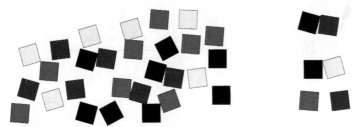

Six tiles of the handful are counted.

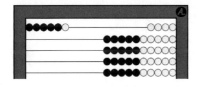

Counted tiles on the abacus.

After he has completed the counting, ask him to compose the number with the place-value cards.

Determining quantity with grouping by tens. Next ask him to put the same tiles into some kind of pattern so anyone can tell how many there are without having to count. If needed, prompt grouping in 5s and 10s. See the figure below. Ask him to compare with his earlier number. [same]

Grouping in 5s and 10s like the AL Abacus, makes the number quickly recognizable.

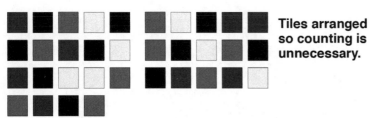

Tiles arranged so counting is unnecessary.

In conclusion. Ask: What is 6 + 6? [1-ten 2]

LESSON 47: NICKELS AND ESTIMATING QUANTITIES

OBJECTIVES:

1. To learn the value of a *nickel*
2. To estimate the number of a collection of objects

MATERIALS:

1. Coins
2. AL Abacus
3. Worksheet 12, Writing More Numbers: Start at Left
4. Tiles
5. Place-value cards

ACTIVITIES FOR TEACHING:	EXPLANATIONS:
Warm-up. Sing the song "Three-ten Days Has September."	

Warm-up. Sing the song "Three-ten Days Has September."

Ask the child to say the even numbers to ten.

Tell the child that you will say two numbers and she is to say the next two numbers. Say: 3, 4; [5, 6] 7, 8; [9, 10] 1-ten 5, 1-ten 6. [1-ten 7, 1-ten 8]

Show the child a penny. Ask the name and value. Show her 2 pennies and ask her to enter the quantity on the abacus and to say what it is worth. [2 cents]

Nickels. Show the child a nickel and tell her it is called a *nickel*. Tell her it is worth 5 cents and show the quantity on the abacus. Show 2 nickels and ask the child to enter the value on the abacus. Repeat for 4 nickels, [2-ten cents] 8 nickels, [4-ten cents] and 6 nickels. [3-ten cents]

Next display 1 nickel and 4 pennies; ask her to enter the quantity on the abacus and say the value. [9 cents] Repeat for other nickel and penny combinations.

Ask her to show the values for 3 nickels and 1 penny, [1-ten 6 cents]; 2 nickels and 2 pennies. [1-ten 2 cents]

Worksheet 12. Give the child the worksheet for practice in writing these numbers; remind her to start at the dots. Tell her to do only the left half of the page.

You might keep extra copies available so the child can practice writing numbers at other times.

Counting ones to 2-ten. Ask the child to count by 1s to 10 by adding 1 bead at a time on the top wire of the abacus. [1, 2, 3, ...10] Then tell her: Add 1 more bead on the second wire. Now how much do you have? [1-ten 1] See the figures below. Ask her to continue adding 1 bead at a time saying how much it is. [1-ten 1, 1-ten 2, ... 2-ten] Continue to 2-ten.

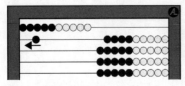

Counting 1 more: 1-ten 1.

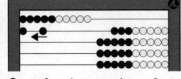

Counting 1 more: 1-ten 2.

ACTIVITIES FOR TEACHING CONTINUED:

Estimating a quantity. Spread out between 60 and 70 tiles so the child can see them. Lay out an additional 10 tiles to the side as a reference and tell her that is what ten looks like. Ask her to make a guess as to how many are in the big pile. Show her guess with place-value cards.

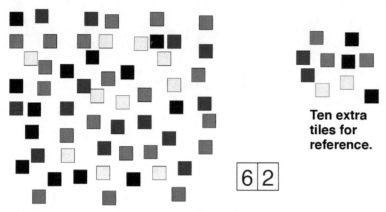

Ten extra tiles for reference.

How many tiles do you think are here?

Next ask the child to help arrange them in a pattern so anyone can tell how many there are without counting. [67 in this example] Discuss how close her guess was. Ask if the reference group of 10 tiles helped her to make a good guess. Emphasize that guesses can be good although they are not exactly right.

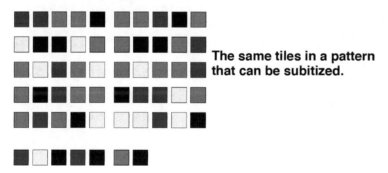

The same tiles in a pattern that can be subitized.

Choosing an estimate. Tell the child to try to take 2-ten 5 tiles by guessing. Then ask her to find out how many she has actually taken. Finally, ask if she thinks she made a good guess.

If the child is interested, repeat the activity with a different number.

In conclusion. Ask: Which is larger in size, penny or nickel? [nickel] Which has a greater value, a penny or a nickel? [nickel]

EXPLANATIONS CONTINUED:

Estimation is used when a rough idea of a quantity is needed rather than an exact figure. An estimate gives an idea of what can be expected without having to go into detail.

This activity is different from the one above in that the child tries to choose a certain amount without counting.

Lesson 48: Dimes and Estimating with the AL Abacus

OBJECTIVES:
1. To continue work with pennies and nickels
2. To learn the value of a *dime*
3. Estimating with the AL Abacus

MATERIALS:
1. Coins
2. Worksheet 12, Writing More Numbers: Start at Left
3. AL Abacus
4. Place-Value cards

ACTIVITIES FOR TEACHING:	EXPLANATIONS:
Warm-up. Sing the song "Three-ten Days Has September." Ask the child to name the current month and the next. Ask the child to say the even numbers up to 10. Show the child a penny. Ask him for its name. [penny] Show 5 fingers and ask the child what coin has that value. [nickel] Repeat for 1 finger. [penny] **Worksheet 12.** Give the child the worksheet for practice in writing these numbers; remind him to start at the dots. Tell him to do the right half of the page. **Dimes.** Show the child a dime and tell him it is called a *dime*. Tell him it is worth 10 cents. Display the penny and dime; tell the child that sometimes people confuse them. Ask how he could tell them apart. [color, the head on only the penny faces right, size, smooth edges on the penny] Lay out a penny, nickel and dime. Ask him how you can tell the coins apart? Explain that the reason the dime is smaller is because it used to be made from silver, which is very expensive. Show 2 dimes and ask the child to enter the value on the abacus. Repeat for 4 dimes, 8 dimes, and 6 dimes.	

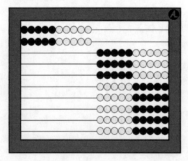

Showing two dimes on the abacus.

Estimating with the abacus. Ask the child to enter 6 on the first row of the abacus. Then ask: Can you enter a number less than 10 on the second row? Enter a number more than 2 on the third row.	The numbers entered are not important.

ACTIVITIES FOR TEACHING CONTINUED:	EXPLANATIONS CONTINUED:

Continue to challenge the child to enter numbers on the abacus that are less or more than your stated amount. See figure below.

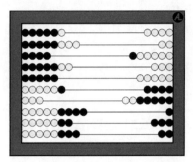

Guess the number of beads.

Tell the child to guess how many beads are entered all together. Ask him to compose his guess with the place-value cards. You take a guess too.

Now ask him to use Take and Give to find the actual number. See figures below. Compare guesses.

If the child is interested, do another estimation.

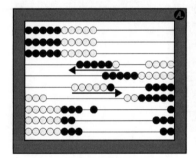 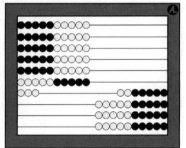

During Take and Give.   **Following Take and Give.**

In conclusion. Which coin is larger in size, penny or dime? [penny] Which coin is worth more, penny or dime? [dime]

LESSON 49: INTRODUCING HALVES AND HALF OF A SET

OBJECTIVES:
1. To find half of a group of items

MATERIALS:
1. AL Abacus
2. Coins
3. Worksheets 13-1 and 13-2, Finding Halves
4. **Scissors**
5. Tiles

ACTIVITIES FOR TEACHING:

EXPLANATIONS:

Warm-up. Sing the song "Three-ten Days Has September."

Ask the child to clap for the numbers in "One, Two, Buckle my Shoe." Then ask her to say only the numbers aloud, emphasizing the second number in each group: one, **two**; three, **four**, and so forth. The remaining words are whispered or said silently.

Say: Enter 100 beads on the abacus and divide them in half. [5-ten] Is there another way? [yes]

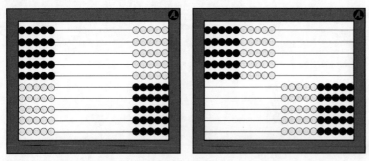

One hundred beads divided in half two ways.

Ask the child to count to 4-ten by moving beads one at a time on the abacus.

Review the values of a penny, nickel, and dime with words, fingers, and the abacus.

Show 10 fingers and ask: What coin has this value? [dime] Repeat for 1 finger [penny] and 5 fingers. [nickel]

Finding the value of multiple coins. Show the child 3 pennies and ask her to show its value with her fingers, on the abacus, and to say the value. Repeat using other coins.

Finding halves. Ask her to cut out the figures on the two worksheets. (You might want to help.) Then ask her to name all the figures she can. Ask her for which two figures she would like to learn the names, then tell her.

ACTIVITIES FOR TEACHING CONTINUED:	EXPLANATIONS CONTINUED:

circle	circle	equilaterial triangle	ellipse
right triangle	hexagon	semicircle	octagon
rectangle	rhombus	pentagon	trapezoid

Halves are part of fractions.

Cut one of the circles into two parts with one part considerably larger than the other part. Ask: Is it cut in half? [no] How do you know? [The two parts are not the same.] Superimpose them so the child can see that they are not the same.

Cut the other circle into equal halves. Again ask, Is this circle cut into half? [yes] How do you know? [The two parts are the same.] Say: Yes, the two halves must be the same!

Ask the child to fold the remaining figures and cut them into halves. Ask her to show the halves by superimposing one on the other.

Half of a set. Show the child 20 tiles. Tell her that you want to give half to her and keep the other half. Ask her how she could do it.

When she has decided on the halves, ask her how she could be sure. [Each half has the same amount.] Ask how many are in each half. [10]

Ask the child to take a handful of tiles, about 8 to 20. Ask her to divide her quantity in half and to tell you how many are in each half. Repeat the activity several times. Let her decide what to do when there is an odd number.

In conclusion. Ask: What is half of 10? [5] What is half 8? [4]

This activity is designed to expand the children's concept of half. Eventually we want them to realize that one half means one part of something or a collection that has been separated into two equal parts. Today's work deals with a single object.

One way to do this systematically is to pick up two tiles at a time one with each hand, and lay them down is separate piles. Remember that a person can only make a discovery once, so let the child struggle some.

ENRICHMENT LESSON 50: MAKING CIRCLES AND ELLIPSES

OBJECTIVES:
1. To construct circles in the sand
2. To construct ellipses in the sand

MATERIALS:
1. **Strings of various lengths (5–25 inches)**
2. Some tally sticks
3. **Sandbox**
4. Math journal (found in the back of the child's worksheets)

ACTIVITIES FOR TEACHING:

Warm up. Review with the child the terms circle and ellipse.

Circles. Lay the strings out flat. Attach a tally stick to each end of the strings either by tape or tying.

Take the child to a sandbox for this activity. Have the child push one of the tally sticks into the sand. Stretch the string so it is not touching the sand. With the other tally stick, start to draw around the first tally stick, keeping the string tight so it is not touching the sand. Go all the way around to create a circle. See figure below.

Repeat making a another circle in the sand using a different length of string and the same center point. Ask: How is the first circle different from the second circle?

One end of the string is attached to the tally stick in the center and the other end to the stick tracing the circle in the sand.

EXPLANATIONS:

This is the first of several enrichment lessons designed to bring the world of math into everyday life. If necessary because of time restraints, the lesson may be omitted without loss of continuity.

This could also been done in the snow, depending on locations and the time of year.

The circle displayed in the picture was dampened with water from a spray bottle to make it more visible.

ACTIVITIES FOR TEACHING CONTINUED:

Ellipse. Keep the center tally stick in the sand. Move the outside stick closer to the center stick and push it into the sand. The picture below shows the sticks about 6 inches apart. Put your finger in the middle of the string. With your finger in the sand draw around both tally sticks until you finish where you started, making an ellipse. Move the sticks closer together and have the child use his fingers this time. Compare the two ellipses to the circle. Ask the child what he notices about all four shapes.

The string is attached to both tally sticks in the center while your finger traces the ellipse in the sand.

While outside, have the child look around for circles and ellipses.

In conclusion. Have the child draw an ellipse and a circle in his math journal. Ask: How does the circle change when the string is longer?

EXPLANATIONS CONTINUED:

A circle is a special ellipse in the same way as a square is a special rectangle.

LESSON 51: COMBINING SEVERAL COINS

OBJECTIVES:

1. To continue work with pennies, nickels, and dimes
2. To associate dimes with 10s and nickels with 5s

MATERIALS:

1. AL Abacus
2. Coins

ACTIVITIES FOR TEACHING:	EXPLANATIONS:
Warm-up. Sing the song "Three-ten Days Has September."	

Ask the child to clap for the numbers in "One, Two, Buckle my Shoe." Then ask her to say only the numbers aloud, emphasizing the second number in each group: one, **two**; three, **four**, and so forth. The remaining words are whispered or said silently.

Tell the child to enter 100 beads on the abacus and divide them in half. [5-ten] Is there another way? [yes]

Ask the child to count to 4-ten by moving beads one at a time on the abacus.

Review the values of a penny, nickel, and dime with words, fingers, and the abacus.

Show 10 fingers and ask: What coin has this value? [dime] Repeat for 1 finger [penny] and 5 fingers. [nickel]

Finding the value of multiple coins. Show the child 3 pennies and ask her to show its value on the abacus and to say the value.

 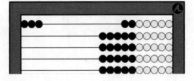

Representing 3 pennies.

Repeat with 4 pennies then with 5 pennies. Repeat again with 2 nickels and with 2 dimes.

 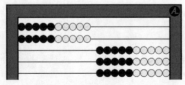

Using 2 dimes to match the quantity 2-ten on the abacus.

ACTIVITIES FOR TEACHING CONTINUED:	EXPLANATIONS CONTINUED:

Enter 10 on the abacus and ask her to find a coin that will match. [dime] Ask if she could do it another way. Point out the 2 fives. [2 nickels] Ask if she could do it still another way. [10 pennies]

Enter 20 and ask the child to name the quantity [2-ten] and to find the matching coins, but this time to use as few coins as possible. If she suggests 4 nickels, ask her to compare the number of coins, 2 dimes versus 4 nickels.

Ways to make 15 cents problem. Tell the child that Bobby wants to buy an apple that costs 1-ten 5 cents. Enter 15 on the abacus. Ask the child how she could pay for it. [1 dime and 1 nickel, 1 nickel and 10 pennies, 3 nickels, 2 nickels and 5 pennies, 1 dime and 5 pennies]

When the child has found one solution, ask if she could do it another way. Continue until she has found all the solutions.

Practice. Enter 4-ten on the abacus and ask the child to show the quantities using as few coins as possible. Repeat again for 2-ten 5.

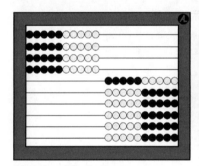 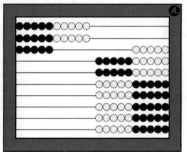

Match with 4 dimes.   2 dimes and 1 nickel.

In conclusion. Ask the child to find 2-ten 3 cents using the fewest amount of coins. How many coins are needed? [5]

LESSON 52: GROUPING BY FIVES

OBJECTIVES:

1. To count by grouping by fives
2. Representing coins on the abacus

MATERIALS:

1. AL Abacus
2. Coins
3. Worksheet 14, Writing More Numbers: Start at Right
4. Tiles
5. Place-value cards

ACTIVITIES FOR TEACHING:	EXPLANATIONS:
Warm-up. Sing the song "Three-ten Days Has September."	
Play the Comes After game for numbers 1 to 10. Also play it for days of the week.	
Ask the child to count by twos to 2-ten as you enter beads on the abacus two at a time.	
Have the child enter 2-ten on the abacus and ask him to show you which coins will give you 2-ten. Make sure to use pennies, nickels and dimes.	
Divide the beads on the abacus in half.	
Worksheet 14. Give the child the worksheet for practice in writing numbers that start at the right. Remind him to start at the dots. Tell him to only do the left half of the page.	You might keep extra copies available so the child can practice writing numbers at other times.
Grouping by 5s. Spread 50 to 100 tiles (64 in this example) in a heap and tell the child: Let's find out how much this is by entering the number on the abacus. Tell him that you are going to take 5. Move 5 tiles as a group. Ask: How much is this? [5] Enter 5 on the abacus. Continue by taking another 5 and ask the child to enter another 5 on the abacus as shown.	

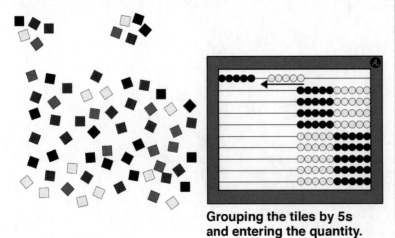

Grouping the tiles by 5s and entering the quantity.

ACTIVITIES FOR TEACHING CONTINUED:	EXPLANATIONS CONTINUED:

Continue until all the tiles have been grouped as shown. The last group may contain less than 5 tiles. Ask the child how many are entered on the abacus [6-ten 4 for this example] and to show the amount with the place-value cards.

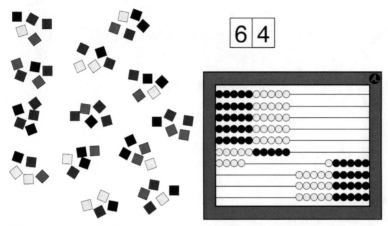

Tiles grouped by 5s.   The final number entered, 64.

Practice. Ask the child to take a handful of tiles and group them by 5s. Show the amount with the place-value cards. Then ask him to enter the quantity on the abacus.

Repeat the activity several more times with different quantities.

Representing quantities with coins. Enter 4 on the abacus and ask the child to find coins that will show that amount. Next enter 5 and ask the same question. [5 pennies or 1 nickel] If he names only one answer, ask if there is another way.

Repeat with 7. [7 pennies or 1 nickel and 2 pennies]

Repeat with 10. [10 pennies, 2 nickels, 1 dime, or 1 nickel and 5 pennies] Continue asking for more solutions until there are no more.

In conclusion. Lay out 10 pennies in no particular order. Ask the child to find the amount and show it on the abacus.

LESSON 53: ASSESSMENT 2

OBJECTIVES:
1. To assess for understanding

MATERIALS:
1. AL Abacus
2. Coins
3. Assessment Checklist 2 (Appendix p. 11)
4. *Math Card Games* book
5. Geoboard and Geometry reflector
6. Three sets of basic number cards, 0 to 10

ACTIVITIES FOR TEACHING:	EXPLANATIONS:
Warm-up. Sing the song "Three-ten Days Has September."	

Warm-up. Sing the song "Three-ten Days Has September."

Play the Comes After game for numbers 1 to 10. Also play it for days of the week.

Ask the child to enter 10 on the abacus with her left hand and 8 with her right hand. Then ask: How much is entered? [1-ten 8]

Ask for the values of a penny, nickel, and dime with words, fingers, and the abacus.

Show 5 fingers and ask the child what coin has that value. [nickel] Repeat for 1 finger [penny] and 10 fingers. [dime]

Ask the child to place her hands above the table. Now ask her to place her hands below the table.

Assessing using games. Have the assessment checklist (Appendix p. 11) next to you while you play the following games. Use the checklist to track what the child understands.

Swim to Ten game. Play the Swim to Ten game found in *Math Card Games*, N34. Encourage the child to visualize her move to realize that the biggest number is not always the best move. Play it several times to allow her the opportunity to learn to strategize.

Can You Find game. Play a variation of the game, Can You Find, N43. Ask the child to show 4-ten on the abacus and find the matching place-value card. Continue with 60, 70, and 80.

Reflections on the geoboard. Place a rubber band around the geoboard near the center between two columns. See the left figure on the next page. Ask the child to build the triangle's reflection as seen in the middle figure on the next page. Ask the child to show the triangle's reflection with the geometry reflector. See the right figure on the next page.

ACTIVITIES FOR TEACHING CONTINUED:

EXPLANATIONS CONTINUED:

The Less game. This simple war game uses tally marks for scoring. Use about 30 basic number cards (3 sets, 1–10), divided into two piles. Each player takes a card, turns it over for both to see and says the number aloud. The player having less writes a tally mark. Set the cards aside. Players take turns deciding whose card is less.

In the event the cards played have the same quantity, both players write a tally mark. Continue until one player reaches 10.

Assessment Checklist 2. Found on Appendix page 11.

If there are concepts that the child struggles with, review by playing the games.

Name	Goal 1. Show their left hand.	Goal 2. Enter a quantity on the abacus and name it.	Goal 3. Find something above/below the table.	Goal 4. Make the reflection of a triangle on the geoboard.	Goal 5. Determine more and less.

LESSON 54: ASSESSMENT 3

OBJECTIVES:
1. To assess for understanding

MATERIALS:
1. AL Abacus
2. Coins
3. Assessment Checklist 3 (Appendix p. 12)
4. *Math Card Games* book
5. Dot and Bead cards
6. Two sets of basic number cards, 1 to 10

ACTIVITIES FOR TEACHING:	EXPLANATIONS:
Warm-up. Sing the song "Three-ten Days Has September."	

Warm-up. Sing the song "Three-ten Days Has September."

Enter 4 on the abacus. Have the child start at 4 and count to ten, adding one bead at a time.

Play the Comes After game for numbers 1 to 10. Also play it for days of the week.

Ask the child to count by twos to 2-ten as you enter beads on the abacus two at a time.

Show the penny, nickel, and dime. Tell the child to point to the coin worth 5 cents. [nickel] Tell him to point to the coin worth 1 cent. [penny] Finally, point to the coin worth 10 cents. [dime]

Show 5 fingers and ask the child what coin has that value. [nickel] Repeat for 1 finger [penny] and 10 fingers. [dime]

Assessing using games. Have the assessment checklist (Appendix p. 12) next to you while you play the following games. Use the checklist to track what the child understands.

Dot Card and Bead Card Memory. Lay the dot cards face down on the left and the bead cards on the right. The child first turns over a dot card, says the number aloud, and looks for its match among the bead cards. For more instructions, see the *Math Card Games* book, N17.

Mixed-Up Cards game. In this game, a set of basic number cards is laid out in order; another set is mixed-up. For instructions, see the *Math Card Games* book, N12.

Mystery Card game. Here the child must think of the missing card. See the *Math Card Games* book, N13.

Harder Mixed-Up Cards game. This game is similar to Mixed-Up cards, but only one set of cards is used. See the *Math Card Games* book, N14.

Missing Card game. Play this game like Mystery Card with the gap removed. See the *Math Card Games* book, N15.

ACTIVITIES FOR TEACHING CONTINUED:

Assessment Checklist 3. Found on Appendix page 12.

Name	Goal 6. Recognizes 8 on dot and bead cards.	Goal 7. Put numbers in order from 1-10.	Goal 8. Start with 4 on the abacus and count by ones to 10.	Goal 9. Find the missing number in a sequence from 1 to 10.

EXPLANATIONS CONTINUED:

If there are concepts that the child struggles with, review by playing the games.

LESSON 55: FINDING CORRECT COINS & TALLY MARK CHART

OBJECTIVES:

1. To find the coins, pennies, nickels, and dimes, to match a written number
2. To introduce the "¢" sign
3. To introduce the term *between*

MATERIALS:

1. Dry erase board
2. Place-value cards
3. AL Abacus
4. Coins
5. Tiles

ACTIVITIES FOR TEACHING:	EXPLANATIONS:

ACTIVITIES FOR TEACHING:

Warm-up. Sing the song "The Months" which is sung to the tune of "Michael Finnegan." Ask the child to name the current month and the next month. Ask what month comes before the current month. Sing the song again if needed.

Play the Comes After game. Ask: What number comes after 7? [8] What number comes after 6? [7] Continue as needed.

Ask the child to say the numbers in the fashion of "One, Two, Buckle my Shoe" by emphasizing the even numbers: one, **two**; three, **four**; five, **six**; seven, **eight**; nine, **ten**.

Finding the correct coins. Write 23¢ on the dry erase board and say that it is the price of an apple or some other item. Point out the ¢ sign and tell the child that it means cents. Ask her to read it [2-ten 3 cents] and to construct the number with the place-value cards. She may also need to enter the quantity on the abacus.

Then ask the child to make that amount with coins. [2 dimes and 3 pennies]

Matching 2-ten 3 with 2 dimes and 3 pennies.

Repeat for 35¢. [3 dimes and 1 nickel]

Ask the child to name the price of some object less than 99¢. Then ask her to find the corresponding coins. Repeat for several prices.

Counting the letters in the alphabet. Ask the child how many letters there are in the alphabet. Let her decide how to keep track by writing tally marks, or entering on the abacus.

111

ACTIVITIES FOR TEACHING CONTINUED:	EXPLANATIONS CONTINUED:

Say the alphabet slowly while the child writes or enters beads on the abacus.

At the end ask her how many letters are in the alphabet. [2-ten 6]

Tally marks chart. On the dry erase board write some of names of the child's friends along the left side. Choose an appropriate question, such as the number of people living in their home, number of animals they have, or how many letters in their names. Ask the child to record the number to the answer next to names as shown below.

Heather	|||
Jon	||||
Andrea	ℍ	
Noel	||
Dana	|||

A chart showing measurement of some meaningful quantities.

Between. Place four tiles in a row: blue, red, yellow and green. See the figure below. Then ask: Which color tile is *between* blue and yellow? [red] Ask: What is *between* the red and green tiles? [yellow]

Red is between blue and yellow. Yellow is between red and green.

Ask the child to think of a number between 2 and 5. [3 or 4] Use the abacus to explain that the number must be less than 5 (enter 5 on the abacus), but more than 2 (slide 3 of the 5 beads slightly to the right, then move the fifth bead another slight distance to the right). See below.

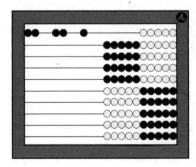

The abacus displaying the numbers between 2 and 5.

Encourage the child to think of questions involving between.

In conclusion. How many dimes and pennies do you need to make 3-ten 4 cents? [3 dimes and 4 pennies] What is between your eyes and your mouth? [nose]

© Activities for Learning, Inc. 2013

LESSON 56: ADDING WITH TALLY MARKS

OBJECTIVES:
1. To add using tally marks
2. To write equations using tally marks

MATERIALS:
1. AL Abacus
2. Tally sticks
3. Dry erase board
4. Worksheet 15, Writing Equations Using Tally Marks

ACTIVITIES FOR TEACHING:	EXPLANATIONS:
Warm-up. Sing the song, "Days of the Week." Ask the child: What day comes after Monday? [Tuesday] What day comes after Saturday? [Sunday] What day comes before Sunday? [Saturday]	

Ask the child to count to 5-ten while entering beads one at a time on the abacus.

Ask the child to say the even numbers up to 10. Then play the Comes After game. Ask: What even number comes after 2? [4] What even number comes after 6? [8] What even number comes after 4? [6]

Adding 2 + 1 with tally marks. Tell the child: Let's add 2 books + 1 more book using tally sticks. See the figure.

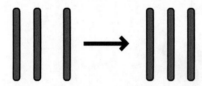

On the dry erase board, write || for the 2 and then the plus sign, +. Ask him what the plus sign means. [and] Write the | for the 1. Ask him to read what is written so far. [two plus one]

Write the = sign. Ask him what the equal sign means. [the same as or equals] See figure below.

$$|| + | =$$

If necessary, remind the child that you are using tally marks, so || is two, not 1-ten 1. Ask him to write what 2 marks and 1 more is the same as. If he is not absolutely certain, ask him to physically add it with the tally sticks. Write |||. Ask the child to read the equation [2 plus 1 equals, or is the same as, 3]

Initially equations will be written horizontally. With the exception of arithmetic paper and pencil procedures, virtually all of mathematics is written horizontally. It also is consistent with the left to right orientation needed for reading.

$$|| + | = |||$$

ACTIVITIES FOR TEACHING CONTINUED:	EXPLANATIONS CONTINUED:

Adding 4 + 1 with tally marks. For the next example, ask the child to add 4 cartons of milk and 1 more carton of milk with tally sticks.

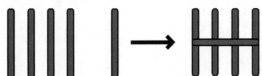

Ask him to write the left part of the equation, using tally marks. Ask the child to read it. [4 plus 1 is the same as.] Then ask what it is the same as. [5] Ask him to write equals 5 in tally marks. Ask him to read it. [4 plus 1 equals, or is the same as 5.]

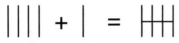

Writing 4 + 1 using tally marks.

Writing a sum shown with the tally sticks. Tell the child that you are going to add two numbers using tally sticks. He is to write it down using tally marks.

Lay out 5 and 3 tally sticks. Ask what it shows. [5 and 3] Ask him to write the equation on the dry erase board.

‖‖ + ‖‖ = ‖‖ ‖‖

Writing the equation using tally marks.

Repeat for 4 + 4.

Worksheet 15. Give the child Worksheet 15, where he writes equations using tally marks. Tell him that he may use tally sticks if he wants.

The solutions for the six problems are as follows:

‖‖ + ‖‖ = ‖‖ ‖	‖‖ ‖ + ‖ = ‖‖ ‖‖
‖‖ + ‖‖ = ‖‖ ‖‖	‖‖ + ‖‖ = ‖‖ ‖
‖‖ + ‖‖ = ‖‖ ‖	‖‖ ‖ + ‖‖ = ‖‖ ‖‖

In conclusion. Ask the child to read his equations on the worksheet.

Lesson 57: More about Evens and Odds

OBJECTIVES:

1. To learn to count by twos in higher numbers
2. To see the relationship between evens and counting by twos

MATERIALS:

1. AL Abacus
2. Tiles

ACTIVITIES FOR TEACHING:	EXPLANATIONS:
Warm-up. Say the rhyme "One, Two, Buckle my Shoe."	

Warm-up. Say the rhyme "One, Two, Buckle my Shoe."

Ask the child to count by twos to ten. Then ask the child to say the even numbers.

Ask the child to count to 3-ten by entering beads on the abacus one at a time. Ask: What number comes after 4? [5] What number comes after 10? [1-ten 1] What number comes after 2-ten 9? [3-ten]

Adding 1 on the stairs. Ask the child to build the stairs on the abacus. Next ask: What happens if you add 1 to any row? [same as row below] See the figure below. Ask: Does that happen every time? [yes] Let the child explore if needed.

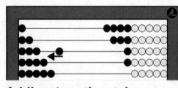

Adding 1 on the stairs.

Evens with tiles and abacus. Ask the child to use the tiles and build the evens like the dot cards. See below.

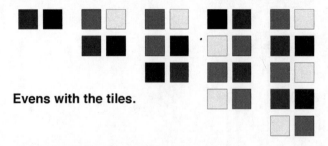

Evens with the tiles.

Save this arrangement for the next activity.

Next ask the child to enter each even number on a row of the abacus. See the figure below.

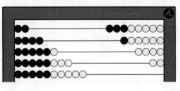

Evens on the abacus.

ACTIVITIES FOR TEACHING CONTINUED:	EXPLANATIONS CONTINUED:

Odds with tiles and abacus. Ask the child to remove one tile from each arrangement. See below. Ask: What do you have now? [odd numbers]

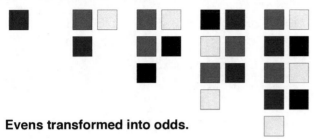

Evens transformed into odds.

Ask her to enter those numbers on the abacus below the even stairs. See the left figure below.

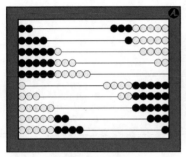

Evens and odd stairs.

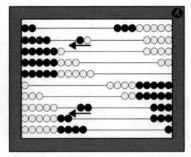

Adding 2 on even/odd stairs.

Ask her: What happens if you add 2 to an even number? [next even number] See the right figure above. What happens if you add 2 to an odd number? [next odd number]

Counting by twos. Ask the child to enter 2 on the abacus and name the quantity. [2] Ask her to add another 2 and name it. [4] Ask her to continue beyond 10. See the figure below. Encourage her to continue as high as she wants.

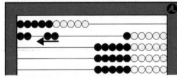

. . . 1-ten 2, 1-ten 4 . . .

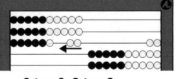

. . . 2-ten 6, 2-ten 8 . . .

Even/odd problem. Ask the child: Is 3-ten 7 an even number? [no, odd] Ask how she knows or ask her to show it on the abacus. See below. Repeat for 1-ten 6.

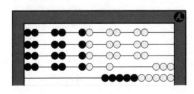

3-ten 7 is an odd number.

In conclusion. Ask the child: What is the difference between counting by 2s and saying the even numbers? [none]

116

LESSON 58: MORE DOUBLING AND HALVING

OBJECTIVES:
1. To write doubles and halving equations
2. To provide practice working with teens
3. To review the term sum

MATERIALS:
1. AL Abacus
2. Worksheet 14, Writing More Numbers: Start at Right
3. Math balance and four weights
4. Dry erase board
5. Math journal
6. Place-value cards and Tiles

ACTIVITIES FOR TEACHING:	EXPLANATIONS:

Warm-up. Sing the song "Writing Numbers."

Ask the child to count to 3-ten by entering beads on the abacus one at a time. Ask: What number comes after 4? [5] What number comes after 1-ten 4? [1-ten 5] What number comes after 2-ten 4? [2-ten 5]

Ask the child to count by twos to 3-ten. Then ask: Are those numbers evens or odds? [evens]

Worksheet 14. Give the child this worksheet for practice in writing these numbers; remind him to start at the dots. Tell him to do the right half of the page.

Doubling 1–5. Tell the child: Put a weight on the left 1-peg of the math balance. Ask him to do it again. Explain that he has doubled 1. Now ask him to make the balance level. Then tell him to write the equation on his dry erase board using tally marks. Also ask him to write the equation with numerals in his math journal. See the figures below.

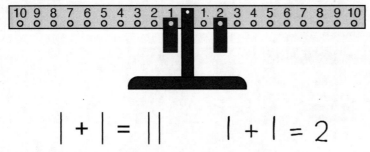

$$| + | = || \qquad 1 + 1 = 2$$

Doubling 1.

After clearing the balance, ask: Now can you put a weight on the left 2-peg and double it? Ask him to level the balance and write the equations. [|| + || = ||||] Continue with doubling 3, 4, and 5.

Doubling 6–9. For doubling 6–9, the child will need a weight on the 10 along with two other weights for the right side. See the figures on the next page for doubling 6. Ask him to use the place-value cards to compose 1-ten 2 before writing it.

| ACTIVITIES FOR TEACHING CONTINUED: | EXPLANATIONS CONTINUED: |

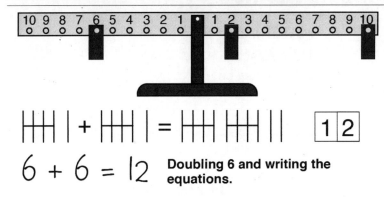

$$6 + 6 = 12$$ **Doubling 6 and writing the equations.**

Continue with doubling 7, 8, and 9. Then ask him to read his equations. Remind him: When you add numbers together, what you get is called the *sum*. Ask him to read the sums from his equations. [2, 4, 6, 8, 10, (1-ten,) 1-ten 2, 1-ten 4, 1-ten 6, 1-ten 8] What is special about the sums? [They are the even numbers.]

Halving 10, 12, 14, 16, 18. Ask the child to take 10 tiles. Then ask him to divide them into half. One way to do this systematically is pick up two tiles at a time, one with each hand, and lay them down in separate piles.

Discourage counting.

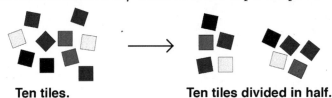

Ten tiles.   **Ten tiles divided in half.**

Ask him to write the equation, starting with 10 =___. [10 = 5 + 5]

Next ask him to combine both piles of tiles and add 2 more tiles. Ask: How many do you have now? [1-ten 2] Ask him to make the number with the place-value cards. Then ask him to divide this pile in half and write the equation. [12 = 6 + 6]

Ask him to continue to 18, by combining the piles, adding 2 more, and dividing in half.

Some children may choose to go beyond 18.

Halving 2, 4, 6, 8. Ask the child to find half of the even numbers 2, 4, 6, and 8 and to write the equations. Tell him this is called halving. Let him choose his own method to determine the answer.

Comparing doubling and halving. Ask: What happens if I take 3 tiles, double it, and then take half? [3 left] If the child is not sure, tell him to try it. Repeat the question with 5: What happens if you take 5 tiles, double it, and then take half? [5 left] Repeat with 10.

In conclusion. Ask: What is the opposite of doubling? [halving] What is the opposite of halving? [doubling]

LESSON 59: INTRODUCING MULTIPLICATION

OBJECTIVES:

1. To introduce multiplication

MATERIALS:

1. AL Abacus
2. Dry erase board
3. Place-value cards
4. Math journal
5. Math balance

ACTIVITIES FOR TEACHING:	EXPLANATIONS:
Warm-up. Sing the song "Three-ten Days Has September." Also sing "The Months."	

Warm-up. Sing the song "Three-ten Days Has September." Also sing "The Months."

Ask the child to count to 4-ten by entering beads on the abacus one at a time. Ask: What number comes after 7? [8] What number comes after 1-ten 7? [1-ten 8] What number comes after 2-ten 7? [2-ten 8] What number comes after 3-ten 7? [3-ten 8]

Ask the child to count by twos to 3-ten.

Ask the child to write the equation for doubling 5 on the dry erase board. [5 + 5 = 10] Continue with writing the equation for doubling 4. [4 + 4 = 8]

Ask: What is half of 12? [6] What is half of 4? [2]

Beginning multiplication. Tell the child to enter 6 on the first wire of the abacus. Then ask her to enter 6 on the second and third wires. See the figure below. Ask: How many times did you enter 6? [3] Tell her: We call this 6 taken 3 times. Write 6 × 3 and tell her this is how we write it.

Sometimes 6 × 3 is thought of as "6 groups of 3." However, consistency with the other arithmetic operations requires a second look. When adding 6 + 3, we start with 6 and transform it by adding 3. When subtracting 6 − 3, we start with 6 and transform it by removing 3. When dividing 6 ÷ 3, we start with 6 and transform it by dividing it into 3 groups or into groups of 3s. Likewise, 6 × 3 means we start with 6 and transform it by duplicating it 3 times.

This model for interpreting multiplying is also consistent with the coordinate system, where the first number, 6, indicates the horizontal number and the second number, 3, indicates the vertical number.

Note that the multiplication sign, ×, is not an "x." Actually, it is the plus sign, +, turned 45°.

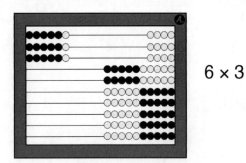

6 × 3

6 taken 3 times.

Ask her to find out how much 6 taken 3 times is equal to and to compose the amount with the place-value cards. If necessary, suggest using Take and Give. Ask the child to write the equation in her math journal:

The more advanced child might notice that two 5s make 10 and with the remaining 5 plus the 3 light-colored beads gives 1-ten 8.

$$6 \times 3 = 18$$

| **ACTIVITIES FOR TEACHING CONTINUED:** | **EXPLANATIONS CONTINUED:** |

Now ask her to enter three 6s on the left side of the math balance. Ask her to balance it. See the figure below. Ask: Is this the same answer you found on the abacus? [yes]

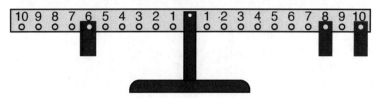

Finding 6 taken 3 times; 6 × 3.

Now ask her to find 9 × 3 on the abacus. Here Take and Give gives the solution, 2-ten 7. Then ask her to show the equation on the math balance. See the figures below.

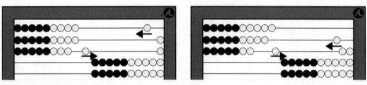

Using Take and Give to find 9 × 3.

When I introduced 5-year-olds to multiplication, they told me, "Don't give us easy ones like 2 × 4, but give us hard ones like 9 × 9." They greatly enjoyed using Take and Give to find the answers.

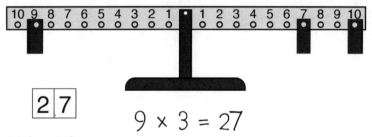

$$9 \times 3 = 27$$

9 taken 3 times.

Since more than four weights will not fit on a peg, the math balance cannot be used for all the examples.

Then ask her to compose the answer with the place-value cards and to write the equation in her math journal. [9 × 3 = 27]

Reading an array. Enter 5 × 7 on the abacus. Ask the child to read what is entered. [5 taken 7 times] Then ask her to write it and find the how much it is. [5 × 7 = 35]

An array is an arrangement of quantities in rows and columns.

More multiplication equations. Ask the child to make her own arrays. Ask her to enter any number on the top wire and then to enter the same number on as many wires as she wants. Tell her to write it in her math journal, find the answer, and finish the equation.

In conclusion. Ask: How much is 3 + 3? [6] Then ask: How much is 3 taken 2 times? [6]

LESSON 60: ADDING AND WRITING DOUBLES EQUATIONS

OBJECTIVES:
1. To add quantities based around doubles
2. To write equations using numerals

MATERIALS:
1. AL Abacus
2. Dry erase board
3. Tally sticks
4. *Math Card Games* book, N43

ACTIVITIES FOR TEACHING:	EXPLANATIONS:
Warm-up. Sing the song "Three-ten Days Has September." Also sing "The Months."	

Enter 8 taken 4 times on the abacus. Ask the child what is shown. [8 taken 4 times] Show 5 taken 2 times. Ask the child what is shown now. [5 taken 2 times]

Ask the child to count aloud as he enters beads on the abacus continue to 5-ten. Ask: What number comes after 8? [9] What number comes after 1-ten 8? [1-ten 9] What number comes after 2-ten 8? [2-ten 9] What number comes after 4-ten 8? [4-ten 9]

Ask the child to say the even numbers up to 2-ten. Repeat for the odd numbers up to 1-ten 9.

Have the child write the equation for doubling 3 on the dry erase board. [3 + 3 = 6] Continue with writing the equation for doubling 2. [2 + 2 = 4]

Ask: What is half of 6? [3] What is half of 4? [2]

Adding doubles with numbers. Draw a part-whole circle set on a dry erase board. Then ask: How many wheels are on 1 car? [4] Ask: How many wheels are 2 cars? [8]

Write the number of wheels for one car in one part-circle and write the number of wheels for the other car in the other part-circle. See the left figure below.

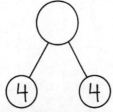

Entering the parts.

Ask the child what is the total amount of wheels on the 2 cars. Ask him to write the total number of wheels in the whole-circle. See the figure on the next page.

ACTIVITIES FOR TEACHING CONTINUED: **EXPLANATIONS CONTINUED:**

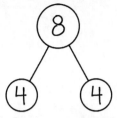

Entering the whole.   **Writing the equation.**

Next ask him to state the equation. [Four and four is the same as eight or 4 + 4 = 8.] Write the equation, using numerals. See the figure above.

Adding 3 + 3. Ask the child to make a triangle with tally sticks. Ask: How many tally sticks did you use? [3] Now ask the child to build two triangles. How many tally sticks do you need to make two triangles? [6] Draw more part-whole circle sets and write 3 and 3 in the smaller circles. Ask the child: What is the whole? [6] Write the equation.

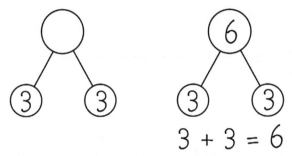

Finding 3 + 3 and writing the equation.

Can You Find game. Practice 10s and 1s by playing the Can You Find game, *Math Card Games*, N43. Ask the child to spread out his place-value cards. As a variation, instead of saying the quantities he is to find, enter the quantities on the abacus.

In conclusion. Ask: How many toes are on my two feet? [10]

LESSON 61: MORE ADDING WITH THE ABACUS

OBJECTIVES:

1. To use part-whole circle sets to solve story problems
2. To add two quantities on the abacus with the larger quantity first

MATERIALS:

1. AL Abacus
2. Dry erase board
3. Worksheets 16-1 and 16-2, Adding With the Abacus, (Worksheet 16-2 is an extra worksheet similar to 16-1)

ACTIVITIES FOR TEACHING:	EXPLANATIONS:
Warm-up. Sing the song "Three-ten Days Has September." Also sing "The Months."	

ACTIVITIES FOR TEACHING:

Warm-up. Sing the song "Three-ten Days Has September." Also sing "The Months."

Ask the child to say the days of the week. Then play the Comes After game with the days. What day comes after Wednesday? [Thursday] What day comes after Friday? [Saturday]

Enter 7 taken 5 times on the abacus. Ask the child: What is shown on the abacus? [7 taken 5 times] Repeat for 5 taken 4 times.

Have the child write the equation for doubling 6 on the dry erase board. [6 + 6 = 12] Continue with writing the equation for doubling 8. [8 + 8 = 16] Ask: What is half of 1-ten 2? [6] What is half of 2-ten? [10]

Ask the child to enter 2-ten on the abacus. Have the child name the quantities aloud as she adds one bead at a time. Continue to 6-ten. Ask: What number comes after 9? [10] What number comes after 1-ten 9? [2-ten] What number comes after 3-ten 9? [4-ten] What number comes after 4-ten 9? [5-ten]

Addition problem. Draw a part-whole circle set on the dry erase board and give her the following problem:

> Jessie has 4 books and receives 2 more new books. How many books does Jessie have now?

Ask: Is 4 a part or a whole? [part] Where should we write the 4? [part-circle] See the left figure below. Is 2 a part or a whole? [part] Where should we write the 2? [other part-circle]

EXPLANATIONS:

Part-whole circles give the child a way to visualize the problem and build conceptual understanding.

Research shows that young children can solve problems better with part-whole circles.

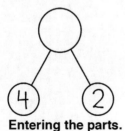

Entering the parts.

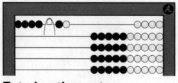

Entering the parts.

ACTIVITIES FOR TEACHING CONTINUED:	EXPLANATIONS CONTINUED:

Ask her to find the whole with her abacus: First, ask her to enter the number of books Jessie had at the start. Place a finger after the 4. Second, ask her to enter the number of new books Jessie received. [6] See the right figure on the previous page.

Then ask her to slide the beads together. Ask: How many books does Jessie have all together? [6] Then ask: Where should we write the 6? [in the whole-circle] See the figures below.

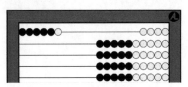
Adding the number of books on the abacus.

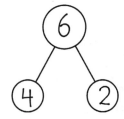

Write or ask the child to write the equation [4 + 2 = 6] and ask her to read it. [4 plus 2 equals 6]

Completing equations. Write the equation

$$5 + 2 = \underline{}$$

Explain to the child that you want to use the abacus to find out how much it is. Ask her to enter the 5. If desired, place your finger after the 5 (or ask her to place a finger) and ask her to enter the 2. Explain that adding means to put them all together.

Ask the child how much the abacus shows now. [7] Ask her to write the 7. Then ask: So how much is 5 + 2? [7]

Repeat for 4 + 1 and 6 + 3.

Worksheet 16-1 and 16-2. Give the child Worksheet 16-1, which has the larger addend given first. It is to be done with the abacus. Worksheet 16-2 is similar and is optional.

The eight addition equations are as follows along with the answers.

16-1	16-2
3 + 2 = **5**	5 + 3 = **8**
4 + 3 = **7**	4 + 2 = **6**
5 + 1 = **6**	6 + 1 = **7**
7 + 2 = **9**	3 + 3 = **6**
4 + 4 = **8**	1 + 0 = **1**
5 + 3 = **8**	7 + 3 = **10**
6 + 1 = **7**	2 + 2 = **4**
8 + 2 = **10**	7 + 2 = **9**

In conclusion. Write 5 + 4 = 9, then ask the child to read it and to explain what it means.

124

LESSON 62: PAIRS THAT EQUAL TEN

OBJECTIVES:
1. To introduce the pairs that total 10

MATERIALS:
1. AL Abacus
2. Two of each basic number card 1 to 9
3. *Math Card Games* book, A2

ACTIVITIES FOR TEACHING:	EXPLANATIONS:
Warm-up. Sing the song "Three-ten Days Has September." Ask: According to the song, which months have 3-ten days? [September, April, June, November] Sing "The Months." Ask: What month comes after January? [February] What month comes after February? [March] Enter 4-ten on the abacus. Have the child name the quantities aloud as he adds one bead at a time. Continue to 9-ten. [4-ten 1, 4-ten 2, 4-ten 3, . . . , 9-ten] Then play the Comes After game: What number comes after 5-ten 9? [6-ten] What number comes after 7-ten 5? [7-ten 6] What number comes after 8-ten 9? [9-ten] Ask the child to child to enter 5-ten. Ask him to enter two beads at a time and say the quantity. Continue to 7-ten. ***Reading the right side of the abacus.*** Enter various quantities from 1 to 10 as shown. Point to each row and ask the child to read the amount entered. [6, 3, 9, and so on] Next point to the right side and ask the child to read the quantities that are not entered. [4, 7, 1, and so on] 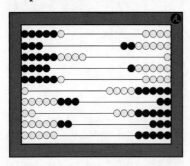 **Reading both sides of a row, the right as well as the left.** ***Find the Pairs game.*** Spread out the basic number cards face up. Demonstrate finding pairs. Pick up a 4 card and enter 4 on the abacus. Then say: I want to find what 4 needs to make 10. Take the remaining beads and slide them near the 4. See the figures on the next page.	The facts totaling 10 are the most basic facts for a child to learn because they often are used to find other facts.

RightStart™ Mathematics Level A second edition

© Activities for Learning, Inc. 2013

ACTIVITIES FOR TEACHING CONTINUED:

EXPLANATIONS CONTINUED:

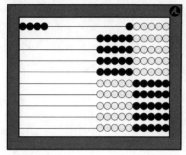

Entering 4.

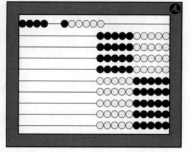

Entering what is needed to make 10.

This game is in the *Math Card Games* book, A1.

Find a 6 card and put it next to the 4. Ask the child to pick up another card and find its pair that makes 10. Place the second pair directly on top of the first pair. Ask the child to find the remaining pairs.

Find the Tens Memory game. Use the same 18 cards to play the memory game that matches pairs that make 10. See game in the *Math Card Games* book, A2.

Tens with the stairs. Ask the child to make the abacus stairs. Then ask him to look at the first wire and name what is on the left side and the right side. [1 and 9] Now ask the child to slide the 9 beads next to, but not touching the 1 and to say the equation. [1 and 9 is 10 or 1 + 9 = 10]

Repeat for the second wire. Ask the child to slide the right 8 beads to the left side and to say the equation. [2 and 8 is 10 or 2 + 8 = 10]

Continue for the remaining rows. The last row will be 10 + 0 = 10.

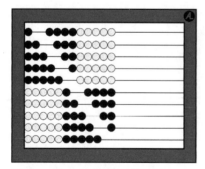

Using the stairs to find tens.

In conclusion. Can you think of two ways of making 10? [for example: 1 & 9, 2 & 8, 3 & 7, 4 & 6, 5 & 5]

LESSON 63: HALVES AND THE GO TO THE DUMP GAME

OBJECTIVES:

1. To find halves on the abacus
2. To practice the combinations that total 10 with the Go to the Dump game

MATERIALS:

1. AL Abacus
2. Six (or four) of each basic number card 1 to 9
3. *Math Card Games* book, A3

ACTIVITIES FOR TEACHING:	EXPLANATIONS:
Warm-up. Sing the song "Three-ten Days Has September." Ask: According to the song, which months have 3-ten days? [September, April, June, November] Which month has 2-ten 8 days? [February]	

Warm-up. Sing the song "Three-ten Days Has September." Ask: According to the song, which months have 3-ten days? [September, April, June, November] Which month has 2-ten 8 days? [February]

Sing "The Months" song. Ask: What month comes after March? [April] What month comes after September? [October]

Ask the child to start at 7-ten and count to one hundred.

Ask: What is 1 + 1? [2] What is 2 + 1? [3] What is 3 + 1? [4] What is 4 + 1? [5]

Ask the child to say the equation for doubling 4. [4 + 4 = 8] Ask: What is half of 8? [4] Ask: What is the equation for doubling 6? [6 + 6 = 1-ten 2] What is half of 1-ten 2? [6]

Halving on the abacus. Ask the child to enter 1-ten 6 on the abacus. Then ask her to find half by using Take and Give to make the rows equal. [8] See the figures below.

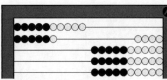

Entering 1-ten 6.   **Take and Give to find half.**

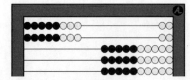

Half of 1-ten 6 is 8.

Enter 1-ten 4 and have her find half. [7]

Repeat for 1-ten 2. [6]

ACTIVITIES FOR TEACHING CONTINUED:	EXPLANATIONS CONTINUED:

ACTIVITIES FOR TEACHING CONTINUED:

Go to the Dump game. Play Go to the Dump game in the *Math Card Games* book, A3. Pairs equaling 10 are placed face up, one on each of two piles. At the end of the game, players combine their two stacks of cards; the winner is the player with the higher stack. The cards are now ready to play the game again without any shuffling.

In conclusion. Ask: What is 5 + 5? [10] What is half of 10? [5] What do you need with 9 to make 10? [1] What is 9 + 1? [10]

EXPLANATIONS CONTINUED:

Go to the Dump is a favorite game of many children.

LESSON 64: COUNTING WITH TALLY MARKS & MORE ADDING

OBJECTIVES:

1. To count using tally marks
2. To continue practicing facts to 10 by playing Go to the Dump

MATERIALS:

1. AL Abacus
2. Dry erase board
3. Place-value cards and Tiles
4. *Math Card Games* book, A3
5. Worksheet 17, Adding the Smaller Number First

ACTIVITIES FOR TEACHING:	EXPLANATIONS:
Warm-up. Sing "The Months" song. Discuss the name of the current month and the next month.	

Warm-up. Sing "The Months" song. Discuss the name of the current month and the next month.

Ask the child to say the days of the week. What day comes after Tuesday? [Wednesday] Thursday? [Friday]

Show 5 taken 2 times on the abacus. Ask the child what is shown. [5 taken 2 times] Repeat for 5 taken 8 times.

Have the child write the equation for doubling 7 on the dry erase board. [7 + 7 = 14] Repeat for doubling 9. [9 + 9 = 18] Ask: What is half of 14? [7] What is half of 18? [9]

Ask the child to start at 7-ten and count to one hundred.

Ask: What is 10 + 1? [1-ten 1] What is 1-ten 1 + 1? [1-ten 2] What is 1-ten 3 + 1? [1-ten 4] What is 4 + 1? [5]

Counting with tally marks. Show the child a heap of tiles and ask him to guess how many he thinks there are. Ask him to enter his guess on the abacus.

Then ask if he could count them by writing tally marks. Suggest that he set aside the tiles he has counted. Let him decide how many to move over at a time. If necessary, remind him to start a new row of tally marks when he reaches 10.

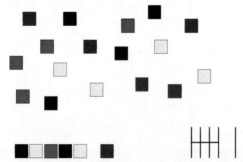

Six of the 2-ten 3 tiles counted with tally marks.

When he has finished counting, ask the child how many tiles there are. [2-ten 3 in this example]

129

| ACTIVITIES FOR TEACHING CONTINUED: | EXPLANATIONS CONTINUED: |

If necessary, point out the 2 tens. Ask him to compare the tally marks with his guess entered on the abacus. Correct the abacus to read the actual number. Ask him to construct the number with place-value cards.

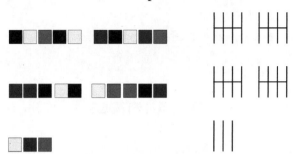

All 2-ten 3 tiles counted with tally marks.

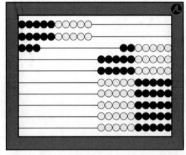

2 3

2-ten 3 on the abacus and the place-value cards.

Practice. Do the activity again with a fresh heap of tiles.

Go to the Dump game. Play the Go to the Dump game found in the *Math Card Games* book, A3.

Worksheet 17. For adding practice, give the child Worksheet 17, which is similar to a prior lesson. However, the smaller addend is first, the worksheet is to be done with the abacus. The problems and answers follow.

    1 + 3 = **4**
    3 + 7 = **10**
    3 + 5 = **8**
    2 + 4 = **6**
    1 + 6 = **7**
    4 + 5 = **9**
    1 + 2 = **3**
    0 + 5 = **5**

In conclusion. Write the number 56 without reading it. Ask the child to show the number on the abacus and to read it. [5-ten 6]

If the child's answers are incorrect and the same as the larger addend, show him how to use a finger to separate both addends on the abacus to come up with the correct answer.

© Activities for Learning, Inc. 2013

LESSON 65: COUNTING TILES & ADDING ONES

OBJECTIVES:
1. To count objects without grouping
2. To introduce partitioning 10
3. To discover the rule for adding 1s

MATERIALS:
1. AL Abacus
2. Dry erase board
3. Tiles
4. Worksheet 18-1, Adding Ones

ACTIVITIES FOR TEACHING:	EXPLANATIONS:
Warm-up. Sing the song "Three-ten Days Has September." Ask: According to the song, which months have 3-ten days? [September, April, June, November] Which month has only 2-ten 8 days? [February]	
Ask the child to say the days of the week. Ask: What day comes after Sunday? [Monday] What day comes after Monday? [Tuesday] What day comes after Thursday? [Friday]	
Show 10 taken 5 times on the abacus. Ask the child what is shown. [10 taken 5 times] Show 5 taken 6 times. Ask the child what is shown now.	
Have the child write the equation for doubling 6 on the dry erase board. [6 + 6 = 12] Continue with writing the equation for doubling 3. [3 + 3 = 6]	
Ask: What is half of 4? [2] What is half of 4-ten? [2-ten]	
Ask the child to enter 4-ten on the abacus. Then ask her to add 2 beads at a time while saying the quantity. [4-ten 2, 4-ten 4, . . . , 6-ten] Continue to 6-ten.	
Counting days and months. Using the abacus, have the child say the names of the week as she moves one bead over for each day. How many days are there in a week? [7]	
Repeat for the months of the year. [12]	
Counting tiles. Take about 20 tiles and lay them on a flat surface. Have the child count and say the number as she touches the tile, then moves it away from the rest of the tiles. Continue until all tiles are touched and moved over. Ask: How many tiles are there? Repeat if necessary.	Counting objects that can be moved is easier for children and should be mastered before attempting counting stationary objects.

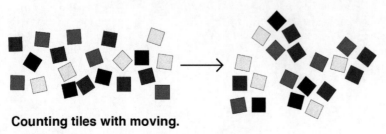

Counting tiles with moving.

| ACTIVITIES FOR TEACHING CONTINUED: | EXPLANATIONS CONTINUED: |

Partitioning 5 and 10. Review the partitioning of 5. Draw several part-whole circle sets on the dry erase board, write 5 in the whole-circles and ask the child what numbers could go into the part-circles. [0 & 5, 1 & 4, 2 & 3, 3 & 2, 4 & 1, 5 & 0]

Now write 10 in the whole-circles and ask the child to think of the parts. Suggest that she use the abacus to find the second number. For example, if 4 is written in one part-circle, enter 10 on the abacus and separate the parts as shown below. Now the parts are seen as 4 and 6. Continue with other ways to partition 10.

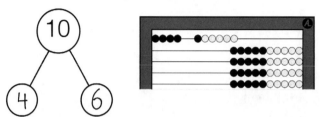

Partitioning 10 into 4 and 6.

Worksheet 18-1. Tell the child to do the worksheet using the abacus when needed. Let her discover that all the problems are adding 1 and that the answer is one number higher than the first addend. The problems are shown below.

$$2 + 1 = 3$$
$$4 + 1 = 5$$
$$1 + 1 = 2$$
$$5 + 1 = 6$$
$$9 + 1 = 10$$
$$7 + 1 = 8$$
$$3 + 1 = 4$$
$$6 + 1 = 7$$

Often a child will not make this discovery on the first try. However, the next time, which will be the following lesson, she will be looking for the pattern. Document that the child has made the discovery!

This is an important discovery since it marks, for most children, when they start to become independent learners, confident in their own abilities and not relying on others for the correct answers.

In conclusion. After the child has completed the worksheet, ask: Did you discover the pattern? Often a child who has made the discovery will say that she did not need the abacus. Be sure to ask why; encourage her to explain it in her own words. After hearing her explanation, you might tell her: Yes, when you add 1 to a number, it is the next higher number.

LESSON 66: PARTITIONING TEN & ADDING ONES

OBJECTIVES:
1. To partition 10
2. To continue working on adding 1s

MATERIALS:
1. AL Abacus
2. Dry erase board
3. Tiles
4. Worksheet 18-2, Adding Ones
5. *Math Card Games* book, A3

ACTIVITIES FOR TEACHING:	EXPLANATIONS:
Warm-up. Sing the song "Three-ten Days Has September." Also sing "The Months."	

Warm-up. Sing the song "Three-ten Days Has September." Also sing "The Months."

Ask the child to say the days of the week. Ask: What day is today? What day was yesterday? What day is tomorrow?

Show 10 taken 3 times on the abacus. Ask the child what is shown. [10 taken 3 times] Show 5 taken 10 times. Ask the child what is shown now.

Have the child write the equation for doubling 9 on the dry erase board. [9 + 9 = 18] Continue with writing the equation for doubling 10. [10 + 10 = 20]

Ask: What is half of 6? [3] What is half of 6-ten? [3-ten]

Enter 2-ten on the abacus. Have child count aloud as he enters one bead at a time on the abacus from 2-ten to 5-ten.

Take a handful of tiles and lay them on a flat surface. Have the child count and say the number as he touches each tile, then moves it away from the rest of the tiles. Continue until all tiles are touched and moved over. Ask: How many tiles are there?

Review partitioning ten. Draw a part-whole circle set and write 10 in the whole-circle. Write a 3 in a part-circle and ask the child to find the other part. [7] Erase and write other numbers in a part-circle. Write the parts in the left part-circle as well as right part-circle.

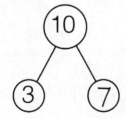

Finding the other part when 10 is the whole.

ACTIVITIES FOR TEACHING CONTINUED:	EXPLANATIONS CONTINUED:

The teddy bear problem. Give the child the following problem, but use the names of friends:

> Bob and Greta have 10 teddy bears between them. How many teddy bears could they each have?

Write the names at the top of two columns on the dry erase board as shown.

<u>Bob</u> <u>Greta</u>

Ask the child how many teddy bears Bob could have. If he says, for example, 3, write 3 in the column under Bob. Then ask how many Greta would have; ask him to use the abacus to find the answer. [7] Write the 7.

<u>Bob</u> <u>Greta</u>
3   7

Continue by asking for another amount that Bob could have. Write the solutions in the columns.

<u>Bob</u> <u>Greta</u>
3   7
6   4

After all possible combinations have been found, help the child reflect on the problem. Discuss how many answers he found.

Worksheet 18-2. Take out the worksheet and tell the child to use the abacus when needed. When he knows the pattern, he will not need the abacus. The problems are shown below.

$5 + 1 = \mathbf{6}$
$4 + 1 = \mathbf{5}$
$6 + 1 = \mathbf{7}$
$8 + 1 = \mathbf{9}$
$7 + 1 = \mathbf{8}$
$2 + 1 = \mathbf{3}$
$9 + 1 = \mathbf{10}$
$3 + 1 = \mathbf{4}$

Go to the Dump game. Play the Go to the Dump game found in the *Math Card Games* book, A3.

In conclusion. Ask: What number comes after 5? [6] What is 5 + 1? [6] Do you see the pattern?

LESSON 67: MORE PARTITIONING TEN

OBJECTIVES:
1. To partition 10

MATERIALS:
1. AL Abacus
2. Tiles
3. **Container to hold tiles**
4. Dry erase board
5. Math balance
6. Worksheet 19, Ten Equals

ACTIVITIES FOR TEACHING:	EXPLANATIONS:
Warm-up. Ask the child to say the days of the week and the months of the year.	

Warm-up. Ask the child to say the days of the week and the months of the year.

Ask: What comes after 4? [5] What is 4 + 1? [5] What comes after 7? [8] What is 7 + 1? [8] What comes after 3? [4] What is 3 + 1? [4] Do you see a pattern? [yes] Have her describe it.

Have the child say the even numbers to 2-ten. Ask: What even number comes after 4? [6] What is 4 and 2 more? [6] What even number comes after 10? [1-ten 2] What is 10 + 2? [1-ten 2] Do you see a pattern? [yes] Have her describe it.

Ask the child to enter various quantities on the abacus, such as 1-ten 8, 5-ten 4, 9-ten 3, and 4-ten.

Counting tiles. Take a handful tiles and lay them on a flat surface. Have the child pick up one tile and put it in a container. Have the child continue putting tiles in the container, counting them as she puts them all in the container. Ask: How many tiles are in the container? Have the child write the number.

Now have the child take them out of the container. Lay the tiles out in groups of five and ten. Ask: How many tiles are there? Is it the same number you wrote down?

Equations for the partitioning of ten. Draw a part-whole circle set; write 10 in the whole-circle and 7 in the left part-circle. Ask the child to find the other part. [3]

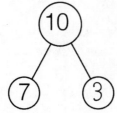

Stating the equation:
Ten equals seven plus three, and writing it.

$$10 = 7 + 3$$

Tell her that we can say the equation as, 10 equals 7 + 3. Then ask her to write it. While she writes, say, 10 equals 7 plus 3. Repeat with different numbers in the part-circles, such as 6 and 4, and 5 and 5.

ACTIVITIES FOR TEACHING CONTINUED:	EXPLANATIONS CONTINUED:

Partitioning ten on the math balance. Ask the child to put a weight on the left 10. Then ask her to use two weights and find all the ways to make it balance. [1 & 9, 2 & 8, 3 & 7, 4 & 6, 5 & 5] Ask: What does this remind you of? [the same pairs as found as the abacus]

Find the missing part. Now write the equation

$$10 = 4 + \underline{\quad}$$

and ask the child to find the missing part on the math balance. [6] Ask her to show the solution on the abacus.

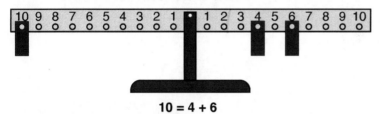

10 = 4 + 6

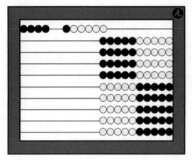

Find the missing part for 10 = 4 + __.

Repeat for the following:

$$10 = 9 + \underline{\quad} \ [1]$$
$$10 = 3 + \underline{\quad} \ [7]$$

Worksheet 19. Give the child the worksheet. The problems and solutions are below.

10 = 9 + **1**
10 = 7 + **3**
10 = 4 + **6**
10 = 8 + **2**
10 = 2 + **8**
10 = 6 + **4**
10 = 5 + **5**
10 = 3 + **7**

In conclusion. Say: Name all the different ways can you think of to make ten. [1 & 9, 2 & 8, 3 & 7, 4 & 6, 5 & 5]

LESSON 68: COMPOSING TENS AND ONES

OBJECTIVES:

1. To build 10s and 1s

MATERIALS:

1. AL Abacus
2. Tiles
3. *Math Card Games* book, N43
4. Worksheets 20-1 and 20-2, Building Tens and Ones
5. **Scissors** & **glue**

ACTIVITIES FOR TEACHING:	EXPLANATIONS:
Warm-up. Sing "The Months." Sing the song "Three-ten Days Has September." Ask: How many days does January have? [3-ten 1] What month comes after January? [February] How many days does February have? [2-ten 8 or 2-ten 9] What month comes after February? [March]	
Show 9 taken 5 times on the abacus. Ask the child what is shown. [9 taken 5 times] Show 5 taken 8 times. Ask the child what is shown now.	
Ask the child to write the equation for doubling 2. [2 + 2 = 4] Continue with writing the equation for doubling 4. [4 + 4 = 8]	
Ask: What is half of 8? [4] What is half of 8-ten? [4-ten] What is half of 2-ten? [10]	
Enter 2-ten on the abacus. Have the child count aloud as he enters beads on the abacus from 2-ten. Continue to 5-ten.	
Take a handful of tiles and lay them on a flat surface. Have the child count and say the number as he touches each tile and moves it away from the rest of the tiles. Continue until all tiles are touched and moved over. Ask: How many tiles are there?	
Can You Find game. Review 10s and 1s by playing the Can You Find game found in *Math Card Games*, N43. Ask the child to spread out his place-value cards. As a variation, instead of saying the quantities that he is to find, enter the quantities on the abacus.	
Building tens and ones. On Worksheet 20-1 have the child cut out the bead strips and numbers by cutting on the heavy lines. Explain that on Worksheet 20-2, he is to compose four numbers using the tens and ones, putting one into each of the four rectangles.	Note that there are many arrangements that could be made—576 to be exact. (The first rectangle can have any 1 of the 4 tens and any 1 of the 4 ones, giving 4 × 4 possibilities. Then the second rectangle can have any 1 of the 3 tens and 1 of the 3 ones, giving 3 × 3 possibilities for each arrangement in the first rectangle. Likewise, the third rectangle can have 1 of the 2 tens and 1 and the 2 ones. So the total number is 4 × 4 × 3 × 3 × 2 × 2 = 576.)
Next he lays out the arrangement of bead strips that corresponds to his numbers. See the figure on the next page for one possible arrangement. Finally, he glues all the pieces in place. (The ones are glued over the zero of the tens.)	

ACTIVITIES FOR TEACHING CONTINUED:

EXPLANATIONS CONTINUED:

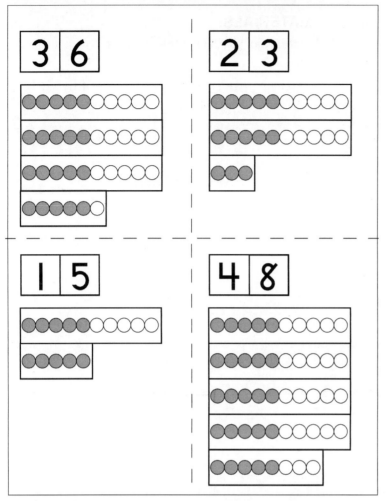

One possible arrangement for building tens and ones from the pieces from Worksheet 20-1 on Worksheet 20-2.

When he has completed the task, ask: What is the largest number you could have made from the pieces you cut out? [48] What is the smallest number you could have made? [13]

In conclusion. Ask: How could you have made your worksheet in a different way?

ENRICHMENT LESSON 69: CALENDAR DAY 1

OBJECTIVES:
1. To explore a calendar
2. To learn more ordinal numbers

MATERIALS:
1. Calendar parts (Appendix p. 13)
2. **Scissors**
3. **A twelve-month calendar preferably with seasonal pictures**

ACTIVITIES FOR TEACHING:	EXPLANATIONS:
Warm up. Sing "Days of the Week" to the tune of "Twinkle, Twinkle Little Star."	

Days of the Week
Sunday, Monday, Tuesday, too.
Wednesday, Thursday–this I knew.
Friday, Saturday that's the end.
Now let's say those days again!
Sunday, Monday, Tuesday, Wednesday, Thursday,
Friday, Saturday!

Sing the song "Three-ten Days Has September." Ask: How many days does April have? [3-ten] What month comes after April? [May] How many days does May have? [3-ten 1] What month comes after May? [June]

Calendar preparation. Have the child cut out all the numbers 1–31 for the days and the tags for the months from Appendix p. 13. Put the numbers in an envelope to save for later.

One purpose of having the child make the next year's calendar is to give him the concept of a year. Drawing pictures appropriate to the months combines math and art.

Arranging the months in order. Sing the song, "The Months," to the tune of "Ten Little Piggies."

The finished calendar can become a gift to the family.

The Months
January, February, March, and April,
May, June, July, and August,
September, October, November, December.
These are the months of the year.

Have the child sing the song again slowly. While singing the song, help the child to find the tags for the months as she says them. See the figure on the next page.

ACTIVITIES FOR TEACHING CONTINUED:

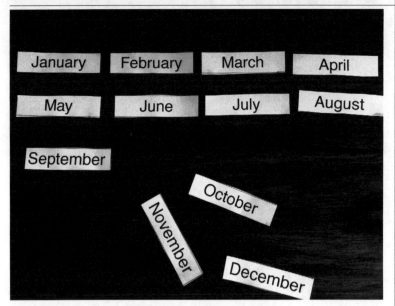

Arranging the tags for the months in order.

Examining the months of a calendar. Show the child a twelve-month calendar. If the calendar has appropriate pictures, talk about how the pictures change with the seasons.

Show her the month of January and say: This is the first month of the year. Can you find where it says January on the calendar? Ask: What is the second month? [February] Turn the page and ask her to find the word February. If the child is interested, continue finding the names for the remaining months.

Calendar games. Pick a tag for a month and ask the child to find that month on the calendar.

Choose a month on the calendar and ask the child to find the tag for that month.

Examining the numbers on a calendar. Ask the child to find the month with her birthday. If she knows her birthdate, ask her to find it on the month.

Ask: How many days does this month have? Where is the first day? [at the 1] Where is the second day? [at the 2] Where is the third day? Where is the fifth day? Where is the tenth day? Where is the sixth day? Where is the last day? Ask: Are the numbers in order?

In conclusion. Ask: What is a calendar? What do we use it for?

EXPLANATIONS CONTINUED:

Ordinal numbers are important, not only for naming a day or an item in a series, but, in English, for naming fractions.

Not all children realize that the numbers on a calendar start each row at the left. They sometimes think the numbers snake back and forth like moving on a board game.

ENRICHMENT LESSON 70: CALENDAR DAY 2

OBJECTIVES:
1. To learn the term *date*
2. To begin making a calendar for the following year

MATERIALS:
1. **Book about the seasons* (optional)**
2. **A twelve-month calendar**
3. Calendar parts, from the previous lesson
4. Twelve copies of Blank Month (Appendix p. 14) Copy onto legal-size to give more space for the month's picture.
5. **Crayons**

ACTIVITIES FOR TEACHING:	EXPLANATIONS:
Warm up. Sing the song, "The Months," to the tune of "Ten Little Piggies."	*Two book suggestions: *Watching the Seasons* by Edana Eckart and *The Reasons for Seasons* by Gail Gibbons.

The Months

January, February, March, and April,
May, June, July, and August,
September, October, November, December.
These are the months of the year.

Ask the child to say the rhyme, "Three-ten Days Has September." Then ask: How many days does January have? [3-ten 1] How many days does March have? [3-ten 1] Which month has only 2-ten 8 or 2-ten 9 days? [February]

Sing "Days of the Week."

Days of the Week
Sunday, Monday, Tuesday, too.
Wednesday, Thursday–this I knew.
Friday, Saturday that's the end.
Now let's say those days again!
Sunday, Monday, Tuesday, Wednesday, Thursday,
Friday, Saturday!

If available, read books about the seasons of the year.

Days of the week. Ask the child to find the month of April on the calendar. Point out the words (or abbreviations) for the days of the week. Ask him to read them in order. [Sunday, Monday, . . . , Saturday] Point out that all the days in the column under the word *Sunday* are Sundays. Ask him to name the *dates* that are Sundays, explaining that dates are numbers. Ask him: Where are the Tuesdays? Ask him to say the dates that are Tuesdays.

This lesson combines math, reading, art, and social studies.

Turn to July and ask: What day of the week is July 1st? What day of the week is July 2nd? What day of the week is July 3rd? What day comes after July 3rd? [July 4th] If appropriate, ask him if he sees anything different for that day.

Most U.S. calendars mark July 4th in some manner.

| ACTIVITIES FOR TEACHING CONTINUED: | EXPLANATIONS CONTINUED: |

ACTIVITIES FOR TEACHING CONTINUED:

Continuing to the next month. Ask the child to point out the last day of July. Ask: What day of the week is it? What do you think the next day is? Ask him to turn to August, the next month, and check if he's right.

Ask: What is the last day of August? What will the next day be? Ask him to turn to September and check if he's right. If he is interested, check other months.

Making the month of January. Explain to the child that he is to make January by arranging the calendar parts on the sample month. Ask him to find the tag for January and to put it on the top line of one of the blank months, Appendix p. 14. See the left figure below.

Find the 1 and put it in the correct place. Ask the child to find the 2 and put it after the 1. Continue with him until he has started the second row. Explain when he has the sample calendar finished, you will give him a blank month so he can copy it. Then let him work independently.

January

S	M	T	W	Th	F	S
	1	2	3	4	5	6
7	8	9	10	11	12	13
14	15	16	17	18	19	20
21	22	23	24	25	26	27
28	29	30	31			

Filling in the sample calendar.

Copying to the blank calendar.

After the name of the month and numbers are copied, ask the child to make a drawing relating to the month.

Completing the year. Tell the child that he will make a full calendar. This project will take a number of days to complete.

Use binder clips to fasten the 12 months when the child completes the project.

In conclusion. Ask: What month comes after January? [February] What day comes after Saturday? [Sunday] What date comes after January 6th? [January 7th] What date comes after January 8th? [January 9th]

EXPLANATIONS CONTINUED:

Checking his work before giving him a blank calendar to write on will avoid excessive erasing and frustration.

A more-advanced child will need only to have the first day of the month checked, especially after the first few.

The remainder of the months can be done daily until finished or whenever it fits in the daily schedule. Have a goal to present the completed calendar to the family as a gift.

LESSON 71: WORKING WITH HUNDREDS

OBJECTIVES:
1. To introduce hundreds

MATERIALS:
1. AL Abacus
2. **Calendar**
3. AL Abacus Tiles
4. Worksheet 21, Writing Numbers
5. *Math Card Games* book, A3

ACTIVITIES FOR TEACHING:	EXPLANATIONS:
Warm-up. Sing "Writing Numbers." Ask the child where to start when she writes 2, [left] 4, [left] and 8. [right]	
Ask the child to say the even numbers to 2-ten.	
Ask the child to count with the abacus starting at 6-ten and continuing to one hundred.	
Ask the child to find the month of November on a calendar. Ask her: How many Thursdays are there? [4 or 5] Then ask her to read those dates. Which is the 1st Thursday? Which is the 4th Thursday? Tell her that day is Thanksgiving.	In the U.S., the fourth Thursday of November is Thanksgiving.
Reviewing one hundred. Ask the child to count by 10s on the abacus. [1-ten, 2-ten, . . . , 1 hundred] How many beads are on the abacus? [one hundred] Ask: How many beads do we need to make 1-ten? [10] How many rows of tens do we need to make one hundred? [10] If she is not sure, ask her to check her abacus.	For some reason, some children when asked how many tens are in one hundred will respond with two tens. Hence, the emphasis on subitizing the number of tens.
AL Abacus tiles. Show the child an abacus tile as shown below. Ask: How many beads are shown on the abacus in this abacus tile? [one hundred]	Working with hundreds is necessary for a child to understand how our decimal system works. Furthermore, children love large numbers.

Abacus tile representing 100.

Show another abacus tile and repeat the question. Then say: How many beads do you think are on both of these abacus tiles? [2 hundred]

Abacus tiles representing 200.

Lay out two more abacus tiles in dot-card formation (two by two) as shown on the next page. Ask: How many do you see now? [4 hundred]

143

| ACTIVITIES FOR TEACHING CONTINUED: | EXPLANATIONS CONTINUED: |

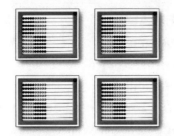

Abacus tiles representing 400.

Lay out seven abacus tiles. [seven hundred] See figure below.

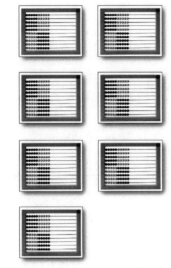

Abacus tiles representing 700.

Practice. Give her ten abacus tiles and ask her to make eight hundred, five hundred, and so forth. Next lay out various hundred configurations and ask her to name them.

If she is interested, you could mention that ten hundreds is called *one thousand*.

Worksheet 21. Give the child the worksheet. Suggest she do half; let her decide which half to do.

Go to the Dump. Play Go to the Dump in *Math Card Games*, A3.

In conclusion. Ask: How many beads are there on the abacus? [1 hundred] How many beads are on two abacuses? [2 hundred] How many beads are on eight abacuses? [8 hundred]

Arranging the hundreds in groups of twos, similar to the dot cards, makes the quantity recognizable without counting. Also, this arrangement is similar to the second side of the AL Abacus.

LESSON 72: RECORDING THE HUNDREDS

OBJECTIVES:

1. To record the hundreds using the place-value cards

MATERIALS:

1. AL Abacus
2. Place-value cards
3. AL Abacus tiles
4. *Math Card Games* book, A3.1
5. Worksheet 21, Writing Numbers

ACTIVITIES FOR TEACHING:	EXPLANATIONS:
Warm-up. Sing "Writing Numbers." Ask the child where to start when he writes 3, [left] 5, [right] and 7. [left]	

Warm-up. Sing "Writing Numbers." Ask the child where to start when he writes 3, [left] 5, [right] and 7. [left]

Ask the child to say the even numbers to 5-ten.

Ask the child to count ones with the abacus starting at 2-ten and continuing to 5-ten. Then play the Comes Before game: What number comes before 5? [4] What number comes before 3? [2] What number comes before 10? [9] What number comes before 1? [0]

Ask the child: What do you need with 3 to equal 10? [7] What do you need with 7 to equal 10? [3] What do you need with 6 to equal 10? [4] What do you need with 4 to equal 10? [6]

Introducing the written 100. Show the child the place-value card for 1 and ask him to enter it on the abacus.

Show him the 10 card. Point to the 1 while saying "one" and point to the 0 while saying "ten." Ask him to enter it on the abacus. See the figures below.

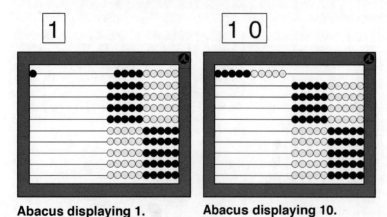

Abacus displaying 1.　　　Abacus displaying 10.

Ask the child to enter 100 on the abacus. Show him the place-value card for 100. Say one while pointing to the 1; say "hun," while pointing to the first 0; and "dred," for the second 0 as shown on the next page.

| ACTIVITIES FOR TEACHING CONTINUED: | EXPLANATIONS CONTINUED: |

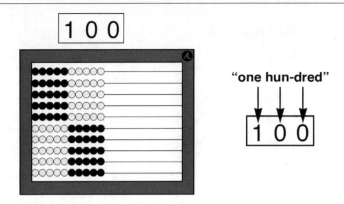

"one hun-dred"
1 0 0

Introducing more hundreds. Ask the child to compose a 2 by entering ones on the first two rows. See the left figure below. Ask him to put the place-value card showing 2 above the abacus.

Then ask him to change the abacus and card to 2-ten. See the right figure below.

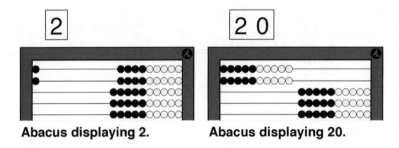

Abacus displaying 2. Abacus displaying 20.

Now ask him to make two hundred with the abacus tiles. Ask: How do you think we write 200? [2 with two zeroes] Ask him to find the place-value card. Again point out the "hun-dred" part by touching each zero in succession. See below.

"two hun-dred"
2 0 0

Show the 500-card and ask the child to build it with abacus tiles. Repeat for 300 and 900.

Handshaking game. Play the Handshaking game from the *Math Card Games* book, A3.1. Suggest players use the abacus stairs as a reference.

Worksheet 21. Have the child finish the worksheet from the previous lesson.

In conclusion. Ask: Which is more, 2 hundred or 2-ten? [2 hundred] Which is more, 6-ten or 6 hundred? [6 hundred] Which is less, 4 or 4-ten? [4]

Encouraging children to see 100 as 1 followed by two zeros allows them to see a number such as 1900 to be viewed as 19 hundred because it is 19 followed by two zeros.

Also, representing hundreds as a number followed by two zeros is consistent for scientific notation, in which 100 is written 1×10^2. Thinking of hundreds only as the "third column" from the right interferes with learning these concepts.

LESSON 73: HUNDREDS PROBLEMS

OBJECTIVES:
1. To solve story problems involving hundreds
2. To learn to play the game, Old Main

MATERIALS:
1. AL Abacus
2. Part-Whole Circle Set (Appendix p. 9)
3. Place-value cards
4. *Math Card Games* book, A4

ACTIVITIES FOR TEACHING:	EXPLANATIONS:

ACTIVITIES FOR TEACHING:

Warm-up. Ask the child to count with the abacus starting at 7-ten and continuing to 1 hundred.

Play the Comes Before game: What number comes before 5? [4] What number comes before 3-ten 5? [3-ten 4] What number comes before 4-ten 5? [4-ten 4] What number comes before 7-ten 5? [7-ten 4]

Ask: What is 6 + 1? [7] What is 1-ten 6 + 1? [1-ten 7] What is 2-ten 6 + 1? [2-ten 7] What is 5-ten 6 + 1? [5-ten 7]

Ask the child: What are the ways to partition 5? [0 & 5, 1 & 4, 3 & 2, 2 & 3, 4 &1, 5 & 0]

Baby chick problem. Provide the child with the part-whole circle set and place-value cards. Ask the child to solve the following problem:

> Two hundred baby chicks hatched on Monday and three hundred more hatched on Tuesday. How many hatched altogether?

Ask: Is 2 hundred a part or whole? [part] Is 3 hundred a part or whole? [part] Ask the child to find the place-value cards for 2 hundred and 3 hundred and to put them in the correct circles. See the left figure below.

Parts for chick problem.
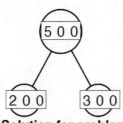
Solution for problem.

Then ask: How many hatched altogether? Give her time to think before asking: What is the whole? [500] Ask her to find the matching place-value card and put it in the whole-circle. See the right figure above.

EXPLANATIONS:

For some children, using the abacus tiles will be helpful. They could be placed in the appropriate circles, 2 and 3 abacus tiles in the part-circles and 5 tiles in the whole-circle.

| ACTIVITIES FOR TEACHING CONTINUED: | EXPLANATIONS CONTINUED: |

Card problem. Read the following problem:

> Morgan is collecting cards and wants to have one hundred cards. Morgan already has 6-ten cards. How many more cards must Morgan collect to have one hundred?

Encourage the child to solve the problem in any way that makes sense to her. After she has found a solution, [4-ten] discuss the parts and whole. See the figures below.

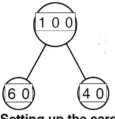

Setting up the card problem.

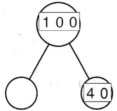

Solution for the card problem.

Stamp problem. Repeat the process for the following problem:

> Jo's family is mailing one hundred invitations. Jo has attached stamps to 7-ten envelopes. How many more envelopes still need stamps?

Ask: What is the missing part? [3-ten envelopes]

Old Main game. Old Main game, found in the *Math Card Games* book, A4, requires players to use the facts that total ten.

In conclusion. Ask: What is 1 + 4? [5] What is 1-ten + 4-ten? [5-ten] What is 1 hundred + 4 hundred? [5 hundred]

LESSON 74: ADDING TENS AND ONES

OBJECTIVES:
1. To learn to add 10s and 1s in problems
2. To learn to add 10s and 1s in equations

MATERIALS:
1. AL Abacus
2. Place-value cards
3. Worksheet 22, Adding Tens and Ones
4. *Math Card Games* book, A3 or A4

ACTIVITIES FOR TEACHING:	EXPLANATIONS:
Warm-up. Ask the child to say the even and odd numbers up to 4-ten. Play the Comes After game, ask: What even number comes after 4? [6] What odd number comes after 3? [5] What odd number comes after 7? [9]	
Ask the child to build the stairs on the abacus. Then ask him to count backward by reading each row starting at the bottom. [10, 9, 8, . . . , 1]	
Ask the child to say the days of the week. Then play the Comes Before game with the days.	
Enter various quantities on the abacus such as 7-ten 2, 9-ten 2, and 10-ten and ask the child to name the quantities.	
Problem 1. Give the child the following problem:	
A class has 2-ten children. One afternoon 7 parents came to visit. How many children and parents are in the room now?	
Ask the child to solve the problem in his own way. Challenge him to do so without counting. Ask him to explain how he solved the problem. [2-ten 7]	Even though a child may know that 2-ten and 7 is 2-ten 7, he often is unsure about 2-ten + 7. Apparently, it takes a while for the meaning of "+" to be really understood.
Draw a part-whole circle set. Discuss with the child which numbers are the parts and which is the whole. Write the numbers in the appropriate circles as shown below. 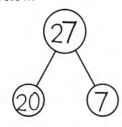 $$20 + 7 = 27$$ **The parts, 20 and 7, and the whole, 27.**	According to research, a young child does not use equations to solve problems. Therefore, solving the problem, then writing the equations is far more beneficial to a child.
Ask the child to write the equation. [20 + 7 = 27] Ask: Is there another way to write the equation? [27 = 20 + 7] This is not the preferred way for this particular problem, but it is not wrong.	
Also ask him to show the problem on the abacus and the answer with place-value cards.	

ACTIVITIES FOR TEACHING CONTINUED:

EXPLANATIONS CONTINUED:

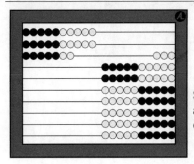

2	7

Showing 2-ten plus 7 on the abacus and with place-value cards.

Problem 2. Read the next problem to the child:

A park has 6-ten trees. This spring the caretaker will plant 7 more trees. When the trees are planted, how many trees will the park have?

Proceed in the same way as in Problem 1. Use the four representations, part-whole circle set, abacus, and place-value cards, and equation. [6-ten 7]

Practice. Write

80 + 1 = ___ [81]

and ask the child to use an abacus and place-value cards to solve the equation.

Repeat for

30 + 8 = ___ [38]

10 + 7 = ___ [17]

Can You Find game. Ask the child to lay out tens and hundreds from the place-value cards. Ask them to find 4-ten, 4 hundred, 6 hundred, and so forth.

Worksheet 22. Give the child the worksheet. The problems and solutions are shown below.

20 + 5 = **25**
60 + 2 = **62**
30 + 4 = **34**
90 + 7 = **97**
50 + 3 = **53**
70 + 8 = **78**
80 + 6 = **86**
40 + 9 = **49**

Games. Remaining time can be spent using the *Math Card Games* book to play Go to the Dump, A3, or Old Main, A4.

In conclusion. Ask: How much is 2-ten and 1? [2-ten 1] How much is 2-ten plus 1? [2-ten 1] How much is 9-ten and 9? [9-ten 9]

LESSON 75: COUNTING BY TENS & MAKING A HUNDRED CHART

OBJECTIVES:

1. To count by 10s and 1s
2. To start making a hundred chart

MATERIALS:

1. AL Abacus
2. Place-value cards
3. Worksheet 23, Making a Hundred Chart

ACTIVITIES FOR TEACHING:	EXPLANATIONS:
Warm-up. Ask the child to say the even and odd numbers up to 50. Play the Comes After game. Ask: What even number comes after 8? [10] What odd number comes after 5? [7] What odd number comes after 3? [5]	

Warm-up. Ask the child to say the even and odd numbers up to 50. Play the Comes After game. Ask: What even number comes after 8? [10] What odd number comes after 5? [7] What odd number comes after 3? [5]

Ask the child to count backward from 10. Then play the Comes Before game. Ask: What number comes before 3? [2] What number comes before 9? [8] What number comes before 6? [5]

Ask the child: How much is 1 + 1, [2] 2 + 1, [3] 3 + 1, [4] 4 + 1, [5] and so forth?

Counting by tens. Tell the child that we are going to count by 10. Ask her to enter 10 on the abacus and to say the quantity. Continue to 10-ten and then ask what is the regular name for 10-ten. [1 hundred]

Next ask the child to spread out the place-value cards from 10 to 100. Enter a group of tens on the abacus ask her to find and show the quantity with place-value cards. See below. Continue until all cards have been found.

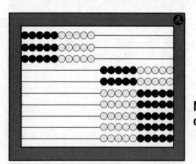

Matching place-value card to quantity.

Counting by ones. Tell the child: Now we will count by ones to 100. How many beads will we move over at a time? [1] Ask her to spread out the place-value cards up to 100 in order as shown on the next page. Ask her to show the correct card after each new bead is entered. Continue to 100.

This activity helps the child experience the pattern in writing numbers; that the numbers 1 to 9 are used with 10 and then repeated with 2-ten and so on.

ACTIVITIES FOR TEACHING CONTINUED:

EXPLANATIONS CONTINUED:

1

2 0		2
3 0		3

1	4

| 4 0 |

5 0		5
6 0		6
7 0		7
8 0		8
9 0		9

The place-value cards in order and the counting at 1-ten 4.

Worksheet 23. The worksheet is an array of 10 by 10 rectangles. The child is to write the numbers up to 100 over the period of several days. She starts by entering 1 on the abacus and writing it in the first square. She continues by adding another bead and writing that number in the next square. Encourage her to use the place-value cards to compose the numbers.

This work can be spread out over three days.

1	2	3	4	5	6	7	8	9	10
11	12	13	14	15	16	17	18	19	20
21	22	23	24	25	26	27	28	29	30
31	32	33	34	35	36	37	38	39	40
41	42	43	44	45	46	47	48	49	50
51	52	53	54	55	56	57	58	59	60
61	62	63	64	65	66	67	68	69	70
71	72	73	74	75	76	77	78	79	80
81	82	83	84	85	86	87	88	89	90
91	92	93	94	95	96	97	98	99	100

The completed hundred chart.

LESSON 76: THOUSAND TRIANGLE

OBJECTIVES:

1. To build the Thousand Triangle (the third iteration of the Tens Fractal)

MATERIALS:

1. AL Abacus Tiles
2. Worksheet 24-1, Thousand Triangle
3. Worksheet 24-2, Fractal Outline
4. **Glue & scissors**
5. Worksheet 23, Making a Hundred Chart
6. *Math Card Games* book, A3, A3.1, or A4

ACTIVITIES FOR TEACHING:	EXPLANATIONS:
Warm-up. Alternate counting: start by saying 1, the child says 2; you continue with 3; he then says 4. Continue to 4-ten.	
Ask the child to count backward from 10. Then play the Comes Before game. Ask: What number comes before 8? [7] What number comes before 6? [5] What number comes before 3? [2]	
Ask the child how much is 2-ten + 1, [2-ten 1] 4-ten + 6, [4-ten 6] and 6-ten + 9. [6-ten 9]	
Building a thousand with abacus tiles. Show the child an abacus tile and ask: How many beads are entered? [one hundred] Give him the remaining tiles. Ask: Can you show me 2 hundred? [2 abacus tiles] Can you show me 4 hundred? [4 abacus tiles]	If the child is uncertain about the number of entered beads on a tile, refer back to the actual abacus.
Next ask him to make a row of four abacus tiles. Then ask him to make a row of three abacus tiles centered above that row. See the figure below. Ask him to center two abacus tiles above the last row and one abacus tile on top.	

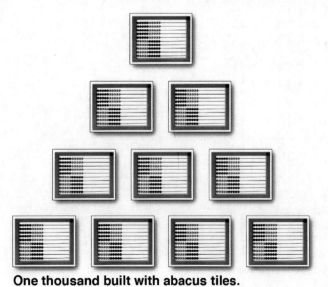

One thousand built with abacus tiles.

| ACTIVITIES FOR TEACHING CONTINUED: | EXPLANATIONS CONTINUED: |

Ask: Which row has 3 hundred entered? [third row] Which row has 1 hundred? [first row] How many are entered in the fourth row? [4 hundred] How many are entered in the first row? [1 hundred]

Continue by asking: How many are in the first two rows? [3 hundred] How many are in the first and third row? [4 hundred] How many are in the last two rows? [7 hundred] How many are in all four rows? [1 thousand (10 hundred)]

Making the Thousand Triangle. Ask the child to cut out the ten Hundred Triangles (not the tiny triangles) from Worksheet 24-1. After they are cut out, say: Show me 2 hundred. [two Hundred Triangles] Show me 4 hundred. [4 triangles] Show me 1 hundred. [1 triangle]

Ask the child to arrange the 10 triangles as shown in the left figure below. Put one triangle in the first row, two in the second row, three in the third row, and four in the fourth row.

This is the third and final iteration of the Tens Fractal. The first and second iterations are found in prior lessons.

Ask him to glue each triangle in place on the outline (Worksheet 24-2) to make the Hundred Triangle. It may be easier to start at the bottom row.

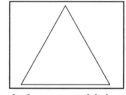

Ten Hundred Triangles form the Thousand Triangle.

Worksheet on which to glue the 10 Hundred Triangles.

Ask the child to compare this Thousand Triangle to the Ten Triangle he did on Worksheet 6 and the Hundred Triangle on Worksheet 9-2.

Hundred chart. The child can continue work on the hundred chart in Worksheet 23.

Sums equaling ten game. With the time left, let the child decide which game to play in the *Math Card Games* book, Go to the Dump, A3, Handshaking game, A3.1, or Old Main, A4.

In conclusion. Ask: How many tens are in one hundred? [10] How many hundreds are in one thousand? [10]

LESSON 77: REGULAR NAMES FOR THE TENS

OBJECTIVES:

1. To review ordinal counting to fifths
2. To learn the regular names for 10s

MATERIALS:

1. Tiles
2. AL Abacus
3. Place-value cards
4. *Math Card Games* book, N43 Level 3
5. Worksheet 23, Making a Hundred Chart

ACTIVITIES FOR TEACHING:	**EXPLANATIONS:**
Warm-up. Ask the child to count by 10s to 100.	
Ask the child to think of an imaginary abacus either on a flat surface or in the air. Tell her to move over 7 imaginary beads. Then ask her to move over the beads she needs to make 10. Ask: How many did you need? [3] Ask her to use her imaginary abacus to find what she needs with 5 to make 10. [5] Repeat for 8. [2]	Manipulating imaginary beads on an imaginary abacus seems to be a necessary step to seeing it mentally.
Reviewing ordinal counting. To review ordinal counting, set out in a row 5 tiles in assorted colors. Tell the child that the left side is the beginning. Then ask: What is the color of the third tile? What color is the fifth tile?	Ordinal counting is a good way for a child to become aware of the "thir" and "fif" sounds needed for thirty, thirteen, fifty, and fifteen.
Do the inverse. Ask: In what positions are the red tile? In what position is the yellow tile?	

Five tiles for ordinal counting.

Regular name for 4-ten. Ask the child to enter 4-ten on the abacus. Tell her that 4-ten has another name, its regular name is *forty*. Tell her that the "ty" in the word forty means ten. Ask: What does forty mean? [4-ten]	Take care to avoid emphasizing the "ty" syllable because it may sound like *teen*.

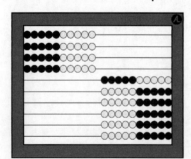

Forty (4-ten) entered on the abacus.

ACTIVITIES FOR TEACHING CONTINUED:	EXPLANATIONS CONTINUED:

Regular names for 60 to 90. Ask the child to show 6-ten on the abacus. Tell her: 6-ten has another name; its regular name is *sixty*. Continue for 7-ten, 8-ten, and 9-ten.

> Remember to avoid emphasizing the "ty" syllable because it may sound like *teen*.

Next ask her to recognize the regular names by asking: Can you enter 40? Can you enter 70? Can you enter 90? Can you enter 8? Can you enter 80? Can you enter 4? Can you enter 40?

> It is not necessary to clear the abacus each time.

Regular names for 30 and 50. Now ask the child to enter 3-ten. Tell her: It is called *thirty*. It might be helpful to explain that its regular name is not "threety," but we use the "thir" sound as in "first, second, third."

> Continue with 30 and 50 only when the child is successful with names 60–90.

Repeat for 5-ten, telling her its regular name is *fifty*.

Regular name for 20. Tell the child that a long time ago, people used to say "twoo" for two. They used to count by saying, one, twoo, three.

> Knowing about "twoo" explains why we need a "w" to spell two.

Ask the child to enter 2-ten and tell her its regular name is *twenty*. You might tell her that a good way to remember twenty is to think of "twoo" or "twin ten." Ask: What is the regular name for 2-ten? [twenty]

Practice. Ask the child to enter 30 on the abacus. Continue with 20, 60, 80, 90, and so forth.

Enter on the abacus any of the 10s between 20 and 90 and ask her to give the regular names.

Ask the child to enter tens on the abacus one at a time and to say the regular name. [10, 20, 30, . . . , 90, 100]

Reading the tens. Show the child one of the 10s place-value cards, for example 50. Demonstrate reading it by pointing to the 5 while saying "fif" and pointing to the 0 while saying "ty."

Reading the 50 card.

Can You Find game. Ask the child to spread out the tens and ones from the place-value cards and play Can You Find Level 3 in the *Math Card Games* book, N43.

Hundred chart. The child can complete work on the hundred chart in Worksheet 23.

In conclusion. Ask the child to count by tens the "math way." [1-ten, 2-ten, . . . , 1 hundred] Then ask the child to count by tens using the regular names. [10, 20, . . . , 100]

LESSON 78: PARTITIONING 50

OBJECTIVES:

1. To combine tens and ones using the regular names
2. To partition 5 and 50

MATERIALS:

1. AL Abacus
2. *Math Card Games* book, N43 Level 4
3. Dry erase board
4. Worksheet 25, Partitioning 50

ACTIVITIES FOR TEACHING:	EXPLANATIONS:
Warm-up. Ask the child to count by 10s to 100 the math way and the regular way.	

Warm-up. Ask the child to count by 10s to 100 the math way and the regular way.

Ask the child to enter 6 on his imaginary abacus. Then ask him how much he needs with 6 to make 10. [4] Continue with: How much do you need with 5 to make 10? [5] How much do you need with 7 to make 10? [3]

Tens and ones on the abacus. Ask the child to enter 40 on the abacus; ask him to say the math name for it. [4-ten] Then ask him to enter 45; if needed, remind him that 45 is 40 and 5. Repeat for other quantities, such as 63, 82, 29, 37, and 58. Omit the teens.

Enter 79 on the abacus and ask the child to name the quantity the math way [7-ten 9] and the regular way. [seventy-nine] Repeat for other quantities such as 48, 29, and 37. Omit the teens.

Can You Find game. From the *Math Card Games* book, play game N43 Level 4. This game provides practice in listening to the regular names and finding the corresponding cards.

The regular teen names will be introduced in later lessons.

The Can You Find game in progress.

ACTIVITIES FOR TEACHING CONTINUED:

Review partitioning 5. Ask the child to a draw part-whole circle set on his dry erase board and to write 5 in the whole-circle. Ask him to partition 5 and write the parts in the part-circles. Then ask him to write the equation. [for example, 5 = 4 + 1] Ask him to show it on the abacus. See the figures below.

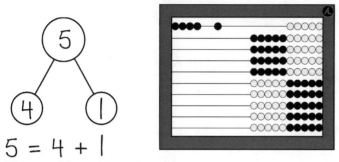

$$5 = 4 + 1$$

Five partitioned into 4 and 1.

Ask the child to erase the parts and find other parts, writing the equations and checking with the abacus.

Partitioning 50. Now ask the child if he could partition 50 into tens. Ask him to write 50 in the whole-circle and 40 in the left part-circle. Then ask him to say and to write the equation. Continue until he finds all the other 10s partitions of 50. [50 = 30 + 20, 50 = 20 + 30, and so forth.]

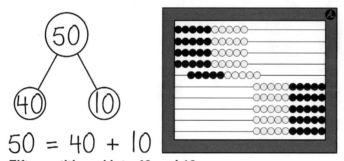

$$50 = 40 + 10$$

Fifty partitioned into 40 and 10.

Worksheet 25. Give the child the worksheet. The answers are as follows:

5 = 2 + **3**
5 = 4 + **1**
5 = 5 + **0**
5 = 3 + **2**
5 = 1 + **4**
50 = 30 + **20**
50 = 40 + **10**
50 = 10 + **40**
50 = 20 + **30**
50 = 0 + **50**

In conclusion. Ask the child to name two ways to partition 50.

EXPLANATIONS CONTINUED:

Do not correct the child if he uses the math name, 5-ten, but use the regular name yourself.

LESSON 79: COUNTING AND COMPOSING TENS TO 200

OBJECTIVES:
1. To introduce the term *dollar*
2. To count 20 dimes to 2 dollars
3. To count by 10s to 200
4. To compose 10s to 200

MATERIALS:
1. AL Abacus
2. Coins
3. AL Abacus tiles
4. Place-value cards

ACTIVITIES FOR TEACHING:	EXPLANATIONS:
Warm-up. Ask the child to count by tens to 100 using the regular names. Ask the child to say the days of the week and the months of the year. Ask the child to enter 30 on the abacus. Then ask her to move over one bead at a time while she says the name. Continue to 60. ***Counting dimes.*** Show the child a dime and ask her if she remembers what it is called. [dime] Then ask how much it is worth. [10 cents] Ask the child to help you lay 10 dimes out in a column leaving a space between the 5th and 6th dime as shown on the right. Ask her to count as you point to each dime. [10 cents, 20 cents, . . . , 90 cents, 1 hundred cents] Tell her that 1 hundred cents has another name, *one dollar.* Ask her to count by herself; challenge her to remember to say "1 dollar" when she reaches 100 cents. Ask the child to make another column of dimes next to the first column. Tell the child: This time we will count to 2 dollars. Count as before to 1 dollar, then continue by saying 1 dollar 10 cents, 1 dollar 20 cents, . . . , 2 dollars. Ask: How many dimes do you need to make 1 dollar? [10] How many dimes do you need to make 2 dollars? [20] How many dimes do you need to make 3 dollars? [30] Ask her to explain her reasoning.	Using money to count by tens is another "real world" way to help the child become familiar with tens.

| ACTIVITIES FOR TEACHING CONTINUED: | EXPLANATIONS CONTINUED: |

Counting by tens to 200. Ask the child to count by tens—using the regular names—by entering tens on the abacus.

Say: Let's go higher than 1 hundred. Lay out an abacus tile and ask: How much does this abacus tile represent? [100] Ask her to enter another ten on the abacus. Tell her that now we have one hundred ten. See the figure below.

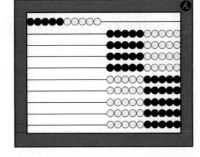

Showing 110.

Enter another 10 and ask the child how much is entered. [1 hundred 20] Continue to 200 and ask her for the other name. [2 hundred] Also discuss if she thinks 2 hundred is a lot.

Recording the numbers. Construct 110 with the abacus tile and abacus. Then ask the child to compose the number with the place-value cards. See the figure below.

| 1 0 0 | 1 0 | 1 1 0 |

Showing 110 with the place-value cards.

Enter other tens on the abacus between 10 and 200 and ask her to compose the number with the place-value cards.

Also compose numbers in the same range and ask her to construct them.

In conclusion. Ask: How much is 100 + 100? [200] What is 100 + 50? [150]

Working with the hundreds gives the child a better understanding of place value.

It is perfectly acceptable to say "one hundred *and* ten" for this number. In the past, students were taught that the "and" indicated the decimal point. That is no longer true; today, most people would read 2.47 as "two point four seven," not "two and forty-seven hundredths."

To ensure proper alignment of the place-value cards, lightly tap the cards on the right side.

LESSON 80: ADDING TENS

OBJECTIVES:

1. To add multiples of 10

MATERIALS:

1. AL Abacus
2. AL Abacus Tiles
3. Dry erase board
4. Worksheet 26, Adding Tens
5. *Math Card Games* book, N43 Level 4

ACTIVITIES FOR TEACHING:	EXPLANATIONS:
Warm-up. Ask the child to say the days of the week and the months of the year.	

Warm-up. Ask the child to say the days of the week and the months of the year.

Ask the child to enter 40 on the abacus. Then ask him to move over one bead at a time while he says the name. Continue to 70.

Ask the child how much is 40 + 1, [41] 60 + 2, [62] and 50 + 3. [53]

Counting by tens. Review with the child counting by 10s up to 2 hundred. Use an abacus and an abacus tile; move over 10 at a time while the child says the quantities as was done in the previous lesson. [10, 20, . . . , 90, 100, 110, . . . , 200]

Problems for adding tens. Give the child the following problem:

On Monday Jack saw 20 monarch butterflies on his way up the hill. Jill saw 30 swallowtail butterflies on her way up the hill. How many butterflies did they see altogether on Monday?

Ask the child to write the numbers in part-whole circle sets on his dry erase board. If necessary ask: What is the whole that we are trying to find? [total number of butterflies] What are the parts? [20 monarch butterflies, 30 swallowtail butterflies] Then ask him to show the addition on the abacus. Ask him to write the equation.

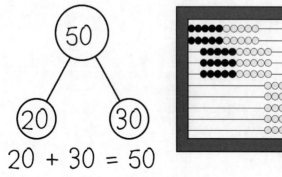

20 + 30 = 50

Solution for the butterfly problem.

ACTIVITIES FOR TEACHING CONTINUED:

Continue with the following problem:

On Tuesday Jack saw 50 robins and Jill saw 40 blue jays. How many birds did they see on Tuesday?

Repeat the prior steps with a part-whole circle set, abacus, and writing of the equation. [90]

Practice. Write the following equation for the child to solve:

$$30 + 30 = \underline{\hphantom{00}} \; [60]$$

Ask the child to explain his solution method. Sometimes a child may not need the abacus for this problem.

Repeat for:

$$70 + 10 = \underline{\hphantom{00}} \; [80]$$
$$40 + 60 = \underline{\hphantom{00}} \; [100]$$

Worksheet 26. Give the child the worksheet. The problems and answers are shown below.

$10 + 20 = \mathbf{30}$
$40 + 20 = \mathbf{60}$
$20 + 20 = \mathbf{40}$
$50 + 50 = \mathbf{100}$
$70 + 10 = \mathbf{80}$
$50 + 20 = \mathbf{70}$
$40 + 10 = \mathbf{50}$
$70 + 20 = \mathbf{90}$

Can You Find game. Play the Can You Find game in the *Math Card Games* book, N43 Level 4. Use the math names for numbers 11 to 19.

In conclusion. Ask the child to say the different ways as he can to make 40 using only 10s. [0 and 40, 10 and 30, 20 and 20, 30 and 10, 40 and 0]

EXPLANATIONS CONTINUED:

This type of problem is more difficult for the child than simple combining because he needs to recognize that robins and blue jays are both birds.

LESSON 81: REGULAR NAMES FOR THE TEENS

OBJECTIVES:
1. To learn that *teen* means one ten
2. To learn the regular names for 13 to 19

MATERIALS:
1. AL Abacus
2. Place-value cards
3. **Five sheets of paper cut in half**
4. **Two different colored crayons**

ACTIVITIES FOR TEACHING:	EXPLANATIONS:
Warm-up. Ask the child to count by 10s to 200.	
Ask the child to enter 37 on the abacus. Then ask: What would the next number be? [38] Repeat for other numbers such as 62, [63] 98, [99] and 25. [26]	Encourage the child to find the answer without adding one on the abacus for the next number.
Words said backward. Tell the child that today she will learn the regular names for the numbers from 1-ten 3 to 1-ten 9. Explain that they can be hard because their regular names are said backward.	
Ask: Can you say *sunset* backward? [set-sun] Can you say *oatmeal* backward? [meal-oat] *Pineapple*? [apple-pine] And mailbox? [box-mail] Also, give her some words said backward and ask her to say them correctly. For example, say: "room-bed," [bedroom] "ball-foot," [football] and "paper-news." [newspaper]	In many Indo-European languages some of the numbers between 11 and 19 are said backward; that is, the ones are said before the ten.
Teens on the abacus. Tell the child that *teen* means ten. So ask her: Can you enter "teen-four" on the abacus? See figure below. Ask: What is entered? [teen-four] Tell her: Now say it backward. [fourteen] Say that fourteen is its regular name.	

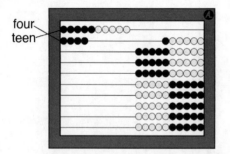

four
teen

Showing the meaning of *fourteen*.

Ask the child to enter "teen-6". Then say: Its regular name is sixteen. Ask the child to show where the six is and where the "teen" is. Ask: What does teen mean? [ten]

Continue with ten 7, ten 8, and ten 9.

ACTIVITIES FOR TEACHING CONTINUED:

EXPLANATIONS CONTINUED:

Say the numbers 14 to 19, omitting 15, in random order and ask the child to enter them on the abacus.

Enter 13 on the abacus. Point to the 3 and say: Here is the "thir." Next point to the 10 and say: Here is the teen. Ask her what the "thir" sound reminds her of. [thirty or third] Repeat for 15.

Say the numbers 13 to 19 in random order and ask her to enter them on the abacus.

Counting. Enter 13 on the abacus and ask the child to say its name. Enter one more bead and ask for the name; [14] continue to 40.

Next enter various numbers from 13 to 19 on the abacus and ask the child to name them.

Numbers 13 to 19 with the place-value cards. Say a number between 13–19 and ask the child to compose it with the place-value cards.

Making a teen number booklet. Give the child the half sheets of paper. Have the child enter a teen number on the abacus and draw it on her paper, using any two crayons she chooses. Then ask her to write the number below it. A sample page with 14 is shown below.

The child can start on the number booklet with numbers 13 to 19. In the following lesson, she will learn the names for 11 and 12, which will be included in the book.

There will be one extra half sheet that can be the cover.

A sample page in the number booklet.

In conclusion. Ask: What is the regular name for 1-ten 7? [seventeen] What is the regular name for 1-ten 5? [fifteen] What is the regular name for 1-ten 3? [thirteen]

LESSON 82: REGULAR NAMES FOR ELEVEN AND TWELVE

OBJECTIVES:
1. To learn the terms *eleven* and *twelve*
2. To review the regular names for 11–19

MATERIALS:
1. AL Abacus
2. Place-value cards
3. *Math Card Games* book, N43 Level 4
4. **Half sheets of paper from previous lesson**
5. **Two different colored crayons**
6. **Stapler**

ACTIVITIES FOR TEACHING:	EXPLANATIONS:

ACTIVITIES FOR TEACHING:

Warm-up. Ask the child to count by tens to 200 using the regular names.

Enter 43 on the abacus and ask the child for its new name. [forty-three] Show 43 with place-value cards; ask when we read the number, which part of the number do we say first. [the 40] Repeat for 68.

$$\boxed{4}\boxed{3} \qquad \boxed{4}\boxed{0}\ \boxed{3}$$

First we read 40 and then 3.

Enter various 2-digit quantities on the abacus and ask the child to name them both ways, such as 27 and 2-ten 7, 51 and 5-ten 1, 68 and 6-ten 8, and 86 and 8-ten 6.

Now enter 14 on the abacus and construct the number with the place-value cards. Ask him to read it. [14] Show the 10 and ask him for another word that means ten. [teen] Then ask which part he needed to read first. [4] Discuss that it is backward, not what we would expect.

$$\boxed{1}\boxed{4} \qquad \boxed{1}\boxed{0}\ \boxed{4}$$

First we read 4 and then teen (ten).

Enter various teen numbers on the abacus and ask him to name them. Also ask him to construct the numbers with place-value cards and to read them.

Eleven. Tell the child the following factual story. Hundreds of years ago some people wanted another name for 1-ten 1. So they put ten pebbles in a row (enter ten on the abacus) and with the extra one, they started a new row (enter one in the second wire).

Point to the top row and say they knew that was ten, like their fingers. But they noticed that they had one left over. (Point to the one in the next row.) They were very interested in the one left over and thought that a good

ACTIVITIES FOR TEACHING CONTINUED:	EXPLANATIONS CONTINUED:

name for this number might be "a one left." However, instead of calling it "a one left," they said it backward and called it "a left one." That is why today we call it *eleven*.

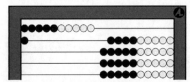

"A one left" became "a left one," which became *eleven*.

Let the child think about the story before asking: What is the regular name for 1-ten 1. [eleven] Ask: How much is eleven? [1-ten 1, or ten-1] You might also tell him that the people in China, Japan, and Korea still call the number "ten-one" in their languages.

Twelve. Tell the child that there is also a story for 1-ten 2. The same people noticed that for 1-ten 2 there were two left. Remember they said "twoo" back then, so they called this number "twoo left," which became *twelve*.

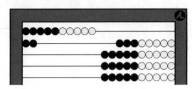

"Twoo left" became *twelve*.

After a pause ask: What is the regular name for 1-ten 2? [twelve] Ask: What does twelve mean? [ten and 2]

Practice. Ask the child to enter 11 then 12 on the abacus. Also ask him to construct them with the place-value cards. Continue by asking him to construct the numbers 11 to 19 in random order.

Counting on the abacus. Tell the child that now he will count up to 20 with the abacus. On the abacus, slowly and rhythmically move over one bead at a time while counting from 1 to 20, using the regular names.

Can You Find game. In the *Math Card Games* book play N43 Level 4. This time use the regular names for numbers 11 to 19.

Number booklet. Ask him to make pages for 11 and 12 for the number booklet. When he has finished all the pages and a cover, ask him to put the pages in order. Staple the pages together.

In conclusion. Ask the child: What is the regular name for 1-ten 2? [twelve] What is the regular name for 1-ten 1? [eleven]

LESSON 83: ADDING ONE TO 2-DIGIT NUMBERS

OBJECTIVES:
1. To add 1 to 2-digit numbers

MATERIALS:
1. AL Abacus
2. Dry erase board
3. Math balance
4. Worksheet 27, Adding One to 2-Digit Numbers

ACTIVITIES FOR TEACHING:

Warm-up. Ask the child to count by tens to 50 on the abacus using the regular names.

Ask the child to count by fives to 50 on the abacus using the regular names.

Ask the child to count from 1 to 50 on the abacus using the regular names.

Adding one on the abacus. Ask the child to enter 37 on her abacus. Then ask her: What number comes after 37 when you are counting? [38]

Now ask her to add 1 more to her 37. Ask: What do you get when you add 1 to the 37? [38] Ask her to write the equation. [37 + 1 = 38] See the figure below.

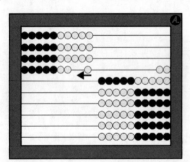

$$37 + 1 = 38$$

Adding 1 is the same as the next number.

Ask: What number comes after 38? [39] Add 1 to 38 on the abacus and write the equation. [38 + 1 = 39]

Repeat one more time: What number comes after 39? [40] Add 1 to 39 and write the equation. [39 + 1 = 40]

Adding one on the math balance. Give the child two weights and ask her to enter 13 on the left side of the math balance. See the first figure at the top of the next page.

Next ask her to add 1 on the left side. Tell her to balance it with 2 weights with one of the weights on the 10. Ask her to say the equation. [13 + 1 = 14] See the figures on the next page for the sequence.

EXPLANATIONS:

Children often do not realize that adding 1 to a number is the same as the next number in the counting sequence. These activities are designed to help with this concept.

ACTIVITIES FOR TEACHING CONTINUED:	EXPLANATIONS CONTINUED:

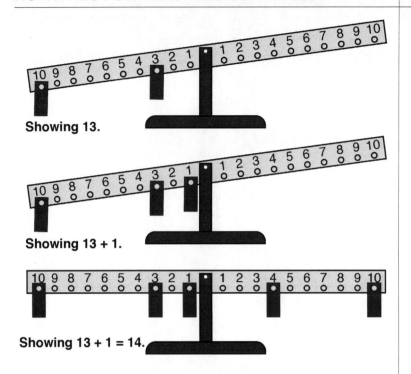

Showing 13.

Showing 13 + 1.

Showing 13 + 1 = 14.

Continue by asking the child to enter 28 and 1 on the left side. Then ask her to balance it and say the equation. [28 + 1 = 29]

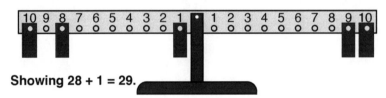

Showing 28 + 1 = 29.

Now tell her to change the left side from 8 to 9. Ask her to make it balance without adding any more weights.

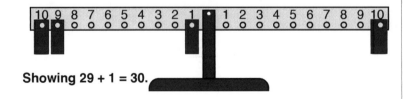

Showing 29 + 1 = 30.

Worksheet 27. Ask the child to do the worksheet. The problems and solutions are given below.

$$43 + 1 = \mathbf{44}$$
$$17 + 1 = \mathbf{18}$$
$$88 + 1 = \mathbf{89}$$
$$35 + 1 = \mathbf{36}$$
$$66 + 1 = \mathbf{67}$$
$$29 + 1 = \mathbf{30}$$
$$54 + 1 = \mathbf{55}$$
$$79 + 1 = \mathbf{80}$$

In conclusion. Ask: What number comes after 15? [16] What is 15 + 1? [16]

LESSON 84: ONE PLUS A NUMBER

OBJECTIVES:

1. To use the commutative property for adding 1 + a number

MATERIALS:

1. AL Abacus
2. Place-value
3. Dry erase board
4. Worksheet 28-1 or 28-2, Adding 1 Plus a Number

ACTIVITIES FOR TEACHING:	EXPLANATIONS:
Warm-up. Ask the child to count from 1 to 60 on the abacus using the regular names.	
Ask the child to enter 64 on his abacus. Then ask: How many tens does 64 have? [6] How many ones? [4] Repeat for 52: How many tens does 52 have? [5] How many ones? [2] Repeat for 12: How many tens does 12 have? [1] How many ones? [2]	
Ask the child: How much is 53 + 1, [54] 39 + 1, [40] 27 + 1, [28] and 86 + 1? [87]	
Entering quantities. Ask the child to enter a number on the abacus to show 4 monkeys. Then ask him to find the matching place-value card and to place it above the abacus.	
Ask him to enter other quantities and to find the matching place-value card, such as:	
6 elephants	
3 zebras	
7 anteaters	
9 antelopes	
Ask the child if those are too easy. Continue with:	
20 tulips	
50 daffodils	
90 irises	
30 crocuses	
Then combine 10s and 1s.	
30 ash trees and 6 more ash trees [36]	
50 oak trees and 3 more oak trees [53]	
10 elm trees and 8 more elm trees [18]	
70 maple trees and 2 more maple trees [72]	
Also ask him to make up his own quantities to enter.	
1 + a number on the abacus. Ask the child to enter 4 + 1 on his abacus. Then ask him to enter 1 + 4 on the second wire on the abacus. See the figure on the next page.	Although this activity emphasizes the commutative property, the word itself should not be taught. Before teaching vocabulary, either the concept or the word must be known.
Ask: What do you notice about 4 + 1 and 1 + 4? [same]	

ACTIVITIES FOR TEACHING CONTINUED:	EXPLANATIONS CONTINUED:

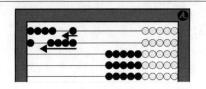

Comparing 4 + 1 and 1 + 4.

__1 + a number.__ On the dry erase board, draw a part-whole circle set and read the following problem:

> Marietta had 1 pencil and received 5 more pencils. How many pencils does she have now?

Ask the child to write the numbers in the correct circles. See left figure below. Ask him to find the whole. [6] Ask him to show it on the abacus and to write the equation. [1 + 5 = 6]

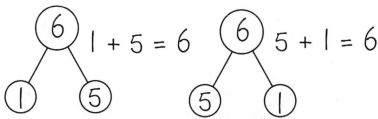

Parts and whole for 1 + 5.   **Parts and whole for 5 + 1.**

Repeat for the second problem:

> Zachary had 5 pencils and received 1 more pencil. How many pencils does he have now?

Ask the child what is special about the answers [6, the same] and why. See right figure above. Then ask him which is easier to add.

__Practice.__ Ask: What is 5 books plus 1 more book? [6 books] What is 1 book added to 5 books? [6 books] What is 7 dogs plus 1 more dog? [8 dogs] What is 1 dog added to 7 dogs? [8 dogs]

Continue with 1 + 9, [10] 1 + 1, [2] and 1 + 5. [6] Also write the following: 1 + 7 = ___, [8] 1 + 4 = ___, [5] and 1 + 6 = ___. [7]

__Worksheet 28-1 or 28-2.__ Give the child one of the worksheets. The problems and solutions are given below.

A child who is not confident with 10s and 1s should be given Worksheet 28-1; otherwise the child can be given Worksheet 28-2.

Worksheet 28-1	Worksheet 28-2
1 + 2 = **3**	1 + 3 = **4**
1 + 6 = **7**	1 + 8 = **9**
1 + 3 = **4**	1 + 21 = **22**
1 + 9 = **10**	1 + 77 = **78**
1 + 4 = **5**	1 + 52 = **53**
1 + 5 = **6**	1 + 35 = **36**
1 + 7 = **8**	1 + 87 = **88**
1 + 8 = **9**	1 + 16 = **17**

__In conclusion.__ Ask: What is 15 + 1? [16] What is 1 + 15? [16] What is 11 + 1? [12] What is 1 + 11? [12]

LESSON 85: USING THE COMMUTATIVE PROPERTY

OBJECTIVES:
1. To continuing using the commutative property

MATERIALS:
1. AL Abacus
2. Worksheet 29, The Commutative Property
3. Dry erase board
4. Tiles

ACTIVITIES FOR TEACHING:	EXPLANATIONS:

Warm-up. Ask the child to say the even and odd numbers. Play the Comes After game; for example, ask: What even number comes after 8? [10] What odd number comes after 7? [9] What odd number comes after 3? [5]

Ask the child to count backwards from 19. Then play the Comes Before game. Ask: What number comes before 16? [15] What number comes before 19? [18] What number comes before 11? [10]

Ask the child to use her imaginary abacus, then ask how much is 5 + 1, [6] 5 + 5, [10] 5 + 3, [8] and 5 + 2. [7]

Worksheet 29. Give the child the worksheet. Use the abacus if necessary. Encourage the use of the imaginary abacus when appropriate. The problems and solutions are as follows:

> 3 + 2 = **5**
> 2 + 3 = **5**
> 8 + 2 = **10**
> 2 + 8 = **10**
> 5 + 3 = **8**
> 3 + 5 = **8**
> 6 + 1 = **7**
> 1 + 6 = **7**

The *commutative property* used to be referred to as the "commutative law." Today we avoid talking about "laws" and "rules" in mathematics because the goal for each child is be able to understand and justify each step in a discussion.

When she is finished, ask the child if she sees any patterns. [The answers in each group of two are the same. The parts are the same, but in a different order.]

Ask her why that is so; ask if she could show why. Discuss it from several different viewpoints. For example, use the problem:

> Jerry has 5 tickets and gets 2 more. Carrie has 2 tickets and gets 5 more. Who has more tickets?

Ask the child to represent the problem using the abacus or tiles. Use the top wire for Jerry's tickets and the next wire for Carrie's tickets as shown on the next page. [the same]

ACTIVITIES FOR TEACHING CONTINUED:

EXPLANATIONS CONTINUED:

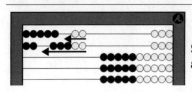

Showing 5 + 2 on the first wire and 2 + 5 on the second wire.

Also ask the child to use part-whole circle sets for the tickets problem and to write the equations. See figures below.

7
5 + 2 = 7
5 2

7
2 + 5 = 7
2 5

Part-whole circle sets showing that identical parts give the same whole.

Pick up 4 tiles with your right hand and 3 with your left hand. Hold them in front of the child. Ask her how many tiles there are altogether [7] and to say the equation. [4 + 3 = 7]

Next cross your arms at the wrist so your hands are now switched around. Ask: Now how many tiles are altogether? [7] What is the equation? [3 + 4 = 7]

Practice. Write 5 + 1 and ask the child: How much is 5 + 1? [6] So, how much is 1 + 5? [6] Ask her how she did it.

Repeat for 6 + 2 [8] and 2 + 6. [8]

Repeat for 5 + 4 [9] and 4 + 5. [9]

Repeat for 10 + 5 [15] and 5 + 10. [15]

Repeat for 18 + 2 [20] and 2 + 18. [20]

In conclusion. Ask: Which is more, 1-ten 4 or 14? [the same]

The purpose of using several representations is not to convince the child of your position, but to enable her to think about the concept in different ways.

LESSON 86: COUNTING OBJECTS BY TWOS

OBJECTIVES:
1. To count objects by twos
2. To review ordinal counting

MATERIALS:
1. AL Abacus
2. Tiles
3. Dry erase board
4. *Math Card Games* book, A14

ACTIVITIES FOR TEACHING:	EXPLANATIONS:
Warm-up. Ask the child to count by 2s starting at 20 and continuing to 60; it may be helpful if he enters 2s on the abacus as he recites the numbers.	

Warm-up. Ask the child to count by 2s starting at 20 and continuing to 60; it may be helpful if he enters 2s on the abacus as he recites the numbers.

Ask the child: How much is 30 + 10, [40] 60 + 10, [70] 80 + 10, [90] and 90 + 10? [1 hundred]

Counting fingers by tens. Suggest to the child that we count the fingers of everyone in the family or of other group. Ask for his ideas for the best way. You might try more than one way and compare answers. At the conclusion, ask: How many fingers are there altogether?

Counting tiles by twos. Place 27 tiles in view of the child. Ask him to guess how many. Then ask him if he could count them by 2s. Demonstrate pairing them and counting, 2, 4, 6, and so forth. When you reach the last single tile, ask him how to count it. [26, then 27] Set them aside; they will be used again later.

Counting separate objects by twos is more difficult than counting by twos on the abacus.

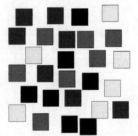

27 tiles to be counted by 2s.

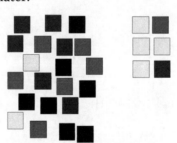

27 tiles with three pairs formed for a count of 2, 4, 6.

Next ask the child to take a handful of tiles. Ask him to count the tiles by 2s. Then ask him to write his answers down on the dry erase board. Have him repeat the activity several times.

When all the numbers are written, ask him to read the numbers and to decide which number is greatest. Also ask which number is least, or lowest.

ACTIVITIES FOR TEACHING CONTINUED:	EXPLANATIONS CONTINUED:

Reviewing ordinal counting. Ask the child what grade comes after kindergarten. [1st] Ask what grade follows next. [2nd] Continue through fifth grade.

Ask the child to construct the stairs on the abacus as shown below.

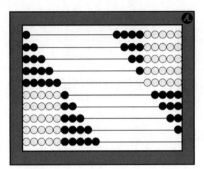

Stairs.

Ask: How many beads are on the 3rd wire? [3] How many beads on the first wire? [1] How many beads on the fifth wire? [5]

To Thirty with Ones and Twos game. Play the game in the *Math Card Games* Book, A14. Use the abacus to play the game.

In conclusion. Ask: When you are in the fifth grade, what is the number of the grade you will be in? [5]

Ordinal counting is a good way for a child to become aware of the "thir" and "fif" sounds needed for "thirty," "thirteen," "fifty," and "fifteen."

174

LESSON 87: WORKING WITH TWOS

OBJECTIVES:
1. To see the pattern of 2s on the hundred chart

MATERIALS:
1. AL Abacus
2. Worksheet 30, Twos on the Hundred Chart
3. **Crayon**

ACTIVITIES FOR TEACHING:

Warm-up. Ask the child to count from 1 to 50.

Alternate saying numbers: start by saying 1, the child says 2, you say 3; she says 4. Continue up to 40.

Ask the child to count by 10s to 200.

Counting by twos. Tell the child that today she will count by twos and find the number on a hundred chart (Worksheet 30) and color it in.

Start by asking her to enter 2 on the abacus. Then ask her to find 2 on the chart and to color that square. See the figure below.

1	2	3	4	5	6	7	8	9	10
11	12	13	14	15	16	17	18	19	20
21	22	23	24	25	26	27	28	29	30
31	32	33	34	35	36	37	38	39	40
41	42	43	44	45	46	47	48	49	50
51	52	53	54	55	56	57	58	59	60
61	62	63	64	65	66	67	68	69	70
71	72	73	74	75	76	77	78	79	80
81	82	83	84	85	86	87	88	89	90
91	92	93	94	95	96	97	98	99	100

The numeral 2 colored on the hundred chart.

Next tell the child to add 2 more and ask: How much do you have now? [4] Ask her to find the 4 on the hundred chart and color it in.

Ask her to continue adding another 2. The results are shown on the next page.

EXPLANATIONS:

Some children will need to use the abacus for this task, others will need only to look at it without touching, and a few will not need it at all.

This is the first time the child is asked to read a standard font where the 9s are rotated 6s.

Rather than color the rectangles, the child may find it easier to circle the number or even underline it.

ACTIVITIES FOR TEACHING CONTINUED:	EXPLANATIONS CONTINUED:

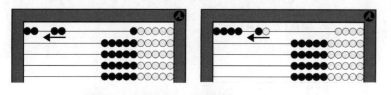

1	2	3	4	5	6	7	8	9	10
11	12	13	14	15	16	17	18	19	20
21	22	23	24	25	26	27	28	29	30
31	32	33	34	35	36	37	38	39	40
41	42	43	44	45	46	47	48	49	50
51	52	53	54	55	56	57	58	59	60
61	62	63	64	65	66	67	68	69	70
71	72	73	74	75	76	77	78	79	80
81	82	83	84	85	86	87	88	89	90
91	92	93	94	95	96	97	98	99	100

Adding more twos and coloring them.

Ask the child to continue to 100. She may discover the pattern and complete the chart without actually doing all the adding. The final chart is shown below.

1	2	3	4	5	6	7	8	9	10
11	12	13	14	15	16	17	18	19	20
21	22	23	24	25	26	27	28	29	30
31	32	33	34	35	36	37	38	39	40
41	42	43	44	45	46	47	48	49	50
51	52	53	54	55	56	57	58	59	60
61	62	63	64	65	66	67	68	69	70
71	72	73	74	75	76	77	78	79	80
81	82	83	84	85	86	87	88	89	90
91	92	93	94	95	96	97	98	99	100

The completed hundred chart showing twos.

In conclusion. Ask: Where are the even numbers on the chart? [colored numbers] Where are the odd numbers? [un-colored numbers] Where are tens? [along the right side]

LESSON 88: ADDING TWOS

OBJECTIVES:

1. To add 2 to 2-digit numbers

MATERIALS:

1. Tiles
2. AL Abacus
3. Dry erase board
4. Worksheet 31, Adding Two to 2-Digit Numbers

ACTIVITIES FOR TEACHING:	EXPLANATIONS:

ACTIVITIES FOR TEACHING:

Warm-up. Ask the child to count by 1s to 50.

Ask the child to count by 10s to 200.

Ask the child to count by 5s to 50.

Ask: How much is 21 + 1? [22] How much is 46 + 1? [47] How much is 88 + 1? [89] How much is 99 + 1? [100]

Adding twos. Place a pile of tiles in front of the child. Ask him to count out 16 tiles, counting by 2s. Also ask him to enter that quantity on the abacus. Now ask him to take 2 more tiles; ask how many he has now. [18] Ask him to enter 2 more on the abacus.

Again ask him to take 2 more tiles and to say how many he has now. [20] Ask him to enter 2 more on the abacus as a check.

Problem. Ask the child to take 10 tiles; verify the amount by counting by twos. Then quickly pick up about 6 of them, hiding them in your hand. Show your closed hand and ask him how many are in your hand.

Ask him to write what numbers he can in a part-whole circle set. See the left figure below.

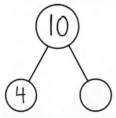 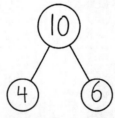

The whole and parts for "quick pickup" problem.

After the child has solved the problem and written the solution in the part-whole circle sets, show him the tiles in your hand. [6] Ask him to explain how he got his answer. Also ask him to write the equations.

$$4 + 6 = 10$$
$$10 = 4 + 6$$

EXPLANATIONS:

Typically, children progress through the following developmental levels for solving addition problems on the abacus:

1. They enter both addends.

2. They enter the first addend and mentally enter the second addend.

3. They use their fingers to enter the addends on an imaginary abacus.

4. They enter the addends on their mental abacus with no physical manipulative.

This "subtraction" problem is actually easier to solve by using addition.

ACTIVITIES FOR TEACHING CONTINUED:	EXPLANATIONS CONTINUED:

Visualization. Now ask the child to enter 8 on the abacus. Ask: How much would you have if you added 2 more? [10]

Repeat for entering 32, then adding 2 more, [34] and 2 more again. [36]

Some children might not need to use the abacus.

Practice. Write the following equations for the child to solve on his imaginary abacus in his mind, if possible.

Some children will need the abacus, which is fine.

$$24 + 2 = \underline{\quad} \ [26]$$
$$46 + 2 = \underline{\quad} \ [48]$$
$$78 + 2 = \underline{\quad} \ [80]$$

Worksheet 31. Ask the child to do the worksheet. The problems and solutions are shown below.

64 + 2 = **66**
32 + 2 = **34**
26 + 2 = **28**
88 + 2 = **90**
42 + 2 = **44**
74 + 2 = **76**
56 + 2 = **58**
18 + 2 = **20**

In conclusion. Ask: How much is 52 + 2 more? [54]

LESSON 89: WORKING WITH A CALCULATOR

OBJECTIVES:
1. To learn to use a calculator

MATERIALS:
1. Casio SL-450S calculator
2. Worksheet 32, Counting by Twos
3. *Math Card Games* book, A13

ACTIVITIES FOR TEACHING:	EXPLANATIONS:
Warm-up. Ask the child to count by 1s to 40.	
Ask the child to count by 10s to 200.	
Ask the child to count by 5s to 60.	
Ask: How much is 4 + 2? [6] How much is 14 + 2? [16] How much is 24 + 2? [26] How much is 34 + 2? [36]	
Introducing the calculator. Give the child the calculator. If necessary, show her how to remove the cover from the front of the calculator and put it on the back.	This Casio calculator has several advantages over TI calculators for a young child. The constant key feature, which frequently causes errors for the unwary on other calculators, is not activated on a Casio until the operation sign is pressed twice. Also, this Casio shows 0 when first turned on.
Encourage her to explore adding numbers of her own choosing.	Encourage the child to learn about the calculator intuitively.
	Intuition as a means of learning is becoming increasingly more important in our technological world. To learn intuitively is to try new procedures by combining common sense with a willingness to take a risk.

The Casio SL-450S calculator.

Counting by 1s on a calculator. Tell the child the calculator can count by 1s. Show the following procedure:

• If the calculator does not show a **0** press **AC**. Tell the child that the **AC** means "all clear."

• Press the **1** key.

ACTIVITIES FOR TEACHING CONTINUED:	EXPLANATIONS CONTINUED:

- Press the + key twice. Point out the letter K, indicating the constant mode.
- Press the = key repeatedly and read the numbers.

For other calculators, press the + once; most do not have the K indicator.

Ask the child to count by 1s up to 30 on the calculator or as far as she would like.

Next ask if she would like to count starting at 50. Tell her to press 50 without hitting the AC key, and the = key as many times as she wants.

Finding the next number. Now ask the child what number comes after 37; [38] ask her to press 37 and then press = to see if she is correct.

Repeat for other numbers: 23, [24] 89, [90] and 11. [12] Encourage the child to think up her own numbers, to key in those numbers, then to say the next number before pressing the =, and check if she is correct.

Counting by 2s. Tell the child that she can also count by 2s on the calculator. Simply press 2 and + twice and then the = key over and over. Ask the child to count by twos up to 30.

Next ask her to enter 4. Ask: What number comes next when counting by 2s? [6] Ask her to check on the calculator. Repeat for 8, [10] 12, [14] 22, [24] and 30. [32]

Solar cells. If time permits, explain to the child that this calculator has no batteries. It operates on light. Show her what happens when the solar collectors are completely covered, that the number slowly fades away and eventually disappears.

Worksheet 32. Give the child the worksheet, where she determines the next number when counting by 2s. When her work is completed, she can check it with the calculator. The numbers and solutions are given below:

6	**8**
10	**12**
14	**16**
18	**20**
20	**22**
26	**28**
32	**34**
38	**40**

Add One or Two game. Play the game Add One or Two found in the *Math Card Games* book, A13.

In conclusion. Ask the child to name as many different things as she can that she could do on a calculator.

LESSON 90: ARRANGING FROM GREATEST TO LEAST

OBJECTIVES:
1. To put numbers in order
2. To compare quantities

MATERIALS:
1. **Sticky notes**
2. Tiles
3. *Math Card Games* book, N44

ACTIVITIES FOR TEACHING:	EXPLANATIONS:
Warm-up. Ask the child to count by 1s to 60.	
Ask the child to count by 10s to 200.	
Ask the child to count by 5s to 100.	
Ask: How much is 23 + 1? [24] How much is 27 + 2? [29] How much is 86 + 1? [87] How much is 99 + 1? [1 hundred]	
Ask the child to name the days of the week and the months of the year.	
Sorting by quantity. Write a color name on four sticky notes; red, blue, green, and yellow. If desired, write the words in the corresponding colors, or use colored sticky notes in the corresponding colors.	
Ask the child to take 3 handfuls of tiles. Explain to the child that he is to sort the tiles by color.	One way to help a child understand greatest quantity, is to organize numerical information into visual forms.

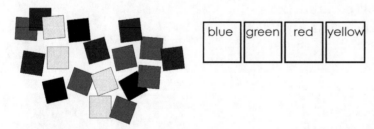

Three handfuls of tiles for sorting.

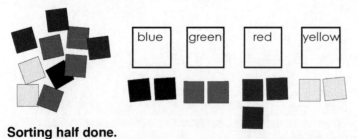

Sorting half done.

The word count can mean "determine the total number"; it does not necessarily imply reciting the number words in order.

When finished, count the quantity of tiles in each pile and write the number on the correct sticky note. Now ask the child to put the sticky notes and tiles in order from greatest to least. Ask: Which pile has the greatest number? Which pile has the least number?

ACTIVITIES FOR TEACHING CONTINUED:	EXPLANATIONS CONTINUED:

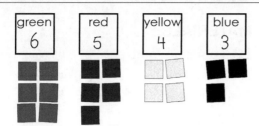

Practice. Repeat the activity again with a different amount of tiles.

Changing a group. Ask the child to take 11 tiles. Then ask him to lay out the tiles so they are easily counted. Now ask the child to change it to 13 tiles. Observe how the child makes 13 tiles. Did he grab two more or put them all back and start over? If the child put them all back, ask: Would it work to just take two more tiles to make 13?

Ask: Which number is greater, 11 or 13? [13]

Ask the child to take 17 tiles. Then ask him to change it to 15. [remove 2 tiles] Ask: Which number is greater, 17 or 15? [17]

Sets in Order game. Play the game, Sets in Order, found in the *Math Card Games* book, N44.

In conclusion. Ask: Of the numbers, 5, 6, 7, which number is greatest? [7] Which number is least? [5] Repeat for 50, 60, and 70.

LESSON 91: THE "ROUND" GEOMETRIC SOLIDS

OBJECTIVES:

1. To find the geometric solids with "round" surfaces
2. To introduce the terms *cylinder, sphere, hemisphere,* and *cone*
3. To discover some of their attributes

MATERIALS:

1. Geometric solids
2. **Flashlight, light source,** or even **sunlight**
3. **A bare wall**

ACTIVITIES FOR TEACHING:	EXPLANATIONS:
Warm-up. Ask the child to count by 1s to 60. Ask the child to count by 10s to 200. Ask the child to count by 5s to 100. Ask: How much is 41 + 1? [42] How much is 12 + 2? [14] How much is 89 + 1? [90] How much is 99 + 1? [1 hundred] Ask the child to name the days of the week and the months of the year. ***Geometric solids.*** Give the child the geometric solids. Give her a few minutes to explore them. Ask: Can you find the five solids that are "round?" They are shown below.  The "round" solids. ***"Round" solids.*** Point out the taller cylinder. Ask the child: Can you think of anything in the kitchen that looks like this *cylinder*? [cans, oatmeal box, salt box] Ask: Do you see another cylinder in the group? [yes] Point out the sphere. Ask: Can you think of something that looks like this *sphere?* [ball] Ask the child to find the sphere that is cut half. Tell her it is called a *hemisphere.* Ask her to find the *cone.* If necessary, tell her it has a point. What can you eat that is a cone? [ice cream cone] What do you find at a party that is a cone? [party hat] ***Rolling the round solids.*** Ask the child to roll one of the cylinders. What direction does it go? [straight ahead] Ask her to try it with the other cylinder. Ask: Is there a difference between the two cylinders? [no]	Often, ice cream cones have flat bottoms making them *truncated* cones. That is, part of the cone is missing.

ACTIVITIES FOR TEACHING CONTINUED:	EXPLANATIONS CONTINUED:

Now ask her to roll the sphere. What direction does the sphere go? [all over] Ask her to roll the hemisphere. [It stays in one place.]

Ask: Which solid do we still need to try? [cone] Ask her to roll the cone. [It makes a circle.]

If possible, ask her to try rolling the solids on a slightly inclined plane.

Ask her to summarize her results by naming each solid and explaining how it rolls.

Finding circles. Ask her to draw a circle with her finger on a flat surface. Tell her: Now we will find circles on the solids. Ask: Do you see any circles on these solids? How many circles does the shorter cylinder have? [2] How many circles does the taller cylinder have? [2]

How many circles does the cone have? [1] How many circles does the hemisphere have? [1] How many circles does the sphere have? [0]

Which solids have the greatest number of circles? [the cylinders] Which solids have the least number of circles? [sphere] How many circles are there on all five of the solids? [6]

Making shadows. Show the child how to make a shadow with the sphere. First shine a light source on the sphere, creating a circular shadow on the wall. Next move the light source around until you see an elliptical shadow. Encourage the child do it.

Ask the child to take a cylinder and make a shadow that is a circle and a shadow that is a rectangle. See figures below.

Cylinder shadow showing a square.

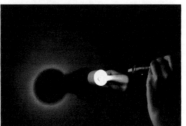

Cylinder shadow showing a circle.

Ask her to find what shapes she can make with the cone. [circle and triangle]

Finally, ask her to make two shapes with the hemisphere. [circle and semicircle]

In conclusion. Ask: How many circles are on a cylinder? [2] How many circles are on a cone? [1]

Varying inclines may give different results.

It is curious that half a circle is called a semicircle, but half a sphere is a hemisphere.

LESSON 92: MORE GEOMETRIC SOLIDS

OBJECTIVES:

1. To introduce more geometric solids
2. To sort the solids by their attributes
3. To introduce the terms *prism, pyramid, cube,* and *face*

MATERIALS:

1. Geometric solids
2. Dry erase board

ACTIVITIES FOR TEACHING:	**EXPLANATIONS:**
Warm-up. Ask the child to count by 1s starting at 10 and ending at 70.	

ACTIVITIES FOR TEACHING:

Warm-up. Ask the child to count by 1s starting at 10 and ending at 70.

Ask the child to count by 10s to 200.

Ask the child to count by 5s to 80.

Ask: How much is 60 + 8? [68] How much is 10 + 3? [13] How much is 50 + 4? [54] How much is 10 + 6? [16]

Ask the child to show parallel lines using his arms. Then ask him to show perpendicular lines.

The "non-round" geometric solids. Give the child the geometric solids. Tell him to name and set aside the round solids from the previous lesson. [cylinders, sphere, hemisphere, cone] How many solids are left? [7]

Sorting by height. Ask the child to make each solid stand so it is as tall as possible. Then ask him to sort them according to height. Next ask him to arrange the groups from greatest height to least. See the figure below.

Solids at their tallest arranged from greatest to least.

Now ask him to stand each solid so it is as short as possible. Again ask him to sort and arrange the groups from greatest to least height. See the figure below.

Solids at their shortest arranged from greatest to least.

| ACTIVITIES FOR TEACHING CONTINUED: | EXPLANATIONS CONTINUED: |

Faces. Ask the child if he sees any solids with sides that are triangles. [pyramid and triangular prism] See the left figure below. Point to the pyramid and ask: How many triangles do you see? [4] Tell him that this is a *pyramid*. Point to the prism and ask: How many triangles do you see? [2] Tell him this is called a *prism*.

Triangular faces.   **Square faces.**

Ask the child to find solids with square sides. [pyramid, cube, and square prism] See the right figure above. Explain that mathematicians call the sides of a solid *faces*. Tell him the shape with 6 square faces is a *cube*.

Ask him if he can find a prism with a hexagon face. How many hexagon faces does it have? [2] Tell the child the last shape is an octagon prism. Ask: How many octagon faces does it have? [2]

Counting faces. Explain that he is to sort the solids by the number of faces, from least to greatest. Show the child the cube and ask: How many square faces does the cube have? [6] An organized approach to counting the faces is to notice the cube has a top and bottom, left and right, and front and back.

Then ask him to write 6 on the dry erase board and place the cube above it. Ask him to find the pyramid and count its faces. [5] Tell him to write 5 near the 6 on the dry erase board. Ask him to count the faces on the triangular prism. [5] Tell him to put it above the 5. Ask him to continue with the remaining solids.

Sorting the solids by number of faces.

In conclusion. Ask: Is a square a geometric solid? [no] Is a cube a geometric solid? [yes]

Some sets of geometric solids have a triangular prism rather than a square prism. If so, the number of solids with square faces would be 2, not 3.

LESSON 93: CONSTRUCTING A CUBE

OBJECTIVES:

1. To construct a cube from 6 squares
2. To introduce the terms *two-dimensional* and *three-dimensional*
3. To understand the difference between two-dimensional and three-dimensional objects

MATERIALS:

1. Worksheet 33, Constructing a Cube
2. **Scissors**
3. Geometric solids
4. **Tape**

ACTIVITIES FOR TEACHING:	EXPLANATIONS:
Warm-up. Ask the child to count by 1s to 70. Ask the child to count by 10s to 200. Ask the child to count by 5s to 100. Ask: How much is 21 + 1? [22] How much is 22 + 2? [24] How much is 88 + 1? [89] How much is 99 + 1? [1 hundred] Ask the child to listen to the pattern and to continue it with the next number: 34, 35, 36; [37] 12, 13, 14; [15] and 20, 30, 40. [50] **Worksheet 33.** Tell the child that she will be making a cube from today's worksheet. First ask her to cut out the single square and set it aside. Then ask her to cut out the six connected squares on the thick lines, keeping it in one piece. Tell her to fold on the dotted lines. To construct the cube, tell her to place the wooden cube on the cutout version on top of the square with the little square in it. See the left figure below. Fold up four squares around the cube. Then tell her to tape the edges together with one piece of tape in the middle of the edges. See the right figure below. Do not tape the top square.	 The paper cube will be the same size as the wooden cube. Placing the tape halfway down makes it easier to remove the solid.

Preparing the paper cube.

Taping the edges of the cube.

Then tell the child to remove the wooden cube from the paper cube.

ACTIVITIES FOR TEACHING CONTINUED:

Inside the cube. Tell the child to put the shorter cylinder in the paper cube. Ask: Does it fit? [yes] Which solid takes up more space in the paper cube, the wooden cube or the cylinder? [wooden cube]

Next tell the child to put the sphere in the paper cube. Ask: Which do you think takes up more space, the sphere or the cylinder? [cylinder] Which takes up more space, the wooden cube or the sphere? [wooden cube]

Tell her that objects that take up space are called *three-dimensional*. Ask: Is the cube three-dimensional? [yes] Is the cylinder three-dimensional? [yes] Is the sphere three-dimensional? [yes] Say that all the geometric solids are three-dimensional.

Comparing a square and cube. Point to the square the child cut out and the cube she made and ask: How are they different? Which one takes up space? [cube] Which one is three-dimensional? [cube]

Ask: Which one can completely lie on a flat surface? [square] Tell the child: The square is *two-dimensional*. Explain that sometimes we say 2D instead of saying two-dimensional. Ask: Is a circle two-dimensional or three-dimensional? [two-dimensional]

Practice. Ask the child to answer either two-dimensional or three-dimensional for each object named:

cube	**three-dimensional**
circle	**two-dimensional**
sphere	**three-dimensional**
pyramid	**three-dimensional**
triangle	**two-dimensional**
rectangle	**two-dimensional**
prism	**three-dimensional**
hemisphere	**three-dimensional**
semicircle	**two-dimensional**

In conclusion. Ask: What is the difference between two-dimensional and three-dimensional?

EXPLANATIONS CONTINUED:

Some children may need to see the objects. For them use the geometric solids and figures drawn on a dry erase board.

LESSON 94: DOZENS & PARTITIONING TEENS INTO TENS

OBJECTIVES:

1. To introduce the term *dozen*
2. To partition teens

MATERIALS:

1. **Egg carton with 2 eggs or other objects**
2. Place-value cards
3. AL Abacus
4. Dry erase board
5. Worksheet 34, Partitioning Teens

ACTIVITIES FOR TEACHING:	EXPLANATIONS:
Warm-up. Ask the child to count by 1s to 80. Ask the child to count by 10s to 200. Ask the child to count by 5s to 100. Ask: How much is 43 + 1? [44] How much is 44 + 2? [46] How much is 78 + 1? [79] How much is 99 + 1? [1 hundred] Ask the child to show parallel lines using his arms. Then ask him to show perpendicular lines. Ask the child to listen to the pattern and to continue it with the next number: 46, 47, 48; [49] 57, 56, 55; [54] and 50, 60, 70. [80] **Dozen.** Show the child an egg carton. Tell him that it holds one *dozen* eggs. Open the carton as shown below. Ask him: How many eggs would fit? [12] Ask: How many eggs are in a dozen eggs? [12] How many buns are in a package of a dozen buns? [12]	While the term dozen has virtually no mathematical significance, 12 continues to be important in a cultural sense. We have 12 in a dozen, 12 months in a year, 12 hours on the clock, and 12 inches in a foot.

An egg carton.

Then ask the child to solve the following problem:

   How many eggs are in 2 dozen eggs?

Let him solve the problem in his own way and to explain how he did it. Ask him to show his solution with place-value cards. [24]

If appropriate, ask him to find the number of eggs in 3 dozen. [36]

Showing the egg carton with two eggs (or similar objects) makes the ten empty spaces more prominent.

ACTIVITIES FOR TEACHING CONTINUED:

Ask the child if it is easier to count by dozens or by tens and why.

Partitioning the teens. Draw a part-whole circle set and write 12 in the whole and 10 in the left part-circle. Ask: What goes in the other part-circle? Ask him to demonstrate the partitioning on the abacus and to explain it.

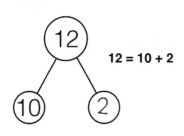 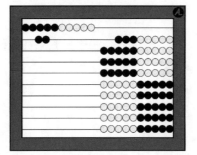

$12 = 10 + 2$

Partitioning 12 into 10 and 2.

Next ask him to say and write the equation. [12 = 10 + 2] Also ask him for the inverse: What is 10 + 2? [12]

Repeat with 15 written in the whole-circle and 10 in the left part-circle. Continue with other teen numbers.

Practice. Ask the child: Sixteen is 10 and what? [6] Fifteen is 5 and what? [10] Thirteen is 3 and what? [10] Nineteen is 10 and what? [9]

Problem. Give him the following problem:

Lee hid a dozen eggs. Lee's friends found 10 of them. How many of them are still hidden?

Ask: What does the word dozen means? [12] How many eggs were found? [10] How many are still hidden? [2]

Worksheet 34. Ask the child to do the worksheet for partitioning the teens into 10 and another number. The problems and solutions are as follows:

15 = 10 + **5**
19 = 10 + **9**
13 = 10 + **3**
11 = 10 + **1**
17 = 10 + **7**
16 = 10 + **6**
14 = 10 + **4**
18 = 10 + **8**
12 = 10 + **2**
20 = 10 + **10**

In conclusion. Ask: How much is a dozen? [12] How much is a half dozen? [6]

EXPLANATIONS CONTINUED:

English-speaking child usually have difficulty conceptualizing the teen numbers as 10 + another number. In other words, the child tends to see 14 as 14 ones, rather than a ten and 4 ones. The following activities are designed to help him make that connection, which becomes harder since he started using the traditional names. Refer back to the math way of saying the numbers, if necessary.

LESSON 95: INTRODUCING SUBTRACTION EQUATIONS

OBJECTIVES:
1. To introduce subtraction
2. To learn the terms *minus* and *subtraction*
3. To learn to write the "-" sign
4. To state and write subtraction equations

MATERIALS:
1. AL Abacus
2. Dry erase board
3. Worksheet 35, Writing Equations

ACTIVITIES FOR TEACHING:	EXPLANATIONS:
Warm-up. Ask the child to count by 1s to 70. Ask the child to count by 10s to 200. Ask the child to count by 5s to 100. Ask: How many eggs are in a dozen? [12] Ask the child to listen to the pattern and to continue it with the next number: 14, 13, 12; [11] 37, 38, 39; [40] 120, 130, 140. [150] Ask the child to count backward from 20 by entering 20 on the abacus, removing one bead at a time, and naming the quantity. [20, 19, 18, . . . , 1] **Introducing subtracting.** Read the following problem to the child: There are 8 crayons on a big cube. Four rolled off. How many crayons are left on the cube? Ask the child to write the story in a part-whole circle set and to write the equation. See the figures below. 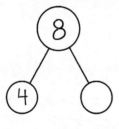 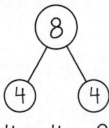 $$4 + 4 = 8$$ Tell the child to point to the two numbers in the equation that are parts. [the 4s] Ask her to point to the whole. [8] Explain that there is another way to write an equation using a whole and parts. Write $$8 - 4 = 4$$ and tell her it is a *subtraction* equation. Read it by saying: 8 *minus* 4 equals 4. Point to the 8 and tell her that is the whole. Explain that the little straight line is called minus. The next number is a part being taken from the whole. The last number is the other part, the part that is left.	It is important for children to understand adding thoroughly before introducing subtraction. If the child struggles with addition, play more addition games from the *Math Card Games* book.

ACTIVITIES FOR TEACHING CONTINUED:

EXPLANATIONS CONTINUED:

Practice. Write 5 in the whole-circle and 3 in the left part-circle (see the figure below). Ask the child to find the other part. [2] Then ask the child to say the subtraction equation [five minus three equals two] and write the addition and subtraction equations. [3 + 2 = 5, 5 − 3 = 2]

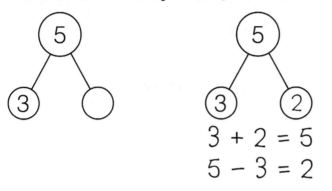

Repeat for 7 as the whole and 6 as a part. See the figures below.

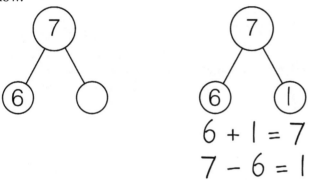

Worksheet 35. Ask the child to do the worksheet where she completes the part-whole circle sets and writes both the addition and subtraction equations. The solutions are as follows:

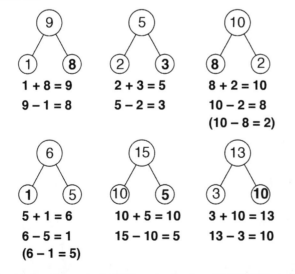

In conclusion. Ask: What is 4 plus 1? [5] What is 4 minus 1? [3] What is 5 plus 5? [10] What is 10 minus 5? [5]

The term "take away" is incorrect English. "Six take away four equals two," is not a logical statement; whereas, "Six minus four equals two" is a complete sentence.

"Take away" is incorrect mathematics because subtraction is not always about going down. Sometimes, we go up, as in making change. Subtraction is also about comparing or finding a difference.

Therefore, the term *minus* (versus take away) should always be used for subtraction, just as *plus* is used for addition.

These activities are not an introduction to "fact families," rather they are an introduction to subtraction. Too often, students manage to memorize where numbers go to fill in worksheets with fact families without really understanding the relationship between addition and subtraction.

LESSON 96: SUBTRACTION AS THE MISSING ADDEND

OBJECTIVES:
1. To solve subtraction problems by adding on
2. To write the corresponding subtraction equations

MATERIALS:
1. Dry erase board
2. AL Abacus
3. Worksheet 36, Subtracting by Adding On

ACTIVITIES FOR TEACHING:	EXPLANATIONS:

ACTIVITIES FOR TEACHING:

Warm-up. Ask the child to count by 1s to 80.

Ask the child to count by 5s to 100.

Ask: How many eggs are in a dozen? [12]

Ask the child to listen to the pattern and to continue it with the next number: 16, 15, 14; [13] 17, 18, 19; [20] 110, 120, 130. [140]

Problem. Read the following problem to the child:

> Little Bo Peep lost nine sheep in the morning. Five of her sheep arrived home before dinner time. How many sheep are still lost?

Ask him to write the quantities using a part-whole circle set. See the left figure below.

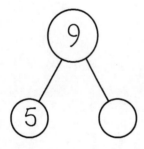

Ask him to start with 5 on his abacus. Then ask him: What is missing to get to 9? [4] See the figure below.

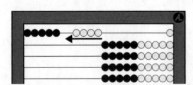

Adding on from 5 to reach 9.

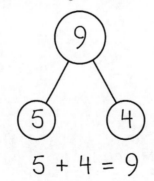

$$5 + 4 = 9$$

EXPLANATIONS:

Ofter children are introduced to subtraction as taking from. However, researcher Karen Fuson found that children can understand subtraction easier by adding on, or counting up from the known part to the whole, rather than counting down from the whole.

ACTIVITIES FOR TEACHING CONTINUED:	EXPLANATIONS CONTINUED:

Ask: What are the parts? [5 and 4] What is the whole? [9] How many sheep are still lost? [4]

Then ask him to write the subtraction equation. [9 − 5 = 4]

Problem. Give the child the following problem:

> Six children are eating at a table. Four children went out to play. How many are still at the table?

Tell the child to use a part-whole circle set to find the missing part. [2] Write the addition and subtraction equations. See the figures below.

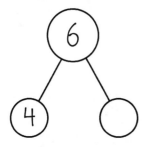
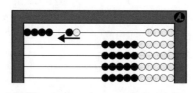

Finding what is needed with 4 to make 6. [2]

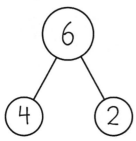

$$4 + 2 = 6$$
$$6 - 4 = 2$$

Worksheet 36. Ask the child to do the worksheet, filling in the part-whole circle sets and completing the subtraction equations. Use the abacus when needed. The solutions are as follows:

This worksheet provides practice finding missing addends to solve subtraction equations.

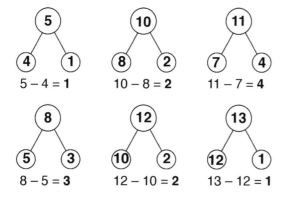

5 − 4 = **1**	10 − 8 = **2**	11 − 7 = **4**
8 − 5 = **3**	12 − 10 = **2**	13 − 12 = **1**

In conclusion. Ask: What is 12 plus 1? [13] What is 12 minus 1? [11] What is 4 plus 4? [8] What is 8 minus 4? [4]

LESSON 97: SUBTRACTION BY GOING DOWN

OBJECTIVES:
1. To practice subtraction by going down

MATERIALS:
1. AL Abacus
2. Dry erase board
3. Envelopes* and corresponding multiplication cards for the 1s, 2s, 5s, and 10s

ACTIVITIES FOR TEACHING:	EXPLANATIONS:
Warm-up. Ask the child to count by 1s from 30 to 100. Ask the child to count by 5s to 100. Ask the child to listen to the pattern and to continue it with the next number: 32, 31, 30; [29] 37, 38, 39; [40] 170, 180, 190. [200] **Review subtracting as going up.** Ask the child to use a part-whole circle set to solve the following problem: Alex has 7 crayons and gave 5 to Joe. How many crayons does Alex have now? Ask her to show how she could use the abacus to find the answer (even if she knew). [2] See the figures below. 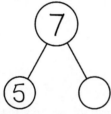 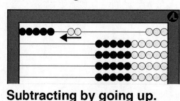 **Subtracting by going up.** Ask her to write the subtraction equation. [7 – 5 = 2] **Subtracting as going down.** Tell her there is another way to subtract on the abacus. Explain: We start with the whole and take away a part. See the figure below. 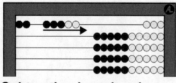 **Subtracting by going down.** Give the child another problem: Robin has a dozen eggs, some brown and some white. If two eggs are brown, how many are white? Ask the child to explain the problem in her own words. Then ask her to write the numbers in a part-whole circle set, find the answer on her abacus [10] and write the subtraction equation. [12 – 2 = 10]	*Included with the multiplication cards are 10 envelopes, each printed with the multiples of a number from 1–10. Insert into each envelope 10 multiplication cards matching the numbers listed on the front of the envelope. A new deck of multiplication cards is collated to make this task easy: the first 10 cards go into the 1s envelope; the next 10 cards go into the 2s envelope; and so forth. This subtraction problem is considered more difficult because it does not entail a physical separation of the collection. Comparing colors is more subtle.

ACTIVITIES FOR TEACHING CONTINUED:	EXPLANATIONS CONTINUED:

Practice. Show the child the envelope with the 2s. Remove the cards and scatter them face up. Turn the envelope face down. Ask the child to find the card with the greatest number. [20] Place it at the start a row.

Next ask her to enter 20 on her abacus. Subtract 2. [18] Ask her to find that card and set it to the right of the 20 card. Ask her to continue subtracting 2 on the abacus and finding the cards. See the figure below.

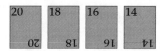

Subtracting 2 and finding the corresponding card.

When she has finished, she could compare with the numbers on the envelope.

Subtract the Same Number Memory game. For this game for two, each player chooses an envelope with cards. The object of the game is to be the first player to complete her row as in the above activity. Players remove their cards from the envelope, shuffle them together slightly, and lay them out face down in four rows with five cards each.

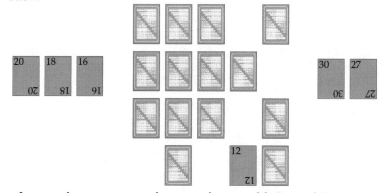

A game in progress using envelopes with 2s and 3s.

Players look at their envelopes to determine their starting number (the greatest number on the envelope) and their subtracting number (the lowest number on the envelope). Begin by looking for starting number. To find their next number, players subtract using their abacuses.

The player says aloud the number she is looking for and turns over a card. If she gets the card she needs, she collects it, lays it in the row, and takes another turn. If she does not get the card she needs, she returns it to its original place face down.

Then the other player takes a turn. Play continues until a player has collected 10 cards.

In conclusion. Ask the child: What is 15 minus 2? [13] What is 13 minus 2? [11]

LESSON 98: COMPARING ADDITION AND SUBTRACTION

OBJECTIVES:
1. To compare addition and subtraction

MATERIALS:
1. AL Abacus
2. Dry erase board
3. *Math Card Games* book, S1

ACTIVITIES FOR TEACHING:	EXPLANATIONS:

ACTIVITIES FOR TEACHING:

Warm-up. Ask the child to count by 1s from 40 to 100.

Ask the child to count by 10s to 200, starting at 100.

Ask the child to count by 5s to 100.

Ask: How much is 16 plus 1? [17] How much is 16 minus 1? [15] How much is 11 plus 1? [12] How much is 11 minus 1? [10] How much is 14 plus 1? [15] How much is 14 minus 1? [13]

Ask the child to listen to the pattern and to continue it with the next number: 84, 85, 86; [87] 67, 66, 65; [64] 80, 90, 100. [110]

Ask the child to count backward by 2s from 20 by entering 20 on the abacus, removing two beads at a time, then naming the quantity.

Comparing addition and subtraction. Write the numbers shown below in part-whole circle sets:

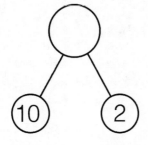 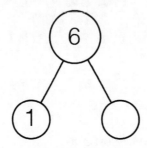

Ask the child to complete the part-whole circle sets. Write an addition equation for the left circles and a subtraction equation for the right circles. See the figures below.

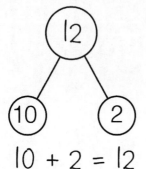 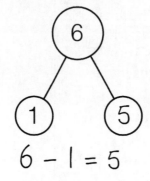

$$10 + 2 = 12 \qquad 6 - 1 = 5$$

ACTIVITIES FOR TEACHING CONTINUED:	EXPLANATIONS CONTINUED:

Ask the child to think of ways that addition and subtraction are different. For some possible questions, ask the following:

1. After addition on the abacus, will your answer be greater or less? [greater] After subtraction, will your answer be greater or less? [less]

2. With addition you start with the parts. What do you start with in subtraction? [the whole]

3. In addition you are putting things together. What happens with subtraction? [taking them apart]

4. In writing equations, you use "+" and call it plus. What do you use in subtraction? ["−"] What do you call it? [minus]

Ten Minus game. Play the game Ten Minus found in *Math Card Games*, S1. This game is the subtraction version of Go to the Dump.

In conclusion. Ask the child: Is 2 plus 2, adding or subtracting? [adding] Is 10 and 4 more, adding or subtracting? [adding] Is 10 minus 2, adding or subtracting? [subtracting] Is taking 3 from 10, adding or subtracting? [subtracting]

Mathematically, the first question is valid only when applied to positive numbers. Since that is the range of numbers at this stage of instruction, the answer is valid.

For this game, the players should use the "going down" subtraction approach on the abacus.

LESSON 99: REVIEW

OBJECTIVES:

1. To prepare for the upcoming assessment

MATERIALS:

1. Worksheet 37-1 and 37-2, Review

ACTIVITIES FOR TEACHING:	EXPLANATIONS:

Review.

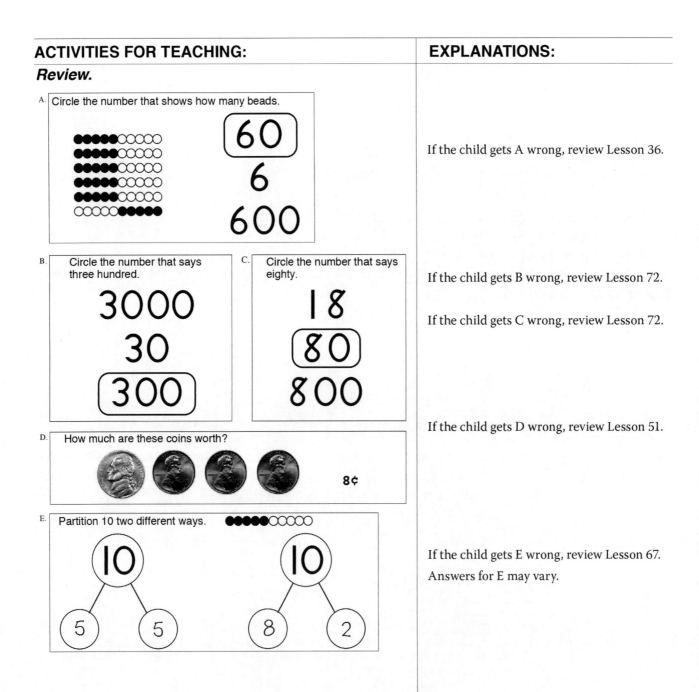

A. Circle the number that shows how many beads.

60
6
600

B. Circle the number that says three hundred.

3000
30
300

C. Circle the number that says eighty.

18
80
800

D. How much are these coins worth?

8¢

E. Partition 10 two different ways.

10 — 5, 5
10 — 8, 2

If the child gets A wrong, review Lesson 36.

If the child gets B wrong, review Lesson 72.

If the child gets C wrong, review Lesson 72.

If the child gets D wrong, review Lesson 51.

If the child gets E wrong, review Lesson 67.
Answers for E may vary.

| ACTIVITIES FOR TEACHING CONTINUED: | EXPLANATIONS CONTINUED: |

F. Chris read 7 pages, some in the morning and 2 pages in the afternoon. How many pages did Chris read in the morning?

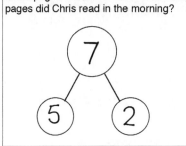

G. Circle all the even numbers.

1
3
8
10

If the child gets F wrong, review Lessons 95 and Lesson 96.

If the child gets G wrong, review Lesson 57.

H. Circle all the rectangles.

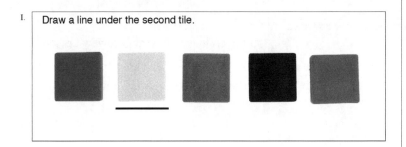

If the child gets H wrong, review Lesson 16, 18, and 19.

I. Draw a line under the second tile.

If the child gets I wrong, review Lesson 86.

Lesson 100: Assessment 4

OBJECTIVES:

1. To check for understanding

MATERIALS:

1. Assessment 4, (found in the back of the child's worksheets)

ACTIVITIES FOR TEACHING:	EXPLANATIONS:

Test.

A. Circle the number that shows how many beads.

80
800
8

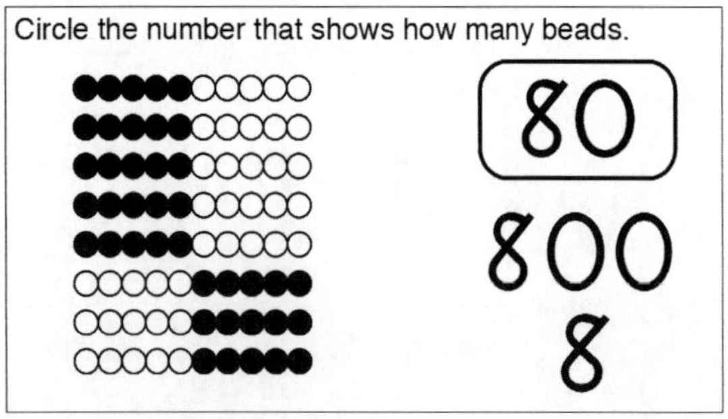

If the child gets A wrong, review Lesson 36.

B. Circle the number that says four hundred.

400
40
4000

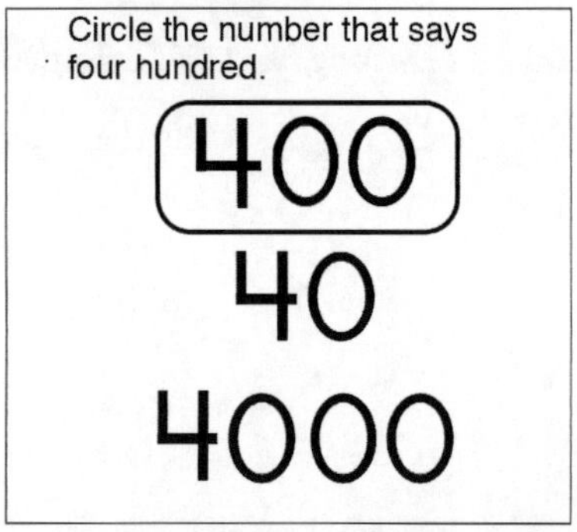

C. Circle the number that says seventy.

17
700
70

If the child gets B wrong, review Lesson 72.

If the child gets C wrong, review Lesson 72.

D. How much are these coins worth?

12¢

If the child gets D wrong, review Lesson 51.

E. Partition 10 two different ways.

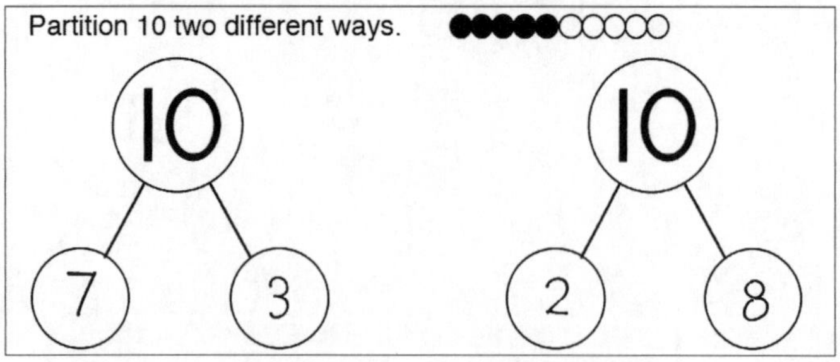

10 → 7, 3

10 → 2, 8

If the child gets E wrong, review Lesson 67.

Answers for E may vary.

201

ACTIVITIES FOR TEACHING CONTINUED:

F. Alex ate 8 crackers, some in the morning and 4 in the afternoon. How many crackers did Alex eat in the morning?

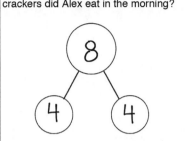

G. Circle all the odd numbers.

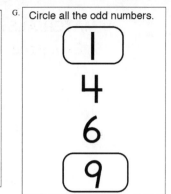

H. Circle all the rectangles.

I. Draw a line under the fourth tile.

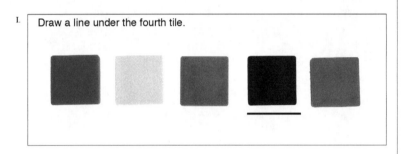

EXPLANATIONS CONTINUED:

If the child gets F wrong, review Lessons 95 and Lesson 96.

If the child gets G wrong, review Lesson 57.

If the child gets H wrong, review Lesson 16, 18, and 19.

If the child gets I wrong, review Lesson 86.

LESSON 101: MEASURING WITH INCHES

OBJECTIVES:
1. To compare lengths
2. To introduce the term *inch*

MATERIALS:
1. Geometric solids
2. Tiles
3. Dry erase board
4. **8 1/2' by 11' sheet of paper**

ACTIVITIES FOR TEACHING:	EXPLANATIONS:

Warm-up. Ask the child to count by 1s from 40 to 100.

Ask the child to count by 10s to 300, starting at 100.

Ask the child to count by 5s to 50.

Ask the child: Is 3 plus 3 adding or subtracting? [adding] Is 10 and 6 more adding or subtracting? [adding] Is 10 minus 4 adding or subtracting? [subtracting] Is taking 2 from 10 adding or subtracting? [subtracting]

After addition on the abacus, will your answer be greater or less? [greater] After subtraction, will your answer be greater or less? [less]

Measuring with tiles. Explain to the child that we can use the tiles to see how long something is. Lay two tiles along an edge of the cube. See the figure below.

 **This edge measures 2 tiles.**

Say: This cube is 2 tiles long. Ask her to measure other edges of the cube. After she has measured them, ask: Are all the edges the same? [yes]

Now tell her to measure all the edges of the square prism. Then ask: Are all those edges the same? [no]

 **This edge is 3 tiles.**

 **This edge is 1 tile.**

ACTIVITIES FOR TEACHING CONTINUED:	EXPLANATIONS CONTINUED:

ACTIVITIES FOR TEACHING CONTINUED:

Introducing inches. Tell her: The length of the edge of a tile is called an *inch*. Ask: How long is each edge of a tile? [1 inch] If a ladybug walked around the tile, how many inches would she walk? [4 inches]

Put two tiles side-by-side and ask: How many inches would the ladybug walk now? [6 inches] See the left figure below.

Distance around is 6 inches.

Distance around is 8 inches.

Now ask her to make a square with four tiles. See the right figure above. Ask: How many inches would the ladybug walk to get around the square? [8 inches]

Ask her to make a "train" with 3 or 4 prisms and to measure how long it is.

Measuring a "train" of prisms.

Ask the child to measure the edges of her dry erase board. [11 and 13 inches]

Also ask the child to measure the longer edge of a piece of paper. [11 inches] If she wants to measure the shorter edge, she will notice that only half of the last tile fits. Then tell her: It is 8 and one-half inches.

If desired, ask the child to measure other objects in the room.

In conclusion. Ask the child: How long is the edge of a tile? [1 inch] What does measuring with tiles tell us? [how long something is]

EXPLANATIONS CONTINUED:

Inches are introduced before centimeters because they are a more convenient size.

A4 paper, used in many countries, is 8.3" by 11.7"; therefore, it is not suitable for this activity.

LESSON 102: MEASURING WITH CENTIMETERS

OBJECTIVES:
1. To introduce the term *centimeter*
2. To compare lengths

MATERIALS:
1. Centimeter cubes
2. Geometric solids
3. Tiles
4. AL Abacus
5. Worksheet 38, Measuring with Centimeters

ACTIVITIES FOR TEACHING:	EXPLANATIONS:
Warm-up. Ask the child to count by 1s from 30 to 100.	

Ask the child to count by 10s to 200, starting at 100.

Ask the child to count by 5s to 100.

In addition, do you start with the parts or wholes? [parts] What do you start with in subtraction? [the whole] In addition, are you putting things together or taking them apart? [putting together] What happens with subtraction? [taking them apart]

Ask the child how long is one edge of a tile. [1 inch] How long is 2 edges of a tile? [2 inches] How long is 3 edges of a tile, [3 inches] and how long is all four edges of a tile? [4 inches]

Introducing the centimeter cubes. Show the child a centimeter cube. Ask him: What shape is it? [cube] How many square faces does it have? [6] Name them. [top and bottom, left and right, front and back]

(Explanation, right column) Introducing measurement with units of different sizes helps the child become aware that the size of the unit matters.

Tell him that we can measure with an edge of the centimeter cube just like we did with a tile. Ask her to measure an edge of the wooden cube with the centimeter cubes. Ask: How many centimeter cubes were needed? [5 centimeter cubes] See the figure below.

Measuring the cube using centimeter cubes.

Introducing centimeters. Tell him: The length of the edge of a centimeter cube is called a *centimeter*. You might comment: It is a long word for a short distance! Ask: How long is each edge of a centimeter cube? [1 centimeter]

ACTIVITIES FOR TEACHING CONTINUED:

EXPLANATIONS CONTINUED:

Ask him to take four tiles of the same color and to make a square with them. Then ask him to measure the sides of the square with centimeters. Ask: How long is the side of the square? [5 cm] If a ladybug walked around the whole square, how far would she walk in centimeters? [20 cm]

Ask: How far is it from one corner of the square to the opposite corner? [7 cm] See the figure below.

The abbreviation for centimeter or centimeters is cm in lower case without a period.

Measuring the square diagonal from corner to corner.

Measuring with the abacus beads. Ask the child to enter 5 on his abacus. Then ask him to use his centimeter cubes and measure how long the beads are. [5 cm] See the figure below.

Yes, the beads on the AL Abacus Standard and AL Abacus Classic are 1 cm wide. This activity will not work with the AL Abacus Junior, where the beads are 1/4 of an inch.

Measuring 5 beads.

Ask: How long do you think 3 beads are? [3 cm] Tell him to check to see if he is correct. Repeat for 10 beads.

Ask him to use the abacus to measure the side of the cube from the geometric solids, [5 cm] the height of the shorter cylinder, [5 cm] and the pyramid edge leading to the point. [8 cm]

Worksheet 38. For this worksheet, the child is to measure the sides of the rectangle and triangle and record his numbers.

The rectangle is **8** and **16**.

The triangle is **15**, **6**, and **11**.

In conclusion. Ask: Which is longer, an inch or a centimeter? [inch] Which is shorter? [centimeter]

LESSON 103: MEASURING LENGTHS

OBJECTIVES:

1. To practice linear comparing
2. To practice linear measuring
3. To apply adding tens and ones

MATERIALS:

1. AL Abacus
2. Tiles
3. Centimeter cubes
4. Worksheet 39, Finding Equal Lengths
5. **Crayons**

ACTIVITIES FOR TEACHING:	EXPLANATIONS:
Warm-up. Ask the child to count by 10s to 100 then count by 5s to 100.	
Ask the child to say the odd numbers to 39.	
Enter multiples of 10 on the abacus and ask the child to name them and to say the next 10, such as 20, [30] 60, [70] and 90. [100]	
Ask the child how many sides are there in a square, [4] in a rectangle, [4] and in a triangle. [3]	
Finding objects by length. Ask the child to take two tiles. Tell her to put them in a row and ask: How many inches long is the row? [2 inches] Ask her to find objects in the room that are 2 inches long.	
Tell her to take one more tile and add it to the row. Ask: How long is your row now? [3 inches] Again ask her to find objects in the room that are 3 inches long.	
Comparing inches and centimeters. Tell her to make a row with centimeter cubes that is 5 centimeters long. Ask: How many centimeter cubes did you need? [5]	
Ask the child to explain her reasoning for the following questions:	
1. Which is longer, 3 inches or 3 centimeters? [3 in.]	A child might not need to use the actual tiles and cubes to answer some of these questions.
2. Which is longer, 5 inches or 5 centimeters? [5 in.]	
3. Which is longer, 6 inches or 3 centimeters? [6 in.]	
4. Which is shorter, 3 inches or 2 centimeters? [2 cm]	
5. Which is longer, 2 inches or 6 centimeters? [6 cm]	
6. How many tiles do you need to be equal in length to 10 cm? [4 tiles]	
7. How long is 4 tiles in centimeters? [10 cm]	

ACTIVITIES FOR TEACHING CONTINUED:	EXPLANATIONS CONTINUED:

ACTIVITIES FOR TEACHING CONTINUED:

Measuring in centimeters. Ask the child to make a green train by laying out four green tiles in a row. See the left figure below. Ask: How long is the green train in centimeters? [10 cm]

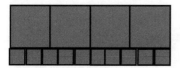 

Train with two cabooses.

Making and measuring a train.

Ask the child to make a red train by using four red tiles. How long is the red train? [10 cm] Ask: If you put the two trains together, how long is it in centimeters? [20 cm] Ask the child to make yellow and blue trains by using the tiles.

Tell the child to attach two little cabooses (centimeter cubes) to the red train. See the right figure above. Ask: How long is the train now? [12 cm] Ask the child the following questions:

If you put the red, yellow, and blue trains together, how long will it be? [30 cm]

If you put 4 trains together, how long will it be? [40 cm]

If you attach 2 cabooses to the red train (see right figure above), how long will the train be? [12 cm]

If you combine 3 trains and 5 cabooses, what will it measure in centimeters? [35 cm]

Worksheet 39. Give the child the worksheet and the centimeter cubes. Explain there are pairs of crayons having the same length. She is to find the matching crayons by measuring them and coloring the pairs the same color.

The matching crayons are shown in the figure below connected by heavy lines.

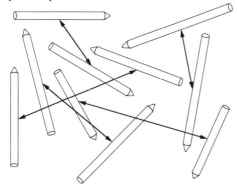

In conclusion. Ask: What is 30 + 20? [50] How much is 10 centimeters plus 20 centimeters? [30 cm]

EXPLANATIONS CONTINUED:

This question is asked repeatedly to make certain that the child understands the very important concept that two inches equals five centimeters.

Encourage the child to measure with the centimeter cubes if she is not sure.

LESSON 104: COMPARING WEIGHTS

OBJECTIVES:

1. To become aware of weight
2. To introduce the term *heavier*
3. To compare weights

MATERIALS:

1. **Two identical glasses, one empty** and **one with water**
2. Geometric solids
3. *Math balance, two weights, **two 4-inch (10 cm) paper cups,** and **two rubber bands**
4. **Small objects to weigh: plastic, metal, etc.**

ACTIVITIES FOR TEACHING:

Warm-up. Ask: How much is 15 plus 1? [16] How much is 15 minus 1? [14] How much is 10 plus 1? [11] How much is 10 minus 1? [9] How much is 12 plus 1? [13] How much is 12 minus 1? [11]

Ask the child: Is 1 plus 1, adding or subtracting? [adding] Is 9 and 2 more, adding or subtracting? [adding] Is 10 minus 1, adding or subtracting? [subtracting] Is taking 2 from 8, adding or subtracting? [subtracting]

Ask the child: After adding on the abacus, will your answer be greater or less? [greater] After subtraction, will your answer be greater or less? [less]

Ask the child: How long is one edge of a tile? [1 inch] How long are 2 edges of a tile? [2 inches] How long are 3 edges of a tile? [3 inches] How long are all four edges of a tile? [4 inches]

Ask: Which is longer, an inch or a centimeter? [inch] Which is shorter? [centimeter]

Comparing weights. Set two glasses, one empty and one half full of water in front of the child. Ask him to carefully lift the empty glass and set it down. Then ask him to lift the glass with water and tell him the second glass is *heavier*. Explain that the glasses look alike, but the one with water feels heavier.

Ask him to find the two cylinders from the geometric solids. Ask: Which one is taller? [the right cylinder shown below] Ask him to lift each one. Which cylinder is heavier? [the left cylinder]

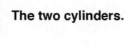
The two cylinders.

EXPLANATIONS:

*To prepare the math balance to be used as a scale, punch holes in two paper cups and insert a rubber band in the holes as shown above. Instead of the rubber bands, twist ties or two paper clips per side will also work.

Clear plastic cups allow the child to see the contents of the cups more easily, but use only cups with plastic code 1. The code is found in the recycling triangle, usually on the bottom. (A cup with plastic code 6 is brittle and often breaks when making the hole, leaving sharp edges.)

ACTIVITIES FOR TEACHING CONTINUED:	EXPLANATIONS CONTINUED:

ACTIVITIES FOR TEACHING CONTINUED:

Comparing weights using the scale. Hang a cup from each 10-peg on the math balance as shown below. Tell the child we will now use the math balance as a scale and we will not be using the numbers.

The math balance converted to a scale.

Ask the child: What do you think will happen if we put a blue weight in each cup? Tell him to try it. [stays balanced]

Comparing the solids using the scale. Ask: What do you think will happen if we put one cylinder from the geometric solids in each cup? Ask him to try it. [The cup with the heavier cylinder sinks.]

Ask him to choose any two geometric solids, guess which is heavier, and then check with the scale. Ask him to try several combinations.

As a challenge, give him several solids and ask him to use the scale to figure out which one is heaviest. Then ask him to put the solids in order from heaviest to lightest.

Four geometric solids in order by weight.

Comparing other objects using the scale. Ask him to compare two other objects, such as a piece of styrofoam and a piece of plastic or metal. Encourage him to find things to compare.

In conclusion. Ask: Can you always tell which of two things is heavier by just looking? [no] How can you find out? [by weighing]

EXPLANATIONS CONTINUED:

If necessary, move the little white weights to adjust the balance.

This can be done by first comparing any two items. Then take the heavier one and compare it with the others.

Your solids may have a different order, because the weights may vary.

LESSON 105: MEASURING WITH GRAMS

OBJECTIVES:

1. To introduce the term *gram*
2. To weigh some geometry solids in grams
3. To review indirectly that ten ones make one ten

MATERIALS:

1. Centimeter cubes
2. Math balance and weights used as a scale
3. Geometric solids
4. AL Abacus

ACTIVITIES FOR TEACHING:	EXPLANATIONS:

Warm-up. Ask: How much is 16 plus 1? [17] How much is 16 minus 1? [15] How much is 11 plus 1? [12] How much is 11 minus 1? [10] How much is 14 plus 1? [15] How much is 14 minus 1? [13]

Ask: Which is longer, an inch or a centimeter? [inch] Which is shorter? [centimeter]

Ask the child how long is one edge of a tile? [1 inch] How long are two edges of a tile? [2 inches] How long are three edges of a tile, [3 inches] and how long are all four edges of a tile? [4 inches]

Ask: Can you always tell which of two things is heavier by just looking? [no] How can you find out? [by weighing]

Weighing with the scale. Give the child the centimeter cubes and one blue math balance weight. Ask: Which is heavier, one centimeter cube or one blue weight? [blue weight]

Tell her each centimeter cube weighs 1 *gram*. Ask her to find how many centimeter cubes it takes to weigh the same as the blue weight using the scale? [10]

Then ask: What does 1 centimeter cube weigh? [1 gram] How much do 2 centimeter cubes weigh? [2 g] How much do 7 centimeter cubes weigh? [7 g] What does the blue weight weigh? [10 g] Tell her: Look closely at the blue weight. What do you see written on it? [10 g] Tell her that means *10 grams.*

Explain that we can also call the centimeter cube, a 1-gram cube. We can also call the larger blue weight a 10-gram weight.

A 1-gram cube and a 10-gram weight.

A weighing problem. Give the child at least 30 1-gram cubes. Ask her to solve the following problem:

> With the hemisphere solid in the left cup, how many cubes are needed to make it balance?

The abbreviation for gram or grams is a lower case "g" without a period.

ACTIVITIES FOR TEACHING CONTINUED:

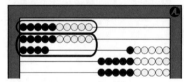

Hemisphere in the left cup and weights in the right cup.

Ask: What is the weight of the hemisphere? [24 g] Ask her to enter her answer on the abacus.

Empty the right cup and modify the problem:

Keep the hemisphere in the left cup. Put one 10-gram weight in the right cup. How many more 1-gram cubes do you need to make it balance?

What is the weight of everything in the right cup? [24 g] Ask her to show the one 10-gram weight and the 1-gram cubes [14] on the abacus. Where are the fourteen 1-gram cubes shown on the abacus? See the left figure below.

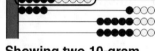

Showing 10-gram and fourteen 1-gram weights.   **Showing two 10-gram weights.**

Empty the right cup and modify the problem again:

Keep the hemisphere in the left cup, and put *two* 10-gram weights in the right cup. How many more cubes do you need to make it balance?

Ask: What is the total weight in the right cup? [24 g] Ask her to show the two 10-gram weights and the 1-gram cubes [4] on the abacus. See the right figure above.

Weighing the cone. Ask the child to weigh the cone, using as few weights as possible. If necessary, guide her to add 10-gram weights until she has too many. Then remove one weight and add 1-gram cubes until it balances.

If time remains, the child may want to weigh other solids or other objects in the room.

In conclusion. Ask the child to show the weight of the 10-gram weight on the abacus. [10] Ask her to show the weight of a the 1-gram cube on the abacus. [1] Ask: What is the weight of one 10-gram weight and four 1-gram cubes? [14] Show it on the abacus.

EXPLANATIONS CONTINUED:

Although the weight of the hemisphere is given here as 24 g, others may vary.

The child need not count the centimeter cubes as she puts them into the cup. She can determine the quantity after removing them once the scale is balanced.

Note: the sphere does not weigh exactly twice the hemisphere.

LESSON 106: PARTS OF A DAY

OBJECTIVES:
1. To provide an overview of time through its various parts
2. To introduce the terms, *morning, noon, afternoon, evening,* and *night*
3. To introduce the analog clock

MATERIALS:
1. **Calendar**
2. Geared clock
3. Worksheet 40, Parts of a Day
4. **Scissors** & **glue**

ACTIVITIES FOR TEACHING:	EXPLANATIONS:
Warm-up. Ask the child: How old are you now? How old will you be next year? Is a year a long time? [yes] Say: Do you remember the calendar you made for the year? Months are parts of a year. Do you remember how many months are in a year? [12] Sing or say the following:	

The Months
January, February, March, and April,
May, June, July, and August,
September, October, November, December.
These are the months of the year.

Then say: Months also have parts. What are the month's parts? [weeks, days] Ask the child to show a week on the calendar. Do you remember how many days are in a week? [7] Sing or say the following song:

Days of the Week
Sunday, Monday, Tuesday, too.
Wednesday, Thursday–this I knew.
Friday, Saturday that's the end.
Now let's say those days again!
Sunday, Monday, Tuesday, Wednesday, Thursday,
Friday, Saturday!

Ask the child to show a day on the calendar. Do all months have the same number of days? [no] How many days in this month? Sing or say the following song:

Three-ten Days Has September
Three-ten days has September,
April, June, and November.
The rest have 3-ten 1 to carry,
But only 2-ten 8 for February,
Except in leap year, that's the time
When February has 2-ten 9.

Parts of a day. Explain that a day has parts. The first part of the day is called *morning.* Ask: What do you need to do first thing in the morning? [get out of bed and eat breakfast]

ACTIVITIES FOR TEACHING CONTINUED:	EXPLANATIONS CONTINUED:

Continue with: Another part of the day is *noon*; that is when we eat lunch. Then later on we have another part called *afternoon*, when you play outside.

We still have two more parts: *evening*, when you eat dinner (supper) and *night*, when you sleep.

Ask: Can you say what you do during the parts of the day? What do you do in the morning? What do you do at noon? What do you do in the afternoon? What do you do in the evening? What do you do at night?

The clock. Show the child the analog clock and explain that we use a clock to help us keep track of the parts of a day. Teach the child the following rhyme:

The Clock

There's a neat little clock
In my school room it stands.
And points to the time,
With its two moving hands.

Tell the child we can use our arms like a clock. Start at the 8 o'clock position and say *morning*, continue around (clockwise for the child) to the top position and say *noon*, continue to the 3 o'clock position and say *afternoon*, continue to 6 o'clock and say *evening*. See below.

Morning   **Noon**   **Afternoon**   **Evening**

Next ask the child to close his eyes and move his arm clockwise all the way around and say *night*.

The day related to the sun. Ask the child to think about the sun. Explain: In the morning the sun is low in the sky, at noon it is high, in the afternoon it is going down, and in the evening the sun sets. Demonstrate with your arm. Ask the child to repeat.

Historically, clocks originated from the sundial. At noon the sun's shadow made a line pointing to the top of the sundial.

Worksheet 40. For this worksheet, the child cuts out the four rectangles with the pictures and words. Next he puts them in order around the clock. Verify the correct placement before he glues them in place.

In conclusion. Ask: What are the parts of a day? [morning, noon, afternoon, evening, night] What tool do we use to help us keep track of the parts of a day? [clock]

ENRICHMENT LESSON 107: HOUR NUMBERS ON A CLOCK

OBJECTIVES:
1. To learn the term *hour*
2. To experience the consecutive numbering around a clock
3. To learn the position of the hour numbers on a clock

MATERIALS:
1. AL Abacus
2. Clock A (Appendix p. 15)
3. Clock cards: one set of hour numbers
4. Worksheet 41, Hours on a Clock
5. **Scissors** & **glue**

ACTIVITIES FOR TEACHING:	EXPLANATIONS:
Warm-up. Ask the child to count by 10s to 200. Enter various teen quantities on the abacus, such as 13, 17, 15, and 12, and ask the child to name them. Ask the child to count by 5s up to 100. Ask: What are the parts of a year? [months, weeks, days] What are parts of a month? [weeks, days] What are some parts of a day? [morning, noon, afternoon, evening, night] **Hours.** Explain to the child that just as we number the days of a month, we number the parts of a day. We call them *hours*. Say: We have 12 hours for the day and 12 hours for the night. Tell the child some clocks will chime the number of times to match the hour. If available, listen for the next chime. **Numbers around the clock.** Tell her to look at Clock A (Appendix p. 15). Explain that the little marks show the hours. Ask her to count the number of hours by starting after the star and ending at the star. [12] Tell her that today she will learn where to put the hour numbers around a clock. Give her a set of hour number cards. Tell her to put them in order as shown below.  **Putting the hour cards in order.** Ask: Where is noon on the clock? [at the top by the star] Tell her the first number starts to the right of the star. Ask her to place the number 1 card on the first mark. Ask her to put number 2 card on the next mark. Continue to 12. See the figure on the next page.	Children are usually very interested in clocks. They are aware that adults' lives revolve around them. Clocks also provide a simple application of numbers 1 to 12. Oftentimes, young children do not realize that the hour numbers on a clock go in order around the clock.

ACTIVITIES FOR TEACHING CONTINUED:

EXPLANATIONS CONTINUED:

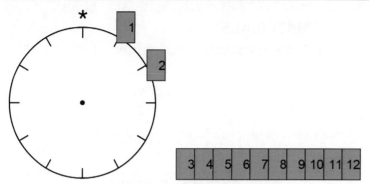

With the cards in order, the child places them around the clock, starting to the right of the star at the top.

Ask: Where is noon on the clock? [top] What number is at noon? [12] Where is dinner (supper) on the clock? [bottom] What number is there? [6]

Ask the child to mix up the cards and put them in the right places around the clock.

Mystery Clock Card game. Keep the hour cards in order around the clock. Ask the child to turn her back while you turn a clock card over. Then ask her to look and say the missing number. She verifies she is correct by turning the card right side up. The number 3 is turned over in the figure below.

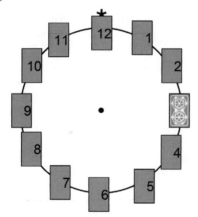

Determining the overturned hour.

If two children play, they take turns turning a card over.

Worksheet 41. Ask the child to cut out the numbers below the clock on the worksheet. Then ask her to put them in order around the clock on the worksheet as shown above. (Some children may first want to put the cards in order in a line.)

Check the placement of the hour numbers before she glues them in place.

In conclusion. Ask: How many hour numbers are on a clock? [12] Which number is at noon? [12]

216

ENRICHMENT LESSON 108: LEARNING HOUR NUMBERS

OBJECTIVES:

1. To learn the terms *hour hand* and *minute hand*
2. To continue to learn the position of the hour numbers on a clock

MATERIALS:

1. **A book about time* (optional)**
2. Geared clock
3. *Math Card Games* book, C2, C4, C5

ACTIVITIES FOR TEACHING:	EXPLANATIONS:
Warm-up. Sing the songs: "The Months," "The Days of the Week," and "Three-ten Days has September."	*A good book about time does not show the hour hand "stuck" at an hour position until the next hour. One suggestion is *DK Readers: Telling Time* by Patricia J. Murphy.

Ask: What are some parts of a year? [months, weeks, days] What are some parts of a month? [weeks, days] What are some parts of a day? [morning, noon, afternoon, evening, night]

Tell the child: Use your arms like a clock. Show morning, noon, afternoon, and evening. Then ask him to imagine night by closing his eyes and making another circle like the hour hand.

Ask the child: How many hour numbers are on a clock? [12] Which number says that it is noon? [12] Where is the 12 on the clock? [top]

Reading about time. If available, read a book about time.

Length of an hour. Ask the child: Do you know how long an hour is? He may know because of the length of a television program. Relate an hour to a favorite program, time to travel a certain distance, or other timed activity.

Hands on a clock. Ask the child to recite the following rhyme after you:

The Clock

There's a neat little clock
In my school room it stands.
And points to the time,
With its two moving hands.

Give the child the geared clock. Tell him that the hands on a clock are pointers that move to tell the time.

| ACTIVITIES FOR TEACHING CONTINUED: | EXPLANATIONS CONTINUED: |

Geared clock.

On this geared clock, the color of the hour hand matches the color of the hour numbers. Likewise, the color of the minute hand matches the color of the minute numbers.

Clocks may vary.

Show him how to move the hands on the clocks. Move them either with the arrow at the end of a hand or with the knob in the back of the clock.

Ask: How many hands does this clock have? [2] Ask him to point to the shorter hand. Tell him that hand is called the *hour hand* because it tells the hour. Remind him that the numbers he put around the clock in the previous lesson were the hour numbers. Ask him: What color is the hour hand? What color are the hour numbers?

The correct terms, *hour hand* and *minute hand*, are more descriptive of their roles and should be used. If the child says, "little hand," tell him that it is the shorter hand, but its real name is hour hand.

Tell him the longer hand is the *minute hand* and it points to the minute marks. Minutes are parts of an hour. Ask him: What color is the minute hand? What color are the minute marks?

Hour number games. The following games found in the *Math Card Games* book provide practice in placing the hour numbers in their correct locations.

    Hour Memory game, C2,

    Placing the Hour Card game, C4,

    Secret Hour Cards game, C5.

In conclusion. Ask: Which hour number is at the top of the clock? [12] Which hour number is at the bottom of the clock? [6]

ENRICHMENT LESSON 109: THE O'CLOCKS

OBJECTIVES:
1. To learn the o'clock positions
2. Ordering and matching the hour clocks

MATERIALS:
1. Cone and a weight from the math balance
2. Geared clock and Dry erase board
3. Clocks on the Hour, cut apart (App. p. 16)
4. **Scissors**
5. Clock Tags, cut apart (Appendix p. 17)
6. *Math Card Games* book, C9.1

ACTIVITIES FOR TEACHING:	EXPLANATIONS:
Warm-up. Sing the songs: "The Months," "The Days of the Week," and "Three-ten Days has September."	

Warm-up. Sing the songs: "The Months," "The Days of the Week," and "Three-ten Days has September."

Tell the child: Use your arms like a clock. Show morning, noon, afternoon, and evening. Then ask her to imagine night by closing her eyes and making another circle.

Ask the child: How many hour numbers are on a clock? [12] Ask: Which hour number is at the top of the clock? [12] Which hour number is at the bottom of the clock? [6]

Reviewing the day. Place the 10-gram blue weight on the cone. Put the weight in the morning part of the day as shown below in the first figure. Ask the child to move the weight to noon, turning it clockwise, as shown in the second figure. Continue turning the weight clockwise to afternoon and evening.

Morning   Noon   Afternoon   Evening

Learning the o'clocks. Point to the two hands on the geared clock and ask for their names. [hour hand and minute hand] Set the clock for 1:00 and tell the child that the clock says 1 o'clock. Tell her to watch the hour hand while you move the hands through a whole hour to 2 o'clock. Ask: What happened? [The hour hand moved from 1 to 2.] Ask her to watch while the hand move the from 2 o'clock to 3 o'clock.

This time tell the child that you are going to move the hour hand to 4 o'clock. Ask her to watch the minute hand this time. Move the hands to 5 o'clock and ask her what the minute hand did. [It moved around the entire clock.] Remind her that the minute hand shows the parts of the hour.

ACTIVITIES FOR TEACHING CONTINUED:

Set the clock to show 6 o'clock and ask the child what time the clock says. [6 o'clock] Repeat for other o'clocks, such as 12 o'clock, 9 o'clock, 7 o'clock, and 2 o'clock. Set the clock for 4:30 and ask her if it is 4 o'clock or 5 o'clock. [neither] Emphasize that the minute hand must point to the top, which is the beginning of the hour, when we can say o'clock.

Writing and reading the o'clocks. Show the child how to write 1:00 on the dry erase board. Tell her that the first number is the hour number; the number after the two dots (colon) is the minute number, the number of minutes after the hour.

Ask her to write 3 o'clock, 7 o'clock, 11 o'clock, and so forth. Write time values, such as 8:00, 12:00, and 2:00, and ask her to read them.

Ordering and matching the hour clocks. Show the child the hour clock figures (Appendix p. 16). Suggest that she put them in order: Ask her to find 1 o'clock and set it aside. Ask her what hour comes next, to find it, and to set it next to 1 o'clock.

When the clocks are in order, give her the twelve hour clock tags and tell her to place the tag below the corresponding clock. See the figure on the below.

Matching the hour-clock cards and the tags.

Next, mix up both the hour clock figures and the clock tag cards. Ask the child to match the tag cards to the clock figures or match the clock figures to the tag cards.

O'Clock Memory game. Play the game O'Clock Memory game found in the *Math Cards Games* book, C9.1.

In conclusion. Ask: What time is noon? [12 o'clock] How long does it take for the hour hand to move from 12 to 1? [1 hour]

EXPLANATIONS CONTINUED:

The tags for the half-hours will be used later.

ENRICHMENT LESSON 110: MORE ABOUT THE O'CLOCKS

OBJECTIVES:

1. To become aware of the length of an hour
2. To learn the terms *midnight* and *day*
3. To learn the o'clock positions on a clock
4. To learn to draw the clock hands

MATERIALS:

1. Geared clock
2. *Math Card Games* book, C9.2
3. Dry erase board
4. Clocks on the Hours and Clock Tags
5. Worksheet 42, Writing and Reading O'Clocks

ACTIVITIES FOR TEACHING:	EXPLANATIONS:
Warm-up. Sing the songs: "The Months," "The Days of the Week," and "Three-ten Day has September."	
Ask the child: How many hour numbers are on a clock? [12] Ask: Which hour number is at the top of the clock? [12] Which hour number is at the bottom of the clock? [6]	
Ask: What time is noon? [12 o'clock] How long does it take for the hour hand to move from 12 to 1? [1 hour]	
Hours in a day. Give the child the clock. Ask: How many hours are there on a clock? [12] Tell him that during every whole day the hour hand goes around twice, or two times, once for the daytime and once for the nighttime. Ask him to figure out the total number of hours that are in one day, using an abacus if necessary. [24 hours]	
Show him 12:00 on the clock and ask: What is the name for this part of the day? [noon] Tell him the other 12:00 is called *midnight*. Ask: What are you usually doing at midnight? [sleeping] Tell him that the calendar day starts at midnight. Ask: How many hours from midnight of one day to midnight of the next day? [24 hours]	Midnight actually is the "middle" of the night. It falls half way between sunset and sunrise (adjusted for how far your location is from the middle of your time zone).
Meaning of day. Explain that the word *day* can mean two things. When we are thinking of a day on a calendar, we mean the whole day, from midnight to midnight. When we say, "daytime" or "day and night," then day means the part of the day that the sun is shining.	It is confusing that the word "day" can mean 24 hours, or only the part of that day between sunrise and sunset.
O'Clock Handshaking game. Play the O'Clock Handshaking game found in the *Math Card Games* book, C9.2.	
Writing the o'clocks. Show 3:00 on the clock and write 3:00 on the dry erase board. Ask the child which number tells the hour? [3] Which number tells the minutes? [00] Remind him that the hour starts at the top, so we write 0s to show no minutes have passed yet. Ask: What do we write between the hour number and the minute number? [:]	

ACTIVITIES FOR TEACHING CONTINUED:

EXPLANATIONS CONTINUED:

Ask the child to set the clock to 7:00 and to write the time. Repeat for 5:00 and 9:00.

Drawing the hands. Next draw a clock on the dry erase board. Show the clock tag saying 5:00. Ask the child to tell you where to draw in the hands. Discuss the details: the hour hand is short and points to the first number; the minute hand is longer and points to the minutes; :00 is the beginning and is at the top.

Start at the number and draw to the center. Also show him how to draw an arrow: start at the point and draw a short line away from the end of the line on both sides. See the figures below.

Steps for drawing the hands on a clock.

Worksheet 42. Give the child the worksheet, where he draws in the hands and writes the time, for o'clocks only. The solutions are as follows:

The numbers to be written in are:

    6:00   12:00   9:00   3:00

In conclusion. Ask: Which is longer, an hour or a minute? [hour] How much time is between 3 o'clock and 5 o'clock? [2 hours] When is midnight? [middle of the night, at 12:00]

LESSON 111: REVIEWING HALVING AND DOUBLING

OBJECTIVES:
1. To review the terms half and double
2. To experience half of a distance
3. To review half of a geometric figure

MATERIALS:
1. AL Abacus
2. Two geometric solids
3. Geoboard
4. Tiles

ACTIVITIES FOR TEACHING:	EXPLANATIONS:
Warm-up. Ask: What time is noon? [12 o'clock] How long does it take for the hour hand to move from 12 to 1? [1 hour]	

Warm-up. Ask: What time is noon? [12 o'clock] How long does it take for the hour hand to move from 12 to 1? [1 hour]

Ask: Which is longer, an hour or a minute? [hour] How much time is between 3 o'clock and 5 o'clock? [2 hours] When is midnight? [middle of the night, at 12:00]

Ask the child to count by 5s to 60.

Enter various quantities on the abacus and ask the child to name them and the next number, such as 17, [18] 11, [12] 66, [67] and 29. [30]

Ask the child to show parallel lines using her arms. Then ask her to show perpendicular lines.

Half of a distance. Designate two objects in the room and tell the child that you will start walking from one object toward the other. Tell her to say "stop" when you are halfway to the other object. Repeat for different distances.

Stopping halfway between two objects.

Set up the geometric solids a good distance apart. Ask the child what would happen if both shapes moved at the same speed halfway towards the other shape. Ask: Which shape would move farther? [They would move the same distance; they would meet at the same point.]

Next ask the child what would happen if the shapes moved at the same speed away from each other. [They would move the same distance.] Which shape would be further from the starting point? [Both would be the same distance from the starting point.]

| ACTIVITIES FOR TEACHING CONTINUED: | EXPLANATIONS CONTINUED: |

ACTIVITIES FOR TEACHING CONTINUED:

Half of geometric figures. Ask the child to use the geoboard to make a rectangle with 2 units on one side and 4 units on another side. Then ask her to use another rubber band and show half. Ask her to do it another way.

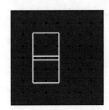 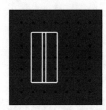 

Building a rectangle 2 by 4 and finding half three ways.

Ask her to make her own rectangles and to find half. Let her discover that she cannot succeed with certain rectangles (those with odd-numbered dimensions) except with diagonals.

In conclusion. Have the child take out 2 tiles. Ask the child to double it. Ask: How many tiles do you have now? [4] Now ask the child to take half the tiles away. How many do you have left? [2] Repeat 2 or 3 times using different even numbers.

LESSON 112: SYMMETRY

OBJECTIVES:

1. To see symmetry in everyday objects
2. To learn the term *symmetry*
3. To play games involving symmetry

MATERIALS:

1. Tiles
2. Geometry reflector
3. **A book about symmetry* (optional)**

ACTIVITIES FOR TEACHING:	EXPLANATIONS:
Warm-up. Ask: Which is longer, an hour or a minute? [hour] How much time is between 1 o'clock and 4 o'clock? [3 hours] When is midnight? [middle of the night, at 12:00]	Several suggestions include: *Is It Symmetrical?* by Nancy Kelly Allen, *Symmetry in Nature* by Allyson Valentine Schrier, and *What Is Symmetry in Nature?* by Bobbie Kalman.
Ask the child to take out 4 tiles. Ask the child to double it. Ask: How many tiles do you have now? [8] Ask him to remove half the tiles. How many do you have left? [4]	
Seeing symmetry. Make the following two designs with the tiles.	

 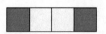

Non-symmetrical design.   **Symmetrical design.**

Although there is symmetry about a horizontal line in these examples, it is not being considered here.

Ask the child if he sees something special about one of the designs. Explain that the right design has the same parts that face each other. Tell the child it is called this *symmetry*.

Ask the child to look around the room to find objects with symmetry. Some possibilities include a face, desk, table, and chairs.

Ask: How could you change the left design to have symmetry? Two solutions are given below. Tell him to check with the geometry reflector.

The child will probably have some difficulty describing the difference.

Two ways to make the left design above symmetrical.

Building the Symmetry game. Place a single tile in the center of the workspace. Demonstrate picking up two identical tiles, one in each hand. Connect them to the original piece symmetrically. See figures on the next page.

Using both hands in unison emphasizes symmetry.

Starting tile.   **After one addition.**

| **ACTIVITIES FOR TEACHING CONTINUED:** | **EXPLANATIONS CONTINUED:** |

The child can continue alone or two people can take turns adding to the design.

Match the Symmetry game. Start with a basic design as shown below. Ask: Is the design symmetrical? [yes]

 Original design.

Add a tile and ask him to add another tile to make the design symmetrical.

The child can use the geometry reflector to check for symmetry.

 **Piece (on the left) added.**

 **Symmetrical again.**

Now ask him to add a tile somewhere on the design. Then you make the design symmetrical again. Tiles can be added in all directions, even stacked.

 **Symmetrical again.**

Players take turns adding a new piece and restoring symmetry. If a player adds a piece without disturbing the symmetry, the other player omits restoring symmetry and adds another piece. See below.

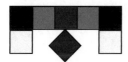 **Still symmetrical.**

Fix the Symmetry game. After a fairly complex symmetrical design is created, play this game. One player turns his back while the other player moves (or removes) one piece to spoil the symmetry. The first player finds the misplaced piece and restores the symmetry.

Next the first player alters a piece while the second player turns her back. Continue taking turns.

Reading about symmetry. If available, read to the child a book about symmetry.

In conclusion. Hold up one hand and ask: Is this symmetrical? [no] Hold up two hands and ask: Are they symmetrical? [yes]

ENRICHMENT LESSON 113: THE HALF HOURS

OBJECTIVES:
1. To become aware of the length of a minute
2. To learn the :30 positions on a clock

MATERIALS:
1. Geared clock
2. Dry erase board
3. Clocks on the Half Hour (Appendix p. 18)
4. **Scissors**
5. Clock Tags, 1:30-12:30 (Appendix p. 17)
6. *Math Card Games* book, C13.1

ACTIVITIES FOR TEACHING:	EXPLANATIONS:
Warm-up. Ask: What time is noon? [12 o'clock] How long does it take for the hour hand to move from 12 to 1? [1 hour] Ask: Which is longer, an hour or a minute? [hour] How much time is between 1 o'clock and 3 o'clock? [2 hours] When is midnight? [middle of the night, at 12:00] Ask the child to count by 5s to 125. **Introducing minutes.** Point to the shorter hand on the geared clock and ask: What is the name of this hand? [hour hand] What does it measure? [hours] Point to the longer hand and ask: What is the name of this hand? [minute hand] What does it measure? [minutes] Explain that each hour has 60 minutes. Ask: Is a minute greater or less than an hour? [less] Say: Yes, it is less than an hour; it is part of an hour? [yes] How many minutes are in a hour? [60] Ask: If you ride in a car for 80 minutes to visit family, is that greater or less than an hour? [greater] Ask: Would you like to see how long a minute is? Tell her she can jump up and down (or some other activity) for a minute. Tell her you will time her. After she has completed the activity, ask: Is a minute a long time? **Becoming aware of the half-hours.** Ask the child to set her geared clock to 1:00 and to watch what happens to the minute hand when the hour hand moves from 1:00 to 2:00. [It moves around the entire clock.] Ask her to guess what the minute hand does if she moves the clock hands from 2:00 to 3:00. [It moves around the entire clock.] Tell her to try it. Now tell her to watch what happens when she moves the minute hand only half way around between 3:00 to 4:00. Ask: Where did the hour hand stop? [halfway between the 3 and 4]	

ACTIVITIES FOR TEACHING CONTINUED:	EXPLANATIONS CONTINUED:

Ask her to try again by moving the minute hand halfway between 4:00 and 5:00. What happens if you move the minute hand? [The hour hand stops halfway between 4:00 and 5:00.]

Half hours. Ask: How many half hours are in a whole hour? [2] Ask: Where does the hour start? [at the top] Ask: Where does the minute hand point when the hour is half gone? [at the bottom]

Ask: How many minutes are in a whole hour? [60 minutes] Now tell her you have a harder question for her: How many minutes are in a half hour? [30 minutes] If necessary, remind her that 60 is 6-ten or encourage her to use her abacus.

Tell the child that now we will name the half hours. Set the clock at 1:00 and say one o'clock, move to 1:30 and say 1:30. Continue for 2:00, 2:30, 3:00, and 3:30.

Continue moving the hands silently, and ask her to tell you to stop when you reach 5:30. Repeat for 6:30 and 7:30.

Writing the half hours. Show her how we write 4:30. Ask her to write and read other times, such as 12:30, 2:30, and 11:30.

Practice. Give the Clocks on the Half Hour figures to the child. Ask her to hold up the time that you say, for example 8:30, 4:30, and so forth.

Ask the child to lay out the half-hour clock figures in a row. Then ask her to match them to the clock tags.

Matching the half hour tags with the clock cards.

Next, ask the child to lay out the tags and match the clocks to the tags.

Half-hour Memory game. Play the Half-hour Memory game in the *Math Card Games* book, C13.1.

In conclusion. Ask: If I count by half hours, what comes after 2:00? [2:30] What is the time a half hour after 2:30? [3:00]

LESSON 114: TANGRAM PUZZLES

OBJECTIVES:

1. To learn the term *parallelogram*
2. To construct new figures from other geometric figures

MATERIALS:

1. Tangrams
2. Geometry reflector
3. Worksheet 43, Tangram Puzzles

ACTIVITIES FOR TEACHING:

Warm-up. Ask: How many half hours are in a whole hour? [2] Ask: Where does the hour start? [at the top] Ask: Where does the minute hand point when the hour is half gone? [at the bottom]

Ask: How many minutes are in a whole hour? [60 minutes] How many minutes are in a half hour? [30 minutes]

Ask the child to find parallel lines and planes around the room. Then ask him to find perpendicular lines and planes.

Tangram pieces. Give the child one set of tangrams.

The seven tangram pieces.

Ask: How many rectangles do you have? [1] How many squares do you have? [1] How do you know it is a square? [It is rectangle with all sides equal.] How many triangles do you have? [5] Can you sort them by size? What do you have? [2 large, 1 medium, 2 small]

Tell the child the last shape is called a *parallelogram.* How many sets of parallel lines are there? [2] How many sets of perpendicular lines are there? [0]

Ask: Which tangram piece does not have symmetry? [parallelogram] Tell him to check with the geometry reflector.

Making figures with small triangles. Ask the child to take the two small triangles and put them together to make a square. Ask: Is it the same size as your square piece? [yes] See the left figure on the next page.

EXPLANATIONS:

Even though a square actually is a parallelogram, for the purposes of naming the pieces in a set of tangrams, *parallelogram* will not include the square.

ACTIVITIES FOR TEACHING CONTINUED:

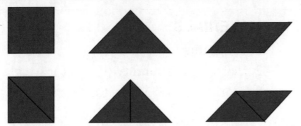

Making figures from the small triangles.

Next ask him to use the small triangles to make the medium triangle. See the second figure above. Lastly, ask him to make the parallelogram with the small triangles as shown above in the right figure.

Making figures with large triangles. Ask the child to take the two large triangles and to make larger versions of the same figures above: a square, a triangle, and a parallelogram.

Worksheet 43. Ask the child to take one of the large tangram triangles and find three smaller tangram pieces that will make the same triangle. Then ask him to record his solution on the first triangle on the worksheet by drawing the lines freehand. Tell him that the dots will help him know where to begin and end his lines. Next ask him to find two more ways to make the large triangle, without using the same three tangram pieces.

For the second row on the worksheet, the child can place the tangram pieces directly on the paper rectangle to solve the puzzle. Then he records his solution. As with the triangles, there are three solutions without using the same three pieces.

Solutions are below. The child's solutions may be in a different order or a different orientation.

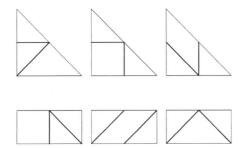

In conclusion. Ask: How many tangram pieces are there? [7] How many are triangles? [5] What are the names of the other pieces? [square and parallelogram]

EXPLANATIONS CONTINUED:

Some children may have more difficulties with these tasks and need to be encouraged. Give them hope they can succeed, but avoid giving hints or rewards.

Give the child plenty of time to solve these puzzles. One of the Standards for Mathematical Practices is that students persevere in problem solving, a skill also necessary for everyday life.

Lesson 115: More Tangram Puzzles

OBJECTIVES:

1. To compare the weights of the tangram pieces
2. To construct new figures from other geometric figures

MATERIALS:

1. Tangrams
2. Math balance and two cups for weighing
3. Worksheet 44, More Tangram Puzzles

ACTIVITIES FOR TEACHING:	EXPLANATIONS:
Warm-up. Ask: How many tangram pieces are there? [7] How many are triangles? [5] What are the names of the other pieces? [square and parallelogram]	

Ask the child to take the two large tangram triangles and make a square and a parallelogram.

Ask: How many minutes are in a whole hour? [60 minutes] How many minutes are in a half hour? [30 minutes]

Weighing the tangram pieces. Ask the child to find the two small triangles. Then ask her to find the square, the medium triangle, and the parallelogram, and to make each with the small triangles.

Now ask: What would happen if we compare the weights of these shapes? Would the small triangles weigh the same? [yes] Ask the child to predict the outcome before comparing the weights on the math balance set up as a scale.

Will one triangle balance the square? [no] Would two triangles balance the square? [yes] How many triangles would you need to balance the parallelogram? [two small triangles] How many triangles would you need to balance the medium triangle? [two small triangles]

Ask: Which figures are double the weight of a small triangle? [medium triangle, square, and parallelogram] Which figure is half the weight of the square? [small triangle]

Ask: Do you think the square is the same weight as the parallelogram? [yes] What else is the same weight as the square? [parallelogram or medium triangle] Why do you think the square weighs the same as the parallelogram? [It can be made from two small triangles.]

ACTIVITIES FOR TEACHING CONTINUED:	EXPLANATIONS CONTINUED:

Weighing the large triangle. Ask: Can you find two figures that weigh the same as the large triangle? [any two of the following: square, parallelogram, medium triangle] Can you find three figures that weigh the same as the large triangle? [two small triangles replacing any one of above answers]

Ask: Which figure's weight is double the parallelogram? [large triangle] What figure weighs twice the small triangle? [medium triangle] What weighs twice the medium triangle? [large triangle]

Ask the child to find what weighs the same as two large triangles. [the five remaining figures]

Worksheet 44. This worksheet is similar to the previous worksheet. The child can solve the puzzle by placing the tangram pieces directly on the worksheet. Then she slides them off and draws the lines to show her solution. The second solution in the first row needs to be solved with pieces different from the first puzzle. There is also a third solution not shown here.

For the second row on the worksheet, ask the child to make the first square with two pieces, the second with three pieces, and the third with four pieces. Some solutions are shown below.

You may want to challenge the child to use five pieces to solve the large square.

For the child who wants to verify her responses, she can use the math balance.

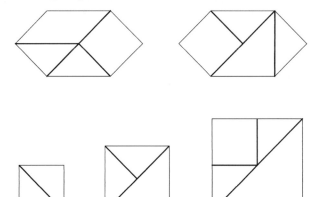

Solutions for the worksheet.

In conclusion. Show the child one small triangle and ask: Which tangram pieces weigh double this piece? [medium triangle, square, parallelogram] What number is double 4? [8] What number is double 20? [40]

LESSON 116: INTRODUCING DIVISION

OBJECTIVES:
1. To introduce division by sharing
2. To solve division problems

MATERIALS:
1. AL Abacus
2. Centimeter cubes
3. Tiles
4. Worksheet 45, Introducing Division

ACTIVITIES FOR TEACHING:	EXPLANATIONS:

ACTIVITIES FOR TEACHING:

Warm-up. Ask the child to build the stairs on the abacus. Then ask: How many beads are on the first row? [1] On the third row? [3] On the fifth row? [5], and so on. End by asking him to name the rows using ordinal numbers. [first, second, third, . . . , tenth]

A sharing problem. Give the child the following problem:

A librarian has 8 books to be given equally to 4 children. How many books does each child get?

Suggest to the child that he use the centimeter cubes to represent the children and the tiles to represent the books. See the figure below.

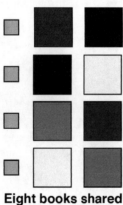

Eight books shared among 4 children.

Ask: How many books did each child receive? [2] How many books are there all together? [8]

Sharing on the abacus. Show the child how to use the abacus to solve a sharing problem. The 4 children are shown by the centimeter cubes placed along the left side of the abacus, one cube at each wire. See the left figure on the top of the next page.

Next enter the 8 beads on the top wire as shown in the second figure at the top of the next page. Use Take and Give to give 1 bead to each of the next three wires. See the next four figures on the next page.

ACTIVITIES FOR TEACHING CONTINUED:

EXPLANATIONS CONTINUED:

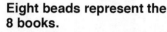

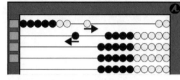

Four cubes representing 4 children.

Eight beads represent the 8 books.

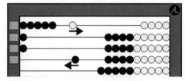

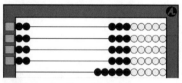

Using Take and Give to share with second child.

Using Take and Give to share with third child.

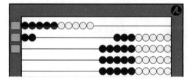

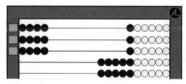

Using Take and Give to share with fourth child.

All beads (books) are shared equally.

If necessary, remind the child to use both hands whenever using Take and Give. Also, more than 1 bead can be moved at a time.

Repeat the process until all the beads are distributed equally. Then ask the child to state the solution. [The librarian gave each child 2 books.]

Another example. Give the child another problem:

Alex has a dozen balloons to share with 3 friends. How many balloons does each friend get?

The abacus setup and solution are shown below. [4]

Ready to find 12 divided by 3.

The answer to 12 divided by 3 is 4, using Take and Give.

Worksheet 45. The solutions are below:

1. Jon gets **3 blocks** and Sara gets **3 blocks**
2. **3 rocks**
3. **6 eggs**
4. **8 seeds**

In conclusion. Ask: In sharing problems, can one person get more than another person? [no] What word tells us that they all get the same amount? [equal]

LESSON 117: INTRODUCING FRACTIONS

OBJECTIVES:
1. To learn the names of the unit fractions
2. To compare unit fractions

MATERIALS:
1. AL Abacus
2. Fraction Charts

ACTIVITIES FOR TEACHING:	EXPLANATIONS:
Warm-up. Ask the child to build the stairs on the abacus. Then ask: How many beads are on the second row? [2] On the fourth row? [4] On the sixth row? [6] End by asking her to name the rows using ordinal numbers. [first, second, third, . . . , tenth]	Ordinal numbers are reviewed here because fractions, other than one half, share the same words.

Assembling the fraction chart. Give the child the fraction charts. Tell her to take the precut chart apart. Then ask her to put it together like the complete chart, but *not* on top of it. The completed chart is shown below.

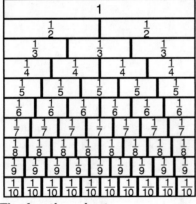

The fraction chart.

The linear fraction model provides a child with a better representation of fractions than circles. With circles it is difficult to show fractions greater than one. Also, with circles the unit of comparison is unclear—are we comparing angles, arcs, or areas of the circles?

The fraction stairs. Tell the child to find only one piece of each size from the fraction chart and to turn them face down. Then tell her to build the fraction stairs by placing the longest piece at the bottom, the next longest piece on top, keeping edges even, followed by the next longest piece, and so on. See figure on the right.

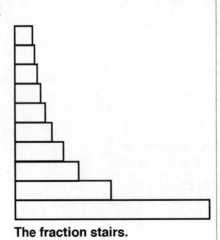

The fraction stairs.

It is important to introduce children to fractions early in their mathematical development. The younger child has little difficulty with the concept that ¼ is less than ½. On the other hand, an older child first encountering fractions feels certain that 4 is always greater than 3.

The mathematical name of the fraction stair curve is *hyperbola*.

ACTIVITIES FOR TEACHING CONTINUED:

Ask the child: Could you climb those stairs? Are they like the stairs on the abacus? [no] How are they different? [The steps get smaller the higher you climb.]

Working with halves. With the pieces face up again, take the 1-piece and ask: Can you find a piece that is half as much? [the ½ piece] Set it below the 1-piece as shown below. Ask: How many one-half pieces do you need to make a whole? [2] Ask her to find the other one-half piece and set it under the 1-piece.

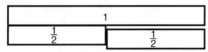

Showing two halves make a whole.

Point out the symbol for ½ and explain that it means 1 divided, or broken, into 2 equal parts.

Working with thirds. Now ask her to find a fraction piece that divides the 1 into 3 equal parts. Tell her to set it under the 1 as shown below.

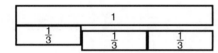

Showing three thirds make a whole.

Tell her to find the other pieces the same size and to set them under the 1. Explain that we call it *one third*. Ask: How many one thirds do you need to make a whole? [3]

Working with fourths. Repeat the activity with fourths, explaining that we call it *one fourth*. See figure below. Ask: How many one fourths do you need to make a whole? [4]

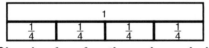

Showing four fourths make a whole.

Working with the remaining fraction names.
Explain: Except for one half, we use ordinal number names for naming fractions. For practice ask questions such as the following: Can you find one sixth? Can you find one eighth? Where is one tenth? Can you find one seventh?

Now ask the child to put the chart together again. Then read together the fractions on the chart. [one half, one third, . . . , one tenth]

In conclusion. Ask: How many halves in a whole? [2] How many thirds are in 1? [3] Which is greater, one half or one third? [one half]

EXPLANATIONS CONTINUED:

Note that this model parallels the way fractions are written. This example of $\frac{1}{2}$ shows the 1 (top piece) divided by (the bottom edge of the 1 piece) into 2 (two pieces below).

Speakers of British English rarely use one fourth; rather they say *one quarter.*

Many other languages distinguish between ordinal number words and fraction words by different suffixes, making it easier for students to understand what a fraction is.

LESSON 118: COMPARING UNIT FRACTIONS

OBJECTIVES:
1. To compare unit fractions

MATERIALS:
1. Fraction Charts
2. *Math Card Games,* F2 and F2.1

ACTIVITIES FOR TEACHING:	EXPLANATIONS:

ACTIVITIES FOR TEACHING:

Warm-up. Using the fraction chart, ask: Can you find one sixth? Can you find one eighth? Where is one tenth? Can you find one seventh?

Ask: How many halves are in a whole? [2] How many thirds are in 1? [3] Which is greater, one half or one third? [one half]

Comparing unit fractions. Ask the child to assemble the fraction chart.

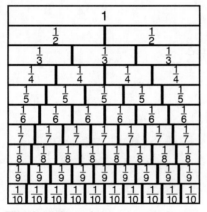

The fraction chart.

Then ask him to answer the following questions while using the chart:

1. Where is one half? [second row]
2. What is the smallest fraction on the chart? [one tenth]
3. Name two fractions greater than one fourth? [one third and one half]
4. Which is more, one half or one fourth? [one half]
5. How can you tell? [Half piece is longer.]
6. Which is more, one third or one fourth? [one third]
7. Which is more, one sixth or one fourth? [one fourth]
8. Which is less, one third or one sixth? [one sixth]

EXPLANATIONS:

A unit fraction is a fraction having 1 as the numerator, such as ⅓.

It is essential that all the fraction pieces be the same color. A fraction piece should be identified by its length, not its color.

Avoid teaching a rule such as: The greater the number, the smaller the fraction. Such rules prevent real understanding.

A child who had learned that rule was asked, "Which is greater, ⅗ or ½?" He replied incorrectly with "½." He was not thinking about fractions, but the rule.

ACTIVITIES FOR TEACHING CONTINUED:	EXPLANATIONS CONTINUED:

Fraction Memory game. Play the Fraction Memory game found in the *Math Card Games* book, F2. The object of this game is to match a fraction piece with the written symbol on a fraction card.

Unit Fraction War game. Next play the Unit Fraction War game found in the *Math Card Games* book, F2.1. Here players compare unit fractions while referring to their fraction charts.

In conclusion. Ask: Which is more, one third or one fourth? [one third] How many thirds are in a whole? [3] How many fourths are in a whole? [4] How many fourths are in a half? [2]

The questions are posed in a slightly different order to expand the child's conceptual understanding.

LESSON 119: MEASURING WITH WATER

OBJECTIVES:

1. To compare volumes of water in different containers
2. To compare fractions in measuring cups

MATERIALS:

1. Geared clock
2. **Two containers of different shapes**
3. Fraction Chart
4. **Set of measuring cups: 1, 1/2, 1/3, and 1/4**

ACTIVITIES FOR TEACHING:	EXPLANATIONS:

Warm-up. Ask the child to count by 10s to 100 then count by 5s to 100.

Ask the child to say the odd numbers to 39.

Ask the child: How many eggs is a dozen? [12] Ask: How many doughnuts is a dozen? [12]

Give the child various hours and half hours for her to set on the clock. Then you set the clock and ask the child to read the time.

Comparing water volumes. Show the child two similar containers and ask: Which do you think can hold more water? Once she has decided, ask how she could find out for sure.

Which container holds more water?

Suggest filling one container with water and ask: How could this help us? If necessary, tell her to pour the water into the other container. Ask her to explain which container has more water. [If the water does not all fit into the second container, the first one is larger. If the water fits exactly, they are equal. If extra space remains in the second container, it is larger.]

ACTIVITIES FOR TEACHING CONTINUED:	EXPLANATIONS CONTINUED:

Comparing unit fractions with 1. With the child looking at the fraction chart, ask: How many halves are equal to 1? [2] How many thirds are in a whole? [3] How many fourths are in 1? [4] How many sixths are equal to 1? [6] How many eighths in a whole? [8]

Comparing halves and fourths. Ask the child to find the 1 fraction piece, the halves, and the fourths. Then ask her to put the halves below the 1 and the fourths below the halves as shown below.

The 1, halves, and fourths.

Ask: What is half of 1? [one half] What is half of a half? [one fourth] How many fourths in a half? [2]

Measuring cups. Show the child the four measuring cups and explain that: One container holds 1 cup; another holds one half of a cup; another is one third cup; and another is a fourth cup. Ask her: Which is which, and to set them out in order. Show the markings on the cups.

Measuring cups.

Ask: How many times do you think you need to fill the half cup with water to fill the whole cup? [2] Tell her to try it.

Repeat with thirds and fourths.

Then ask: How many fourths do you need to fill the half cup? [2] Again tell her to try it. Discuss how this water activity matches the fraction pieces.

In conclusion. Ask: Which is more, one third or one fourth? [one third] How many thirds are in a whole? [3] How many fourths are in a whole? [4] How many fourths are in a half? [2]

LESSON 120: NON-UNIT FRACTIONS

OBJECTIVES:
1. To learn to write fractions
2. To name and write non-unit fractions

MATERIALS:
1. Fraction Chart
2. Dry erase board

ACTIVITIES FOR TEACHING:	EXPLANATIONS:

ACTIVITIES FOR TEACHING:

Warm-up. Ask: Which is more, one third or one fourth? [one third] How many thirds are in a whole? [3] How many fourths are in a whole? [4] How many fourths are in a half? [2]

Ask the child to assemble the fraction chart.

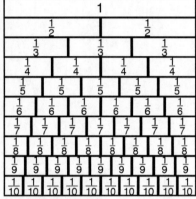
The fraction chart.

Ask him to answer the following while using the chart:

1. Where are the thirds? [third row]

2. How many fourths are equal to one whole? [4]

3. How many eighths are in a whole? [8]

4. How many tenths are in 1? [10]

5. Which is more, one third or one fourth? [one third]

6. Which is more, one sixth or one fourth? [one fourth]

Equal fractions. Ask the child to lay out the 1-piece face down. Now ask: Can you show dividing the 1 into thirds? If the child does it correctly as shown in the left figure, use a ½ and two ¼ pieces to make the right figure and ask: Is this also correct? [no] Why not? [not equal]

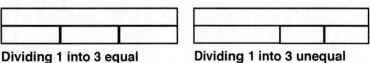

Dividing 1 into 3 equal pieces.

Dividing 1 into 3 unequal pieces.

EXPLANATIONS:

Most young children enjoy assembling the fraction chart and learn much by doing it repeatedly.

While it may seem obvious that 4 fourths make 1, there are many people of all ages who do not understand this concept. Mere words do not work; experience with the fraction chart is key.

If the child initially makes the right figure, ask: Are the pieces equal? [no] If necessary, explain that they must be equal.

| ACTIVITIES FOR TEACHING CONTINUED: | EXPLANATIONS CONTINUED: |

Writing unit fractions. With the 1-piece above the one third pieces, show how we write fractions. Write 1 and say: 1 is the whole. Write the short line under the 1 saying: This means divided by. Then write the 3 and say: 3 is the number of parts. See figure below.

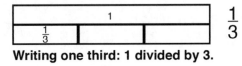

Writing one third: 1 divided by 3.

Ask the child to write various unit fractions on a dry erase board. Name various fractions that he wrote and ask him to find the pieces. Then ask him to read the fractions he wrote.

Non-unit fractions. Ask the child to find a one fifth piece. Ask him to find another one fifth piece. Tell him: Now we have two fifths. Show him how to write it as shown below.

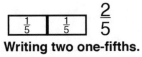

Writing two one-fifths.

Ask him to find three fourths and write the fraction. $[\frac{3}{4}]$ Repeat for two sixths $[\frac{2}{6}]$ and four eighths. $[\frac{4}{8}]$

Can You Find the Fractions game. With the fraction pieces scattered, ask the child to find the pieces and build the fraction chart as you name them as follows:

1. Can you find 1 half? Can you find 1?
2. Can you find 2 thirds? Can you find 2 fourths?
3. Can you find 1 fifth? Can you find 1 sixth?
4. Can you find 2 fifths? Can you find 1 fourth?
5. Can you find 3 sixths? Can you find 4 sevenths?
6. Can you find 2 eighths? Can you find 1 third?
7. Can you find 3 ninths? Can you find 1 half?
8. Can you find 1 fourth? Can you find 3 ninths?
9. Can you find 2 fifths? Can you find 3 eighths?
10. Can you find 4 tenths? Can you find 2 sixths?
11. Can you find 3 sevenths? Can you find 2 tenths?
12. Can you find 3 eighths? Can you find 3 ninths?
13. Can you find 4 tenths?

At the end of this exercise, the all the fraction pieces will be picked up and the fraction chart assembled.

In conclusion. With the child referring to the chart, ask: Which is greater, 1 half or 3 fourths? [3 fourths] Which is greater, 1 half or 2 fourths? [same] Which is less, 2 sevenths or 2 eighths? [2 eighths]

LESSON 121: MAKING ONE WITH FRACTIONS

OBJECTIVES:
1. To learn which pairs of fractions equal 1

MATERIALS:
1. Fraction Chart
2. Dry erase board
3. Fraction cards: 1/3, 2/3, 1/4, 3/4, 1/5, 2/5, 3/5, 4/5, 1/6, 5/6, 1/8, 3/8, 5/8, 7/8, 1/10, 3/10, 7/10, 9/10, and two 1/2s
4. *Math Card Games* book, F3

ACTIVITIES FOR TEACHING:

EXPLANATIONS:

Warm-up. With the child referring to the chart, ask: Which is greater, 1 half or 3 fourths? [3 fourths] Which is greater, 1 half or 2 fourths? [same] Which is less, 2 sevenths or 2 eighths? [2 eighths]

Ask the child to assemble the fraction chart.

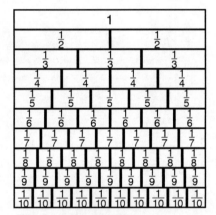

The fraction chart.

Ask her to answer the following while using the chart:

1. What is 1 third and 1 third? [2 thirds]

2. What is 2 eighths plus 1 eighth? [3 eights]

3. How many sixths are in a whole? [6]

4. How many tenths are in 1? [10]

5. Which is more, 1 fourth or 1 third? [1 third]

6. Which is more, 1 sixth or 1 fourth? [1 fourth]

Making 1. Draw a part-whole circle set and write 1 in the whole-circle. Next write 3/4 in a part-circle. See the left figure on the next page. Ask: What is the other part? [1/4] After the child says it, tell the child to write it in the other part-circle. See the right figure on the next page.

Change the 3/4 to 3/5 and ask the child to find and write what is needed to equal 1. [2/5]

There are several ways that the child might use to find the missing part. She might merely look at the fourths row or remove 3 fourths to see what is needed.

For a fraction such as 4/10, show the child to find 4 with her left hand and count the remainder with her right hand (6).

ACTIVITIES FOR TEACHING CONTINUED:

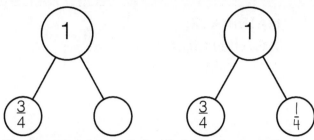

Finding what is needed with 3 fourths to make 1.

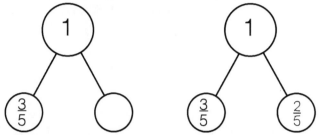

Finding what is needed with 3 fifths to make 1.

Find the Fraction Pairs game. Spread the fraction cards out face up. Use the 20 cards listed in the materials list. Tell the child to find as many pairs equalling one as possible, but each pair must be different. Use the fraction chart. There are 10 different pairs.

These pairs are needed for the next game.

Concentrating on One game. Play the Concentrating on One game found in the *Math Card Games* book, F3. This is a memory game where players look for pairs equal to 1.

In conclusion. Ask: How many thirds do you need to make a whole? [3] Which is greater, 4 fourths or 5 fifths? [same] Which is more, 1 fourth cup of juice or 1 third cup of juice? [1 third cup]

EXPLANATIONS CONTINUED:

Be sure the child refers to the fraction chart when she looks for the matches. Avoid teaching a rule to find the other pair. For example, to find the pair for 2/5, the rule says to subtract 2 from 5 to get the top number, 3, and use 5 for the bottom number.

Such procedures reduce this game to an exercise of a meaningless computation game unrelated to fractions. The fraction chart makes this process visual.

LESSON 122: HALVING FRACTIONS

OBJECTIVES:
1. To compare halves, fourths, and eighths

MATERIALS:
1. Fraction Chart
2. *Math Card Games* book, F7

ACTIVITIES FOR TEACHING:	EXPLANATIONS:
Warm-up. Ask the child to count to 100, starting with 60.	

Warm-up. Ask the child to count to 100, starting with 60.

Ask the child to solve the following problem:

> Jamie has 6 baseball cards. How many more must he get in order to have 10? [4 cards]

Ask the child to assemble the fraction chart.

Halves of fractions. Tell the child to lay out the 1-piece. Then ask: What is half of 1? [one half] How many halves does it take to equal 1? [2] Tell him to find the 2 halves and set them below the 1. See the figure below.

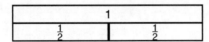

The 1 and halves.

Ask: What is half of a half? [one fourth] How many fourths do you need to equal one half? [2] Tell him to lay out two fourths for each half. See the figure below.

The 1, halves, and fourths.

Ask: What is half of a fourth? [one eighth] How many eighths do you need to equal one fourth? [2] Tell him to lay out two eighths for each fourth. See the figure below.

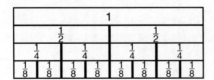

The 1, halves, fourths, and eighths.

This fraction arrangement is the basis of the ruler for measuring inches.

ACTIVITIES FOR TEACHING CONTINUED:	EXPLANATIONS CONTINUED:

With the child referring to the fraction arrangement he has made, ask the following questions:

1. Which is more, 1 fourth or 1 half? [1 half]

2. Which is greater, 2 fourths or 2 halves? [2 halves]

3. Which is more, 1 half or 3 eighths? [1 half]

4. Which is more, 5 eighths or 3 fourths? [3 fourths]

5. Which is more, 4 eighths or 2 fourths? [same]

Fraction War game. Play the Fraction War game, found in the *Math Card Games* book, F7.

This game is a favorite of many children.

In conclusion. Ask: How many fourths do you need to make a whole? [4] How many fourths make a half? [2] How many eighths do you need to make a whole? [8] How many eights make a half? [4] Is 5 eighths greater or less than a half? [greater]

LESSON 123: COUNTING AND CARDINALITY REVIEW

OBJECTIVES:
1. To review the counting and cardinality topics

MATERIALS:
1. Tiles
2. Centimeter cubes
3. Place-value cards
4. AL Abacus
5. Dry erase board
6. *Math Card Games* book, A3

ACTIVITIES FOR TEACHING:	EXPLANATIONS:

ACTIVITIES FOR TEACHING:

Number of objects. Put about 25–30 tiles in a heap and ask the child: How many tiles are here? Ask her to find the answer two different ways. [count or group in fives and tens]

Put the tiles back into the heap. Give her one additional tile and tell her to put it with the other tiles. Ask: Now how many tiles do you have? If she counts all the tiles, add one more and ask: Can you tell without counting how many tiles there are?

Ask her to take 10 tiles and set them aside.

Compare numbers. Arrange 8 centimeter cubes and 5 blue tiles as shown below. Then ask: Are there more centimeter cubes or more tiles? [centimeter cubes] How many more? [3] How many more tiles do you need so both piles will have the same number? [3]

Comparing numbers.

Ask her to put the centimeter cubes into a line and ask: How many cubes are there now? [8] Spread them out and repeat the question. [8]

From the place-value cards show her the 6 and the 9. Ask: Which number is greater? [9]

Number names. Ask the child to count by ones to 100, preferably without the abacus.

Ask the child to count by 10s to 100.

Tell the child that you are going to say a number and she is to say the next two numbers. What two numbers come after 6? [7, 8] What two numbers come after 11? [12, 13] What two numbers come after 18? [19, 20] What two numbers come after 29? [30, 31]

EXPLANATIONS:

In RightStart™ Mathematics, counting is introduced as a quantity naming activity always based on place value—never as a memorized list of words.

Lessons 123, 125, 127, 129, and 131 are review lessons for the end of year assessments. If preferred, these reviews may be taught sequentially, then the assessments may be presented as a single final test.

ACTIVITIES FOR TEACHING CONTINUED:	EXPLANATIONS CONTINUED:

Ask the child to enter the following numbers on the abacus: 7, 11, 31, and 78.

Write the following numbers and ask the child to enter them on the abacus: 30, 0, 12, and 56.

Enter the following on the abacus and ask the child to name the numbers: 13, 19, 42, and 99.

Enter the following on the abacus and ask the child to write the numbers: 8, 15, 27, 49, and 63.

Go to the Dump game. Play the game Go to the Dump game from *Math Cards Games* book, A3.

LESSON 124: COUNTING AND CARDINALITY ASSESSMENT

OBJECTIVES:
1. To assess the counting and cardinality topics

MATERIALS:
1. End of Year Assessment 1 (found in the back of the child's worksheets)
2. Tiles and Place-value cards
3. AL Abacus
4. Dry erase board
5. *Math Card Games* book, N31

ACTIVITIES FOR TEACHING:	EXPLANATIONS:

Assessment 1. Have the child take out the End of Year Assessment 1 from the back of his worksheets. On the first page of the assessment the child will record his work. The second page is done orally or visually and assessments notes can be recorded.

Problems 1–6.

1. Lay out 5 tiles and have the child write the quantity on his worksheet.

2. Have him add one more tile and write the quantity.

3. Tell the child to circle the group that has more. Have him write how many more are in the larger group. Have him write the number of how many more he needs so they are the same.

4. Using the place-value cards, show the child the 9 and the 6. Tell him to write which is less.

5. Have the child write the two numbers that come after 12. Have the child write the two numbers that come after 19. Have the child write the two numbers that come after 38.

6. Enter the following on the abacus and ask the child to write the numbers: 8, 15, 27, 49, and 63.

Problems 7–11. Make assessment notes as the child does the work.

7. Ask the child to enter the following numbers on the abacus: 8, 11, 31, and 78.

8. Write the following numbers and ask the child to enter them on the abacus: 30, 0, 12, and 56.

9. Enter the following numbers on the abacus one at a time and ask the child to say the numbers: 13, 19, 42, and 99.

10. Ask the child to count by 1s to 100.

11. Ask the child to count by 10s to 200.

249

ACTIVITIES FOR TEACHING CONTINUED:

EXPLANATIONS CONTINUED:

1. How many tiles are there? ___5___

2. How many tiles are there now? ___6___

3. Circle the group that has more.

How many more are in the larger group? ___2___

How many do you need so they are the same? ___2___

4. Which is less? ___6___

5. What comes after 12? 13 14

What comes after 19? 20 21

What comes after 38? 39 40

6. Write the numbers entered on the abacus.

___8___ ___15___ ___27___ ___49___ ___63___

Child's answers to End of Year Assessment 1.

Race to Ten game. Play Race to Ten game in the *Math Card Games* book, N31.

LESSON 125: OPERATIONS AND ALGEBRAIC THINKING REVIEW

OBJECTIVES:

1. To review the operations and algebraic thinking topics

MATERIALS:

1. AL Abacus
2. Dry erase board
3. *Math Card Games* book, A44

ACTIVITIES FOR TEACHING:	EXPLANATIONS:
Addition and subtraction with objects. Ask the child: Can you show adding 5 apples and 2 apples on the abacus? What is the sum? [7] Ask the child to add 4 plus 4 on the abacus. What is the sum? [8]	

Addition and subtraction with objects. Ask the child: Can you show adding 5 apples and 2 apples on the abacus? What is the sum? [7] Ask the child to add 4 plus 4 on the abacus. What is the sum? [8]

Ask the child: Can you show 9 minus 4 on your abacus? [5] How much is 6 plus 2? [8] How much is 6 minus 2? [4] Ask her to write the equations for 5 plus 2 and 5 minus 1. [5 + 2 = 7, 5 − 1 = 4]

Solving addition and subtraction problems. Ask the child to solve the following problems using the abacus or any other manipulatives she chooses:

1. Ten children are at a swimming pool. A set of twins come to the pool. How many children are at the pool now? [12 children]

2. Eight robins are on a bush. Five fly away. How many robins are left? [3 robins]

3. A (two-story) house has 4 rooms on the first floor and 3 rooms on the second floor. How many rooms does the house have? [7 rooms]

4. Six children are playing in the sandbox. Four are girls. How many are boys? [2 boys]

Partitioning. Draw a part-whole circle set and write 10 in the whole-circle. Ask the child to name all the ways she could partition 10. [0 and 10, 1 and 9, 2 and 8, . . . , 10 and 0]

You may want the child to write out the partitioning of 10 in the part-circles.

Facts up to 5. Ask: How much is 3 + 2? [5] How much is 2 + 2? [4] What is 5 − 4? [1] If she takes more than 3 seconds to answer each question, suggest she look at the abacus, then ask similar questions.

ACTIVITIES FOR TEACHING CONTINUED:	EXPLANATIONS CONTINUED:

ACTIVITIES FOR TEACHING CONTINUED:

Addition War game. Play the game Addition War from *Math Cards Games* book, A44 Variation 1.

The child can help prepare the cards by removing with numbers greater than 6 (or 7) from the deck.

EXPLANATIONS CONTINUED:

LESSON 126: OPERATIONS & ALGEBRAIC THINKING ASSESSMENT

OBJECTIVES:

1. To assess the operations and algebraic thinking topics

MATERIALS:

1. End of Year Assessment 2
2. AL Abacus
3. *Math Card Games* book, N34

ACTIVITIES FOR TEACHING:	**EXPLANATIONS:**

ACTIVITIES FOR TEACHING:

Assessment 2. Have the child take out the End of Year Assessment 2. On the first page of the assessment the child will record his work. The second page is done orally or visually and assessments notes can be recorded.

Problems 1–8.

1. Tell the child to show adding 5 basketballs and 2 more basketballs on the abacus. Have him write the total on his worksheet.

2. Tell the child to add 2 plus 2 on the abacus. Tell him to write the sum.

3. Have the child find 8 minus 3 on his abacus and record his answer.

4. Ask the child to write how much is 8 plus 2 on his worksheet.

5. Ask the child to write the answer to 5 minus 2.

6. Have the child write the equation for 4 plus 2 and include the sum.

7. Have the child write the equation 4 minus 1 and include the difference.

8. Have the child partition 10 three different ways on his worksheet.

Problems 9–12. Ask the child to solve the following problems using the abacus or any other manipulatives he chooses:

9. Thirteen children are at a park. A set of twins leaves the park. How many children remain at the park? [11 children]

10. Ten bees are by the honey pot. Five fly away. How many bees are left? [5 bees]

11. A house has 5 rooms on the first floor and 4 rooms on the second floor. How many rooms does the house have? [9 rooms]

12. Nine children are playing softball. Six are girls. How many are boys? [3 boys]

ACTIVITIES FOR TEACHING CONTINUED:	**EXPLANATIONS CONTINUED:**

Problems 13–15. Ask the child to answer orally:

13. How much is 2 + 3? [5]

14. How much is 5 + 3? [8]

15. What is 4 − 3? [1]

---

1. What is the total number of basketballs? _7_____

2. What is the sum? _____4_____

3. What is the answer? _____5_____

4. What is the answer? _____10_____

5. What is the answer? _____3_____

6. Write the equation. _____4 + 2 = 6_____

7. Write the equation. _____4 − 1 = 3_____

8.

Answers will vary for the partitioning of 10.

Child's answers to End of Year Assessment 2.

Swim to Ten game. Play the game Swim to Ten from *Math Cards Games* book, N34 Variation.

LESSON 127: NUMBER AND OPERATIONS IN BASE TEN REVIEW

OBJECTIVES:

1. To review the number and operations in base ten topics

MATERIALS:

1. AL Abacus
2. Dry erase board
3. Place-value cards
4. *Math Card Games* book, N40

ACTIVITIES FOR TEACHING:	EXPLANATIONS:
Numbers 11–19. Ask the child: Can you enter ten 1 on the abacus? What is its regular name? [eleven] Repeat for ten 2, [twelve] ten 3, [thirteen] and ten 8. [eighteen]	

Numbers 11–19. Ask the child: Can you enter ten 1 on the abacus? What is its regular name? [eleven] Repeat for ten 2, [twelve] ten 3, [thirteen] and ten 8. [eighteen]

Enter 16 on the abacus and ask the child to say the number both the math way and the regular name. Repeat for 15 and 19.

Ask the child to draw a picture of 14 beads or tiles dry erase board so it can be quickly recognized without counting.

Tens and ones. Ask the child to spread out the place-value cards. Ask her to make the number thirty-nine. Ask: How many tens does it have? [3] How many ones does it have? [9] Ask her to enter it on the abacus.

Say: I am thinking of a number that has 7 tens and 3 ones. Can you make it with the place-value cards? Can you read it? [seventy-three]

Enter 67 on the abacus and ask the child to write the number. Repeat for 17 and 71.

Parts and wholes. Draw the part-whole circle sets as shown below and ask the child to write the missing numbers:

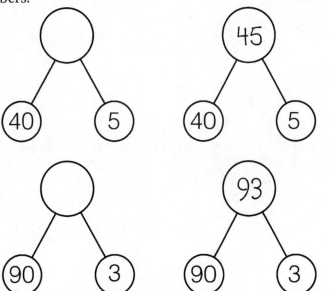

ACTIVITIES FOR TEACHING CONTINUED:	EXPLANATIONS CONTINUED:

Continue with the following part-whole circle sets:

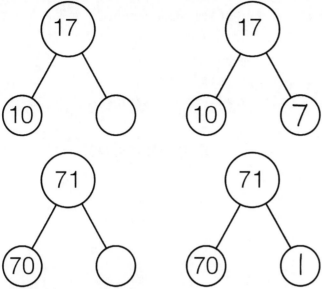

Finding the missing part.

Completing equations. Ask: What is 10 plus 6? [16] What is 30 plus 8? [38] Write the following equations and ask the child to read and complete them either orally or written:

$$20 + 8 = \underline{\quad} \ [28]$$
$$37 = 30 + \underline{\quad} \ [7]$$

Tens and Ones Bingo game. Play the game Tens and Ones Bingo from *Math Cards Games* book, N40.

Use the 9s of the multiplication cards (9, 18, 27, . . . , 90).

LESSON 128: NUMBER & OPERATIONS IN BASE TEN ASSESSMENT

OBJECTIVES:
1. To assess the number and operations in base ten topics

MATERIALS:
1. End of Year Assessment 3
2. AL Abacus
3. Place-value cards
4. Dry erase board
5. *Math Card Games* book, A44

ACTIVITIES FOR TEACHING:	EXPLANATIONS:
Assessment 3. Have the child take out the End of Year Assessment 3. The first page of the assessment is to be done orally or visually and assessments notes can be recorded. On the second page the child will record his work.	

Problems 1–7.
1. Ask the child to enter ten 1 on the abacus. Ask: What is its regular name? [eleven]
2. Ask the child to enter ten 2 on the abacus. Ask: What is its regular name? [twelve]
3. Ask the child to enter ten 3 on the abacus. Ask: What is its regular name? [thirteen]
4. Ask the child to enter ten 8 on the abacus. Ask: What is its regular name? [eighteen]
5. Enter 15 on the abacus and ask the child to say the number the math way and the regular way.
6. Enter 17 on the abacus and ask the child to say the number the math way and the regular way.
7. Enter 19 on the abacus and ask the child to say the number the math way and the regular way.

Problems 8–12. Spread out the place-value cards.
8. Ask the child to make the number twenty-six.
9. Ask: How many tens does it have? [2 tens]
10. Ask: How many ones does it have? [6 ones]
11. Ask him to enter it on the abacus.
12. Say: I am thinking of a number that has 6 tens and 4 ones. Have the child make it with the place-value cards. Ask him to read it. [sixty-four]

Problems 13-14. Ask the child to complete the oral equations.
13. Ask: What is 10 plus 4? [14]
14. Ask: What is 40 plus 0? [40]

ACTIVITIES FOR TEACHING CONTINUED:

EXPLANATIONS CONTINUED:

Problems 15–16. Give the child the worksheet to record his answers.

15. Enter 76 on the abacus and ask the child to write the number on his worksheet.

16. Enter 18 on the abacus and ask the child to write the number.

Problems 17–20. Have the child complete the part-whole circle sets on his worksheet.

Problems 21–22. Have the child complete the equations on his worksheet.

15. Write the number on the abacus. _76_

16. Write the new number on the abacus. _18_

17–20. Write the missing numbers.

35 → 30, 5

82 → 80, 2

16 → 10, 6

61 → 60, 1

21–22. Write the answers.

30 + 8 = _38_

47 = 40 + _7_

Child's answers to End of Year Assessment 3.

© Activities for Learning, Inc. 2013

Lesson 129: Measurement and Data Review

OBJECTIVES:
1. To review the measurement and data topics

MATERIALS:
1. Tiles
2. Centimeter cubes
3. AL Abacus
4. Worksheet 46, Sorting Coins
5. Coins

ACTIVITIES FOR TEACHING:	EXPLANATIONS:

ACTIVITIES FOR TEACHING:

Comparing a centimeter cube and a tile. Show the child a centimeter cube and a tile. Ask: How are the cube and the tile different?

Comparing cube and tile laying flat.

Discuss the difference in color. [blue and yellow (in this example)] Which is longer? [tile] Which is taller or higher? [centimeter cube]

Take a tile and set it on its edge and ask: How are the cube and the tile different?

Comparing cube and tile standing up on end.

Discuss the difference in color. [blue and red] Which is longer? [cube in horizontal direction, but tile in width] Which is taller or higher? [tile]

Which is more, a side of a tile or three beads on the abacus? [three beads] Which is more, a side of a cube or a bead on the abacus? [the same]

Comparing weights. Ask the child: Which weighs less, the math balance or a piece of paper? [paper] Which weighs more, the paper or a pencil? [pencil]

ACTIVITIES FOR TEACHING CONTINUED:

EXPLANATIONS CONTINUED:

Classifying coins by count. Give the child Worksheet 46 along with a handful of coins. Have her sort the coins. Next, tell her to put them in order either from greatest to least or least to greatest. Finally write the number of coins at the bottom of the worksheet. See the figure below.

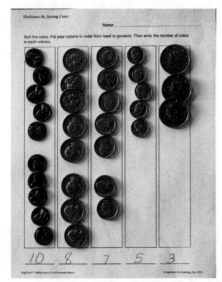

Coins sorted and arranged by quantity.

LESSON 130: MEASUREMENT AND DATA ASSESSMENT

OBJECTIVES:
1. To assess the measurement and data topics

MATERIALS:
1. End of Year Assessment 4
2. AL Abacus
3. Tiles
4. Centimeter cubes
5. Coins

ACTIVITIES FOR TEACHING:	EXPLANATIONS:

ACTIVITIES FOR TEACHING:

Assessment 4. Have the child take out the End of Year Assessment 4. The child will record his work on the top half of the first page and the second page of the assessment. The remaining portion of page one is to be done orally or visually and assessments notes can be recorded.

Problems 1–2.

1. Have the child circle the taller tree on the worksheet.

2. Have the child circle the shortest building.

Problem 3. Give the child some coins. Have the child sort the coins, then put them in order from least to greatest on page 2 of the assessment worksheet. Have him write the number of coins below the column of sorted coins. [Answers will vary.]

Problems 4–6. Give the child an abacus, a tile, and a centimeter cube.

4. Ask: Which is less, the edge of a tile or three abacus beads? [the edge of a tile]

5. Ask: Which is more, the length of a centimeter cube or abacus bead? [the same]

6. Ask: Which weighs more, the abacus or a piece of paper? [abacus]

ACTIVITIES FOR TEACHING CONTINUED:

EXPLANATIONS CONTINUED:

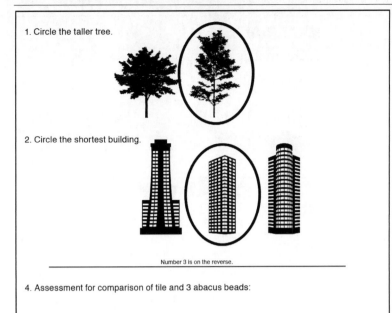

1. Circle the taller tree.

2. Circle the shortest building.

Number 3 is on the reverse.

4. Assessment for comparison of tile and 3 abacus beads:

5. Assessment for comparison of the length of a cube and an abacus bead:

6. Assessment for weight comparison between a piece of paper and an abacus:

Child's answers to End of Year Assessment 4.

LESSON 131: GEOMETRY REVIEW

OBJECTIVES:
1. To review the geometry topics

MATERIALS:
1. Geometric solids
2. Tiles

ACTIVITIES FOR TEACHING:	EXPLANATIONS:
Describing objects and their positions. Give the child the geometric solids and ask him to do the following:	This activity reviews both the position words and the names of geometric shapes through recognition.

Describing objects and their positions. Give the child the geometric solids and ask him to do the following:

1. Find the larger cylinder.

2. Put the cube behind the cylinder.

3. Place the cone above the cube.

4. Place the hemisphere in front of the cone.

5. Put the taller prism beside the cylinder.

The collection will look similar to the figure below.

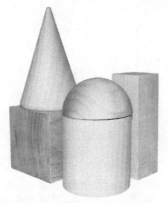

One possible arrangement.

What's my shape? Give the following descriptions about the geometric solids and ask her to find the figure:

6. I have only one circle. What am I? [cone, hemisphere]

7. I have two circles. What am I? [cylinders]

8. I am round all over. What am I? [sphere]

9. I have two hexagons. What am I? [(hexagonal) prism]

10. I have two triangles. What am I? [(triangular) prism]

11. I have four triangles. What am I? [pyramid]

12. I have six squares. What am I? [cube]

This activity reviews both the position words and the names of geometric shapes through recognition.

ACTIVITIES FOR TEACHING CONTINUED:

Faces and sides. Tell the child to find the shape you name and say the number and name of each face:

1. Pyramid. [4 triangles and 1 square]

2. Triangular prism. [2 triangles and 3 rectangles]

3. Cube. [6 squares]

For the same figures, ask the child to find the number of sides:

4. Pyramid. [5 sides]

5. Triangular prism. [5 sides]

6. Cube. [6 sides]

Ask: How many sides does a rectangle have? [4] How many sides does a triangle have? [3]

Building squares and rectangles. Tell the child to take 14 tiles and make as many squares of different sizes as she can. See below.

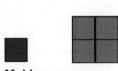

Making squares.

Now ask her to make as many rectangles of different sizes as she can that are not squares. See below.

Some possible rectangles.

EXPLANATIONS CONTINUED:

Some geometric solids have a three-sided pyramid, without a square. The total number of sides then is four.

LESSON 132: GEOMETRY ASSESSMENT

OBJECTIVES:
1. To assess the geometry topics

MATERIALS:
1. End of Year Assessment 5
2. Geometric solids
3. Tiles

ACTIVITIES FOR TEACHING:	EXPLANATIONS:
Assessment 5. Take out the End of Year Assessment 5. It is to be done orally or visually and assessments notes can be recorded.	

Problems 1–12. Give the child the geometric solids. Read the following list to the child, making assessment notes as the child progresses.

1. Find the sphere.
2. Put the cube behind the sphere.
3. Place the pyramid above the cube.
4. Place the cone beside the sphere.
5. Put the shorter cylinder next to the sphere.

Say the following and ask the child to find the geometric solids.

6. I have six squares. What am I? [cube]
7. I have two hexagons. What am I? [(hexagonal) prism]
8. I have only one circle. What am I? [cone, hemisphere]
9. I am round all over. What am I? [sphere]
10. I have two triangles. What am I? [(triangular) prism]
11. I have four triangles. What am I? [pyramid]
12. I have two circles. What am I? [cylinders]

Problems 13–14.

13. Ask the child: How many faces are on the wooden cube? [6]
14. Ask: How many sides does a triangle have? [3]

Problems 15–16. Place about 20 tiles in front of the child.

15. Tell the child to take 14 tiles and make as many squares of different sizes as he can.
16. Now ask him to make as many rectangles of different sizes as he can that are not squares.

Congratulations!

Your child has completed
RightStart™ Mathematics Level A
and is now ready for
Level B Second Edition.

Certificates of completion are in the back of the child's worksheets.

Certificate of Achievement

Presented to

_____

for completing

**RIGHTSTART™ MATHEMATICS
LEVEL A**
Second Edition

On this_____day of_____

_____,Teacher

Joan A. Cotter, Ph.D.

Tracy Mittleider, MSEd

To move on to RightStart™ Mathematics Level B Second Edition, all you need is the Level B Book Bundle. This can be purchased at RightStartMath.com or by calling 888-272-3291.

APPENDIX

YELLOW IS THE SUN

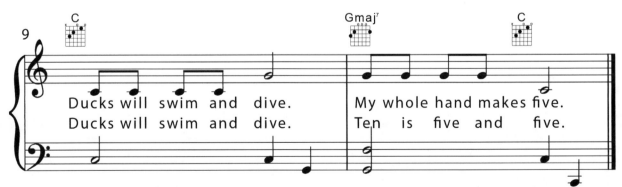

Lyrics by Joan A. Cotter

Composed by Rosine Hermodson-Olsen
Arranged by Barbara Ask

FINGER CARDS

STRIPS FOR SORTING

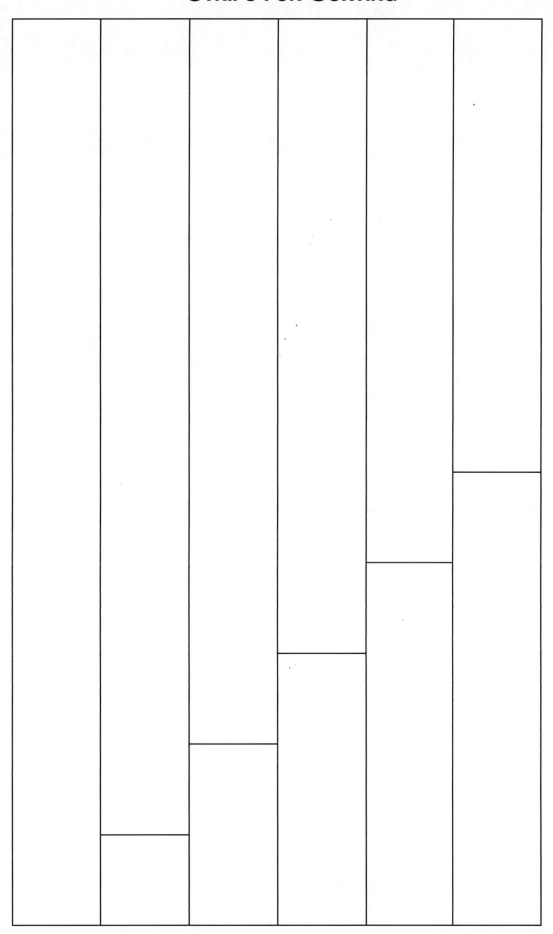

WRITING NUMBERS

Be - fore you write a num - ber, stop. And take a hop to the top. Start at the left to make 2, 3 or 4, Al - so se - ven which you can't ig - nore. Start at the right for 5, 6, 8, or 9. Don't lift your pen and you'll do just fine. Ze - ro and one not left, not right—a rid - dle. They be - gin at the top, smack in the mid - dle.

Lyrics by Joan A. Cotter

Composed by Rosine Hermodson-Olsen
Arranged by Barbara Ask

RECTANGLES

DOT CARDS

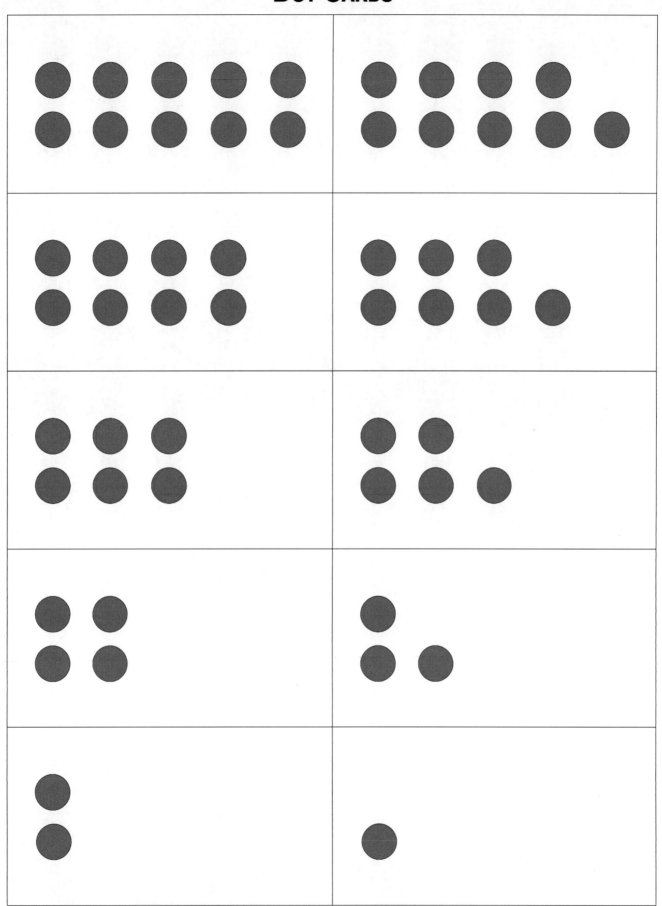

BEAD CARDS

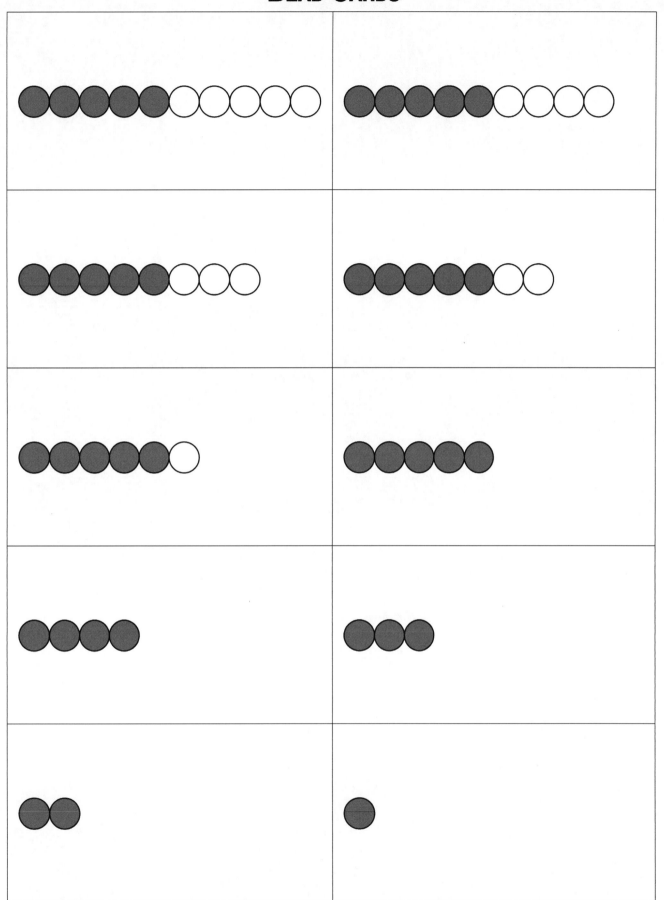

RightStart™ Mathematics second edition, A

ASSESSMENT CHECKLIST 1

Name	**Goal 1.** Understand quanity of a number.	**Goal 2.** Recognize and build the given shapes on the geoboard.	**Goal 3.** Build patterns on the geoboard.
Rosie 10/26/17	1,3,4,2,9,8,7,5,6,0 dot cards are dificult	does not know triangle, rectangle good, can't do square or quad.	very difficult

PART-WHOLE CIRCLE SET

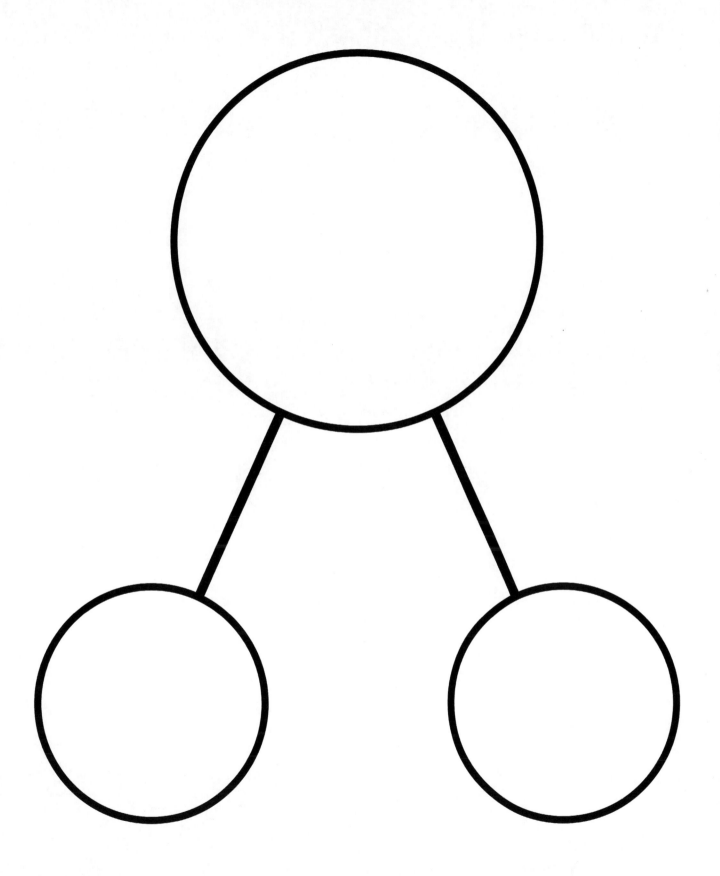

THREE-TEN DAYS HAS SEPTEMBER

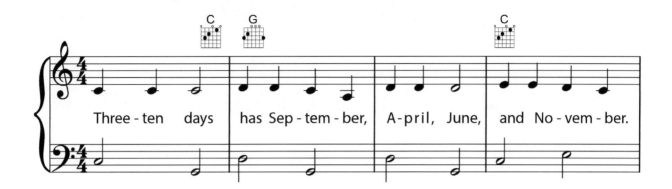

Three - ten days | has Sep - tem - ber, | A - pril, June, | and No - vem - ber.

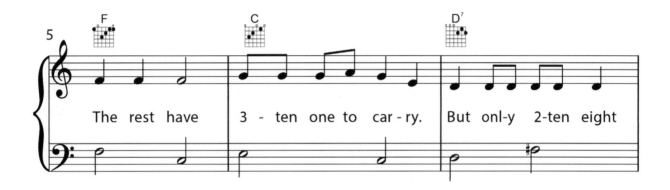

The rest have | 3 - ten one to car - ry. | But onl-y 2-ten eight

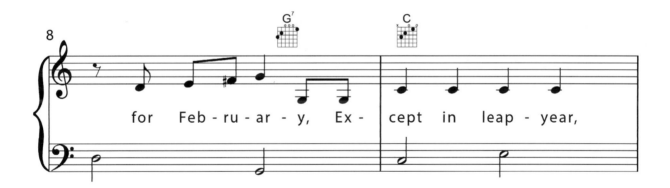

for Feb - ru - ar - y, Ex - | cept in leap - year,

that's the time when | Feb - ru - ar - y's | 2 - ten nine.

Lyrics by Joan A. Cotter

Composed by Rosine Hermodson-Olsen
Arranged by Barbara Ask

ASSESSMENT CHECKLIST 2

Name	Goal 1. Show their left hand.	Goal 2. Enter a quantity on the abacus and name it.	Goal 3. Find something above/ below the table.	Goal 4. Make the reflection of a triangle on the geoboard.	Goal 5. Determine more and less.

ASSESSMENT CHECKLIST 3

Name	**Goal 6.** Recognizes 8 on dot and bead cards.	**Goal 7.** Put numbers in order from 1–10.	**Goal 8.** Start with 4 on the abacus and count by ones to 10.	**Goal 9.** Find the missing number in a sequence from 1 to 10.

CALENDAR PARTS

1	2	3	4	5	6	7	8
9	10	11	12	13	14	15	16
17	18	19	20	21	22	23	24
25	26	27	28	29	30	31	

January	February
March	April
May	June
July	August
September	October
November	December

	S	M	T	W	Th	F	S

Clock A

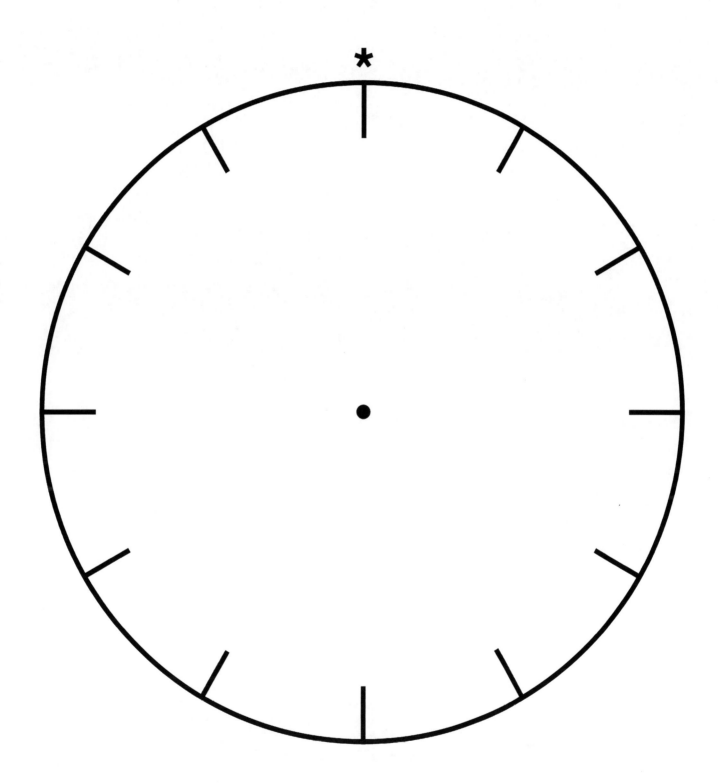

CLOCKS ON THE HOUR

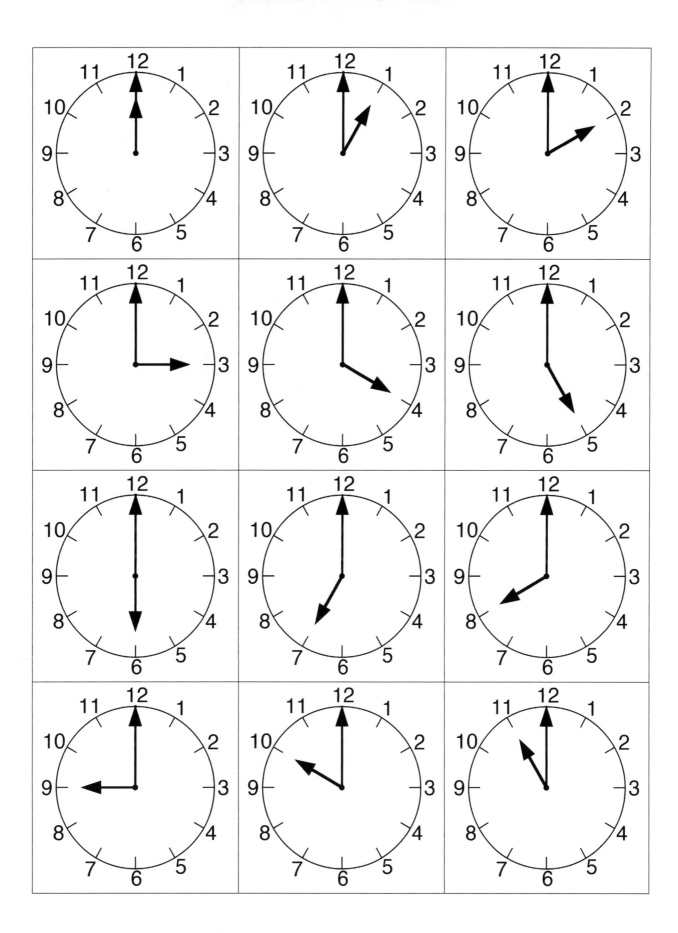

CLOCK TAGS

1:00	2:00	3:00
4:00	5:00	6:00
7:00	8:00	9:00
10:00	11:00	12:00

1:30	2:30	3:30
4:30	5:30	6:30
7:30	8:30	9:30
10:30	11:30	12:30

CLOCKS ON THE HALF HOUR

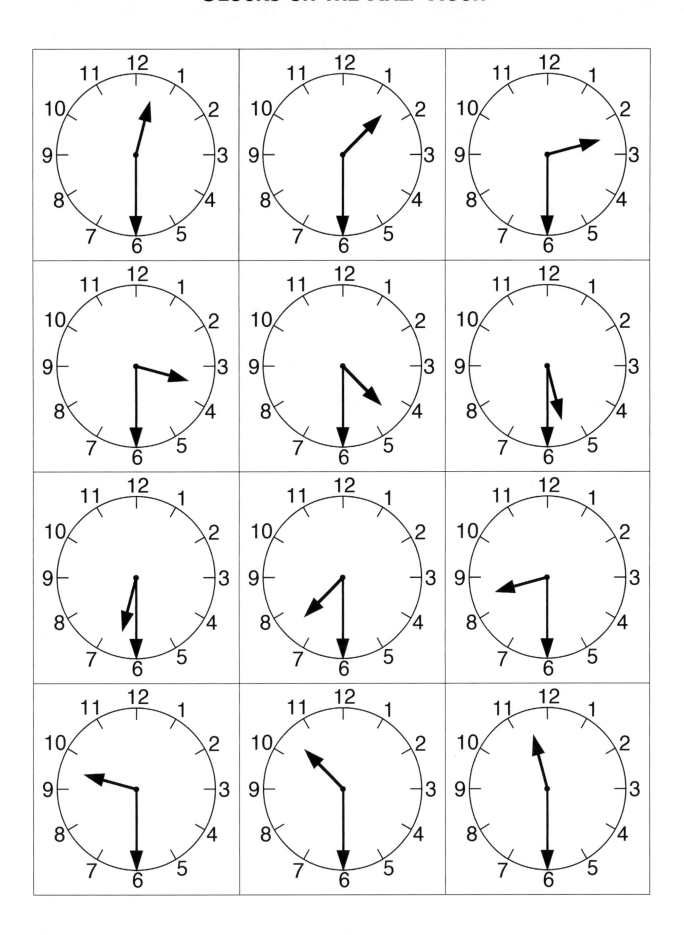

RightStart™ Mathematics second edition, A

TALLY STICK CARDS

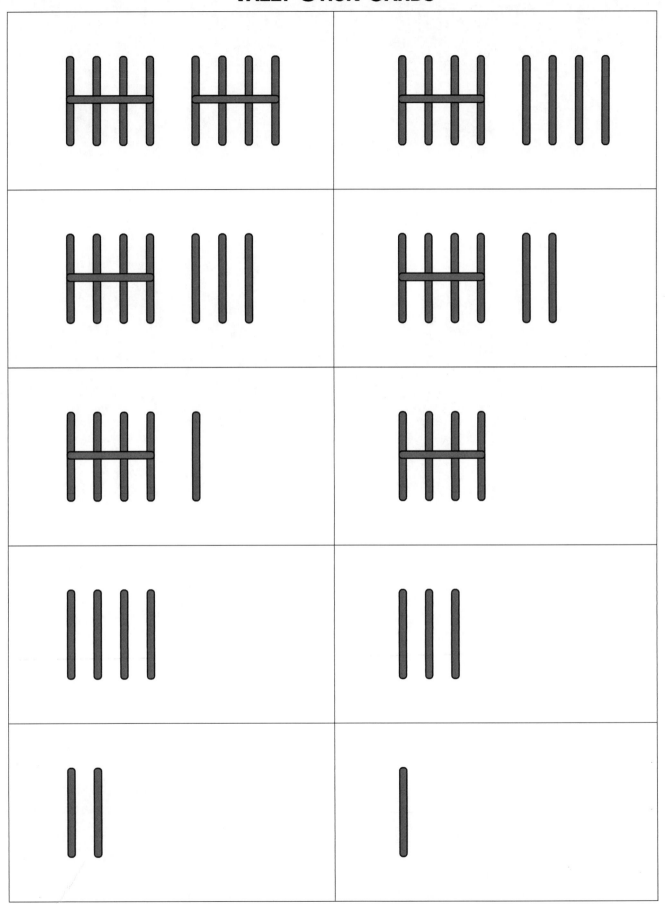